Balkrishna Doshi

PATHS UNCHARTED

Reprinted in 2023 by
Mapin Publishing Pvt. Ltd
706 Kaivanna, Panchvati, Ellisbridge
Ahmedabad 380006 INDIA
T: +91 79 40 228 228 • F: +91 79 40 228 201
E: mapin@mapinpub.com • www.mapinpub.com

First published in India in 2019 by
Mapin Publishing Pvt. Ltd

First published privately by
Vastu-Shilpa Foundation for Studies and Research in
Environmental Design
'Sangath', Thaltej Road
Ahmedabad 380054 INDIA
T: +91 79 27451555 • F: +91 79 27452006
E: vsf@sangath.org • www.vastushilpa.org

ISBN: 978-93-85360-62-6

Design: Khushnu Panthaki-Hoof
Copyediting: Marilyn Gore / Mapin Editorial
Proofreading: Mithila Rangarajan / Mapin Editorial
Editorial Supervision: Neha Manke / Mapin Editorial
Production: Mapin Design Studio
Printed at Thomson Press (India) Ltd.

PATHS UNCHARTED

Balkrishna Doshi

MAPIN
PUBLISHING

Dedicated to

My mother, Radha

For her constant presence and guidance

Kamala, fondly Kamu, my wife

For her friendly and wise counsel in steering our destined path

Acknowledgments

Recollecting one's life is an inherently random and selective process. As much as I have enjoyed doing this, it must have been an arduous and demanding task for those who helped me to give this book its shape.

First, I want to thank Pranali Parikh for deciphering my diaries and lecture notes, transcribing the audio tapes, and eventually compiling it all into one single text.

The person who most deserves a big thank you is Munna, aka Muktirajsinhji Chauhan. He sifted through the 70,000-word file, edited it for the ease of reading, and ensured smoother transitions between places, people and events.

For a little more than two decades now, Rajeev Kathpalia, my partner, has closely shared with me the pleasures and pains of keeping the spirit of Sangath alive as our practice evolved. He has been supportive of this book and a constant source of encouragement, creative discussions and valuable feedback over the years. I am very thankful to him.

My heartfelt thanks to my granddaughter Khushnu Panthaki Hoof—partner and personal critic—who, over the last decade, compiled sketches and notes, composed the book, tied up the loose ends and helped me publish the book.

Vasudevan Akkitham, Neelkanth Chhaya and Sen Kapadia kindly agreed to read the draft at various stages. I thank them for their comments and suggestions.

I am also thankful to Saryu Ahuja, who was kind enough to go through a very early version and offer her insightful observations for improvement.

Very special thanks are due to Niranjan Bhagat, for reading the final draft and encouraging me to publish.

My sincere thanks go to Hemang Desai for his valuable suggestions, and for editing the manuscript at a critical time.

For the work leading to this final version, I would like to thank Manasi Pandey for assisting me.

I am also thankful to Joseph Varghese, for patiently coordinating this effort, retyping and shuffling the base notes over the last few years.

And of course, a wholehearted thank you is due to all the Sangathees, of Vastu-Shilpa Consultants as well as Vastu-Shilpa Foundation, and CEPT faculty and colleagues for their unceasing support over the years.

Last but not the least: I am grateful to my daughters, sons-in-law and grandchildren who prodded me to complete this book, and all those who have traversed life's path with me, some time, somewhere. They have been a true source of inspiration and encouragement in my wanderings.

Doshi

Preface

I grew up in a joint family in a modest house in Pune. Most days, there were at least 15 of us sharing meals, rooms and the facilities. My mother died shortly after I was born. My father—busy with his furniture business and religious and social work—did not spend much time with the family.

I recall my mother's face only from the photographs I saw of her much later. Even now, I miss her very much. I suspect this longing for maternal love made me withdraw into myself. Perhaps my desire to rediscover this intimacy gave rise to my habit of scribbling whatever came to my mind, right from a very young age.

The scribbles and drawings on scraps of paper seemed to satisfy my desire for identity and self-awareness. They seemed to create for me a private intimate world, even in the midst of the daily hustle and bustle of a large household. These have now become a good record of my life, from those days in Pune to those in Ahmedabad now.

Fortunately, quietly jotting one's thoughts in a journal or loose papers anywhere is not considered impolite in most social settings. Thus, I could indulge in it almost all the time. As a result, every time I wrote, I rejoiced in my inwardly absent, yet physically present state. I could be with myself, within my own inner world, and all alone even in a crowd.

These notes are my links to my straying and uncharted life. I feel my life has been interconnected randomly. Yet I see a thread—a sequence—through all these events, as if it contained a purpose. Every moment there is a new opportunity, and many doors to choose from.

The seemingly impossible chain of events in my life—from the places I have been, to the people I have met and the work I have been fortunate to do—has convinced me that there has been an unseen force, charting my path without my knowledge.

I like to believe that my mother has been guiding me on these paths otherwise unknown to me. I remember that, as a child, when I was bedridden for months—very lonely and sad—I had felt her hands caress my wounds. I heard her voice assuring me that I would get well and that she would always be with me.

Did she really set me up on this journey, or was it a natural course of life? I would find it difficult to answer but I do believe that our destiny is not entirely in our hands. Looking back, I like to believe that my journey has been a rather extraordinary one.

It has taken me from the back lanes of Pune to Ahmedabad, via almost all the beautiful places in our world on all the continents. I have been lucky to see almost all of the great architectural accomplishments worth talking about, met so many of the best of the architects, visual and performance artists, critics, theoreticians and historians of our time—not to forget some remarkable patrons.

For some years I have been often asked, 'Why don't you write your experiences?' I hesitated for a long, long time. But after I turned 80, I often found myself recalling the twists and turns that my life has taken, and felt the need to record them, which I did on a series of tapes.

The idea of sharing this journey in print came later. I am doing this in the hope that—for all the chaos that seems to characterize the story of my life—there is perhaps an order, with its own dynamics and logic, which connects all the events; that there must be a reason in there, and, hopefully, a message or a lesson I may add. Therefore, I had the journal entries, lecture audio tapes and videos transcribed and edited to allow for easier reading.

I would like to add here that this book focuses on the path my life has taken over the years: my personal circumstances, experiences, people I have met, places I have been to and the lessons I have learnt. It deals with my growth as a person in search of his ultimate destiny.

The references to my own work here are incidental to circumstances, my concerns at the time, the choices I was making, and lessons I was learning. I hope to write about architecture and planning projects very soon, in another book.

Here they are then, the scribbles from my inner sanctuary. I hope you enjoy reading them.

Balkrishna Doshi,

Ahmedabad, August 26, 2018

Prologue

This is not a note on how to read this book but my own introspection towards understanding the twists and turns of my life's journey so far. I hope that it will also make the effort of sharing my journal more meaningful for all who choose to read this, especially young professionals and students embarking on a challenging yet fascinating life as a designer, architect, planner, or just for their own development.

Frankly, at this stage in life, I even hesitate to call myself an architect because the more I think I know what architecture is, the less I feel I know about its true calling. Every time I felt I had mastered it, each newly completed project made me aware of how much more there was to architecture. As a result, I increasingly see myself more as a person seeking my destiny rather than being just an architect, planner or such.

This is not to deny the fact that I have been mainly occupied with the practice of architecture, and setting up and nurturing CEPT University at Ahmedabad. However, when I see what my gurus—who are not only architects—have accomplished, I feel that their accomplishments have much to do with the kind of persons they were, wiser from all their varied experiences garnered from working in their chosen fields as well as the social and cultural milieu from which they came.

Have I consciously or unconsciously been looking up to my gurus? They have come not just from the field of architecture, but also fine and performing arts, social sciences, as well as more spiritual ways of living.

What am I seeking? Is it being at peace with myself and the world around, through architecture and planning—the mediums that I know best?

How did all this come together? How does it all connect? What led me to each of the new places I went to and people I met, which opened new doors and new opportunities? How and why did I accept opportunities of which I knew almost nothing? Was it my belief in there being a higher purpose to all living beings, some kind of divine calling, even if they do not know it themselves?

I am now trying to find answers to these questions. Perhaps, I will never find final answers to my questions. Nevertheless, the very act of raising these questions and seeking clues to their answers has helped me to better understand myself, and the path I have walked in my life so far.

When I look back at each of the choices that became the turning point in my life, I find that these were guided by my beliefs and the ways in which I have dealt with life and work. Whether these beliefs stemmed from my upbringing, the milieu in which I matured, the gurus I met, or the hidden opportunities that I intuitively grabbed, is difficult to say.

So much in life, as it unfolds daily, is spontaneous on the face of it. However, I believe it is influenced by our past lessons, memories, and hopes for the future, and that it is impossible to separate the exact causes. Nevertheless, I want to understand how I got here and therefore I have attempted to identify what has driven the twists and turns in my life, my work and the decisions I have made.

These are **Breaking Free**, **Constantly Striving for Excellence and Beyond**, **Living and Working as an Enterprise** and **Being Connected** with people you know and the larger community.

As you will read in the following pages, there was very little in the circumstances of my birth and my background, which would have hinted at anything about the path I have taken.

One thing is certain: all my life I have been seeking more fulfilling work and I have had the courage to break free from extant circumstances. These were governed more by the family traditions and expectations, at least in the early years. Later, I believe these had more to do with striving to be a better professional. Put differently, it might all be about what I would love to do next as I learned more about life and work.

Another important trait I notice as I look back is a willingness to learn, being forever a student, and put in the hard, dogged work it calls for. As an example, I can mention starting the School of Planning some 10 years after starting the School of Architecture. I knew nothing about planning, especially development planning, but I was ready to learn from esteemed colleagues.

I have never been afraid of asking questions, however ignorant they might make me seem, because I know that one is surely wiser for having asked them. If that meant I had to work harder and longer to learn more, so be it.

It has helped that I have been relatively more open and accessible to persons from all walks of life, be they my former students, colleagues, fellow professionals, or even strangers in accidental situations. I have learnt a lot from them all, and I hope I have become a better architect and person for it.

When I left my ancestral home in Pune, it was to study art, but I chose architecture at J.J. School in Mumbai. When I came across an opportunity to go to London and study to become an Associate of Royal Institute of British Architects, RIBA, at London, I dropped out of J.J. School. Once in London, when I learnt of an opportunity to work in Le Corbusier's office, I did not wait to complete studies at RIBA.

As I now see it, at each of these stages, I was taking risks, big risks, rather than enjoying the comfort of familiar settings. It is almost like being an entrepreneur obsessed by the next big thing. However, my willingness to work harder and learn constantly made me somewhat fearless regarding the risks I was taking. It is what I would like to call flying without fear.

Even as I started by breaking myself free of the extended family I grew up with, I seem to have constantly connected with all kinds of individuals and groups. These groups may be social, cultural, spiritual or professional in nature, each with its own traditions and aspirations.

I became aware of the close give-and-take relationship between the land, resources, climatic conditions and people very early in my life. I also realized that our world consisted of distinct regions, each with its own characteristics that included distinct architectural practices unique to each region. I believe this has helped me understand the goals and roles for each one of us, both individually and collectively, with regard to our natural and human habitat.

Understanding the close interdependent relationship between these two habitats made me aware of the issues of sustainable development very early in life. However, in those days, we always perceived these simply as living in harmony with nature. Moreover, there was hardly any waste generated, as one rarely consumed anything beyond one's basic needs.

Tempered by both the traditional ways as well as Gandhiji's immense influence then on daily life, being frugal was second nature to all of us. Frugality also seemed right because there were many whose needs were greater than ours.

This, in turn, promoted the virtue of being generous and giving because that was a more responsible way of living as a member of the larger community. Put differently, either by giving proactively or forgoing passively, one was supporting the fulfilment of others' needs, making more available to the community.

Being frugal and forgoing is the way I have lived all my life. Frugal habits have allowed me to choose what I want to do because my needs are minimal. It has also allowed me to forgo money I believed I should not accept on moral or ethical grounds.

For example, I taught at the School of Architecture, Ahmedabad, and administered the School, first as its Honorary Director and then as its Dean for more than 20 years. However, whatever I was paid for my time, I gave back as scholarships for the students. I believe teaching is a service to Saraswati, the Goddess of Education, and I did not think it was right to be paid for it.

Perhaps frugal habits have also greatly influenced my architecture, which has mostly been severe in terms of the choice of materials, finishes, and scale. Frankly, I found it difficult to design using materials like very expensive varieties of marble or provide unduly large spaces where they were not warranted.

I like to believe that these beliefs were shaped by the incidents from the epics like the Mahabharata, Ramayana and other mythological stories I heard from my Dada (grandfather) in my mother tongue, and other elders of the extended family at Pune. One of these, which I often recall, is the story of Karna, who was never accepted as one of the Pandavas—the sons of Pandu—despite being the first-born son of King Pandu's wife, Kunti, since he was born of a boon granted by the Sun God before she was married to the king.

In time, Karna became very famous for his charitable acts but ended up in the enemy camp during the great war of Kurukshetra. After a serious injury in battle, as he lay on his deathbed, a mendicant Brahmin came up to him. The Brahmin said that he had heard a lot about Karna's generosity and asked for an offering. Karna was very heartbroken because in those circumstances he had nothing to offer. Then he suddenly remembered that one of his teeth was made of gold. Unable to move, he asked the Brahmin to fetch a stone using which he removed it and offered it to the Brahmin.

Seeing it covered in blood, the Brahmin said, 'It is covered with blood and impure; so I cannot accept it.' Moved, Karna started to cry. His tears cleansed the tooth and he offered it to the Brahmin. Of course, the Brahmin was no other than the great god Indra, who had been testing Karna. Impressed by Karna's generosity even in such circumstances, he revealed himself and blessed Karna.

Perhaps I recall all this because I am that stage in life, where my own elders were in Pune. I am now the oldest person in my extended family and find myself constantly reflecting on the past and future. Over the last few years, I have found myself reaching out much more to connect with my own extended family including colleagues and students, now spread across four generations.

I often think of the roles that my own elders—Dada in particular—have played in my life. For example, even as they had familial expectations of me, they accepted my adventurous ways not only without any acrimony but also with a generosity unique to our culture and traditions. I now understand what *runanubandh* means. It is not so much being indebted from times before us but being connected to all people and all places across all time—past, present and future—in a common destiny. That is what makes a community, and us human, forever.

I fully grasped this during my discussions with Rasikbhai Parikh in Ahmedabad in the late 1950s. Rasikbhai, whom I addressed as Motabhai—meaning "elder brother" in Gujarati—was my uncle-in-law. More importantly, he was a reputed scholar who was well-versed in the matters of Indian arts, history, culture, politics, religion and philosophy.

Motabhai made me aware of the significance of my childhood experiences as part of a deeply religious extended family. He explained that I had unknowingly imbibed virtues—such as sharing, reverence, forgiveness and tolerance—simply by being around and sometimes participating in various religious rituals and ceremonies; not to forget the stories from the epics my elders told us every evening.

However, the real meaning of all this exposure was in forging the values of life. Our ultimate aim is to find *moksha*, salvation, from the endless physical, material cycles of our lives. Motabhai's explanation for life and death, our duties and responsibilities, and the concept of karma made me aware of the subtlest cells of the body and its connectedness to the cosmic forces. This lent a unique twist to my understanding of the work of both Le Corbusier and Louis Kahn.

I admire the freedom, the joy, the play, the rhythm, the texture, the colour, the volume and the light, which created a unique symphony in Corbusier's work, and lent it a mood that connected me to the world around. Yet, I felt that there was, in spite of its looseness, variety and open-mindedness, a feeling that something was amiss. The spaces, volumes and the forms seemed devoid of something. It was much later that I realized my mistake: Le Corbusier's works are divine, and I had been looking for the mundane.

Of course, his work in Chandigarh strongly connects to the cosmic forces, as if from another planet. I did feel the need for human intervention, and his provision of a veranda at the High Court or at the extension around the Capitol Complex make me feel safe and secure. In Kahn's work, I saw precision and sensibilities of geometry and rhythm; but they still had Lou in them, which is something I cannot do—be there and be myself at the same time.

What I learnt from Motabhai was to act with porosity and allow change if it happened. 'Time and eternity are measurable paradoxes, others are immeasurable, to mark our existence and our emotions. It is essential to find some porosity that allows a chance to intervene.'

Over time, seeking answers to such questions became my main struggle. Even though greatly influenced by both Corbusier and Kahn, I tried to find a space in between the two, where I could express myself and within which I could place my architecture. It was after a long struggle and without being too assertive that I started to design my buildings.

Traditions of the Indian arts emphasize anonymity about the creators of artistic works. One rarely ever knows who designed or sponsored most great historic architecture. If you search carefully you may, in a corner of a wall or at the base of a column or on one of the layers of a plinth, find an inscription or markings that might offer clues about the designer or the patron.

This stems from a belief in the impermanence of all things. Hence, authorship, ownership, a rigid structure, or a space too well defined does not touch us. Encroachment and abuse constantly change what was there, the pristine state; finally, what endure are the main structure and the basic tenets of its making. Ruins always appeal to us more. They touch our hearts, perhaps because of their enigmatic state—that of having been complete and, yet, now being incomplete.

I had to struggle to learn this and, in my later projects, I feel I have partially succeeded. The struggle is caused by the conflict between my upbringing within a Hindu view of life and my training in the Western tradition, which sees architecture as a product meant to provide us stability, comfort and delight. Perhaps I will continue this struggle all my life. That may be my destiny!

In the following pages, I have captured this struggle and my daily life as it has unfolded over the last eight decades in as much detail as I can recall. It is also an account of all the key events of my life, as I moved from one place to another and from one phase of life to another, meeting some of the most remarkable persons from all walks of life across the globe.

How did that come about? I hope that these notes will help to partly answer the questions I raised earlier and link, however tenuously, the seemingly disparate twists and turns my life has taken.

Paths Uncharted:

Notes from my diaries

Looking back, I have come to believe that, over the years, my life has been a rather unusual journey. A series of events that have coalesced like drops of water to gradually become a spring, then a river, and then joined many other rivers towards the oceans.

In the process, these drops of water have traversed many lands, some open, some confined. There were times when the flow ebbed, even stopped, but those pauses gave rise to lakes, small and big. Then there came floods that rose above the lake banks, broke free, flowing once again.

Over the years, I have been to many lands, forests and gardens in all the seasons. In the process, like a river, I have gathered waters from a multitude of regions, climates and cultures enriched by the wisdom and traditions of wise men.

These travels have helped to answer innumerable questions. Just as the muddy water of a river clears up as it flows on, I have gained insight and clarity about the world around me. I now know what it means when one says everything is interrelated. In my field, it can signify the interconnectedness between the design of a pin to a design of a city and everything in between. All that one needs to understand is the differences in the scales and their sphere of impacts.

I realize that even though each object should have its own identity, it cannot be conceived in isolation since identity is a mere comparison. What is immediately around is often our short-sighted perception: 'the disenchantment of the one who believes the truth is what he sees.'

All the choices of technologies or materials are born out of the people's own nature and needs. Their own evolution gives it a character and demonstrates to us its purpose or use. Hence, what we need to do is to allow the goal of existence to clarify its meaning and application.

Time or style is a limited notion. It can easily be set aside if we realize that all that we perceive is viewed through our memories and the present. There are layers that must be seen together and not as fragmented issues—irrespective of whether they are of art, architecture, or life itself. It is essential that we look at these from a distance with eternity or timelessness.

I have memories of living in villages and small towns, the daily life, traditional houses, local customs, religious values and an economy based on agriculture. I also have memories of life in Paris, and of working at 35 Rue de Sevres, and very different impressions of the artistic attitudes to urban life and the world of tomorrow.

Between these two realms—searching for the constants between these two worlds, rural and metropolitan—lies my architectural career. In my life and my work, the effort has been to combine the virtues of both and to find a balance between these two worlds.

I was born into an extended Hindu family in Pune where several generations lived together in our ancestral home. The head of the family, my Dada, Gokuldas Narayandas, was more than 75 years old when I was a child. Thus, members of the extended family ranged in ages from a few days to more than 80 years, spanning the whole range in between at different stages of life.

So, there were widowers, middle-aged parents, newlyweds, and adolescents—all living under one roof and interacting closely on a daily basis. It was natural in such circumstances that one frequently witnessed life events such as birth, marriage and death. These events made one constantly conscious of the transitory nature of life.

Celebration of festivals, ceremonies and rituals connected to various life events, daily trips to temples, and annual pilgrimages were a constant feature of life and all of us—young and old—were actively involved in these activities. Days, months and seasons passed, so also good times and bad times.

The character and form of the house too changed over time, in an organic process of growth. Initially, there were just a few rooms; more were added as the need arose. It grew from one storey to several. Uses of old rooms were changed too, forcing changes in the movement patterns; it all felt a bit strange to begin with but, eventually, the changes were absorbed to our daily lives and became the 'new old'. Thus, the house offered spatial and aesthetic surprises all the time. At any point of time, there was something new, something different about it.

I have often wondered what gave it a lasting identity amidst all these changes, and come to believe that it was the kitchen, dining and prayer rooms—which remained unchanged—that dominated the domestic ambience, like a hearth in earlier times. From these experiences, constant evolution and transformation have become an integral part of my perception of life and my aesthetic experience.

During those years, I often went to nearby villages and temples to attend certain ceremonies with other members of the family. The rituals always appeared to be similar but their purpose, their manner of performance and scale, and sometimes their location, differed.

They occurred in all kinds of locations such as on a riverbank, or in the courtyard of our home, or within the precinct of a local shrine. These events, scattered as they were all over, did not seem odd at all. In fact, they offered opportunities to understand the uncertainties and constant flux of life better.

When I look back and reflect on these things now, I realize the whys and wherefores of the acceptance of life. That it stems from constant sharing life and living space with many. Actually, I have realized that sharing multiplies the joys of celebrations and diminishes those of sad events.

There is a secret reality
a divine reality which
is present in all things
and manifest at appropriate
time

Frequent occurrence of the life's events in a large family helps us better understand the uncertainties in life, and notions of success and failure. This shapes one's world view, makes one more accepting, more patient, and shifts life's focus from material to spiritual values.

The constant reference to life after death and reincarnation also brings hope. It is believed that, in the process of reincarnation, every being continues to carry certain memories and experiences of past lives. The present is then seen only as a transitional phase.

I now realize that life is full of surprises and paradoxes. Everything that occurred in the past can happen again in another time, place, and form. Once past, events become memories.

Such experiences of the world around and beyond, of good, bad, then and now make us acutely conscious of the meaning and purpose of the vast world around us. The immense diversity of the flora and fauna makes us more sensitive to our surroundings.

Such are the contexts and circumstances in which I grew up, and which formed the bedrock of my beliefs and outlook. This is where my roots lie.

I am constantly fascinated, almost like a child, by the ways in which the world around me works. I see a river and think of its journey from its point of origin all the way to the point where it meets the ocean; or the way in which mighty trees grow from a small seed. I see an ant, a snake, or a giraffe, and think about how perfectly its form is suited to life in its particular habitat. That surely is a very valuable lesson in design.

I often recall and think about the tales from epics that Dada and other elders told us children in Pune: the epic characters and their conduct, and the moral and ethical lessons that generations of Indian people have derived from them. I also remember the mythical stories I enjoyed as a child, and think back on how they can trigger lots of thoughts, images and actions despite talking of fictional people, animals and places.

For instance, if I'm sitting under a tree, I might think that may be a monkey is going up the tree. I may think about a crocodile going up too. Then, I might remember Saint Kabir saying, 'Isn't it a miracle that the river is on fire and fish is climbing the tree?' I then see a fish climbing the tree.

Then, I might recall the landscapes in the film *The Lord of the Rings*. I see the valleys; I see those big birds flying and what not. I can fly with them and see what they see. I can touch down to the ground and continue going deep down. Then I would remember step wells and then something else would emerge.

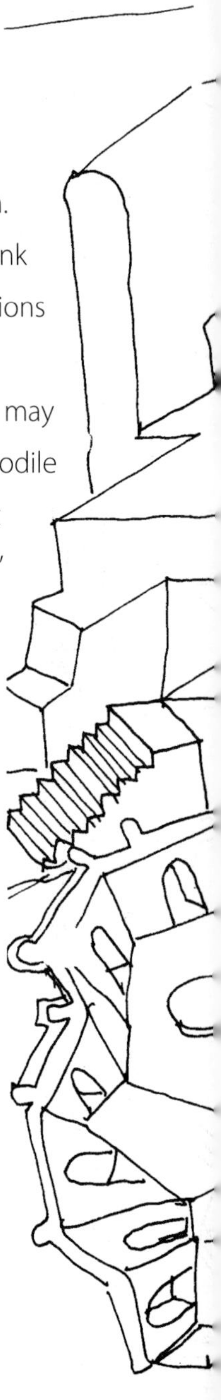

Interestingly, years later, some of these tales did find a place in my life and work. For example, one of the tales I had heard as a child was about God's avatar as a tortoise (*kurma*).

When my colleagues and students questioned me about the unusual form and ground relationship of my design for the Amdavad Ni Gufa, I wrote a fictitious story to explain how the design came about which drew heavily on the myth of Vishnu's *kurma* avatar.

I also often have dreams like this story. I do not like confinement. Even if such things do not actually happen, it does not matter, because I am happy having thoughts of such possibilities.

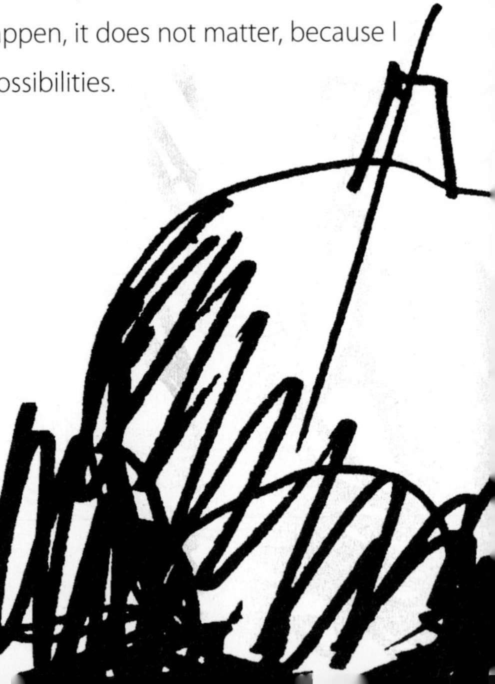

If you are highly motivated, your thoughts about your aspirations and dreams travel, reach out, and are eventually made a reality by cosmic forces.

A series of seemingly disparate coincidences have marked my life.

Now when I think about them, I sense an undercurrent, a binding thread that joins them together.

Were these coincidences just a series of flukes?

I do not think so.

For example, I received the Fellowship of Graham Foundation for Advanced Studies in Arts because I happened to meet Dr Sigfried Giedion, the Swiss architectural historian and critic, in Le Corbusier's office just a few days before I left Paris. He was a very close friend of Le Corbusier.

I was showing him the design of the Capitol Complex at Chandigarh and discussing various related issues. I remember him asking me as to why, despite having praised Piazza San Marco so much, Corbusier makes no such reference at Chandigarh. My explanation was that perhaps he was thinking of the Himalayas in the background and wants to create a grand and open gesture in response.

Since the office was closing, he invited me to join him for a beer at his hotel on Rue St Jacob so we could continue talking. There he asked me about my plans after Paris. I told him about my desire to go back to India and the options I was considering once there. We talked some more in general about world architecture for about an hour and then parted. That was in 1955.

Then in 1957, out of the blue, I received a letter from the Graham Foundation, signed by Professor Jose Luis Sert, then Chairman and the Dean of the Harvard School of Design. He wrote, 'Dr Giedion has highly recommended that we ask you if you would like to apply for this Fellowship which is worth $10,000, and if you do, would you send me a note on what you propose to do?'

I was surely interested but had never before written such a note—what might be called a proposal today. Luckily, Prithvish Neogy who had recently joined as Director of Sanskar Kendra—the museum designed by Corbusier at Ahmedabad—was staying at my house at the time, and helped me to prepare the note, which I then mailed.

I also wrote to Le Corbusier informing him about this offer. I learnt later that, on receiving my letter, Le Corbusier immediately wrote to Prof. Sert recommending me for the fellowship. He actually mentioned that he requested him 'to check in the Volume VI of *Oeuvres Completes Le Corbusier* (that) the work done by Doshi in my workshop; Shodhan Villa on page 135 and Mill Owners' Association building on page 145,' as also in other places.

He went on to add that, 'it is a pleasure for me to recommend Doshi, who has excellent moral values, intellectual capabilities and a good technical sense.' Moreover, that, 'it is in his (Doshi's) interest to receive "the American shock" much as contact with him will be beneficial to those who deal with him (there in the US).'

This is what I mean. How did all these places, people and events fall in place or line up to make that fellowship happen? Such occurrences amaze me no end and I feel that there are larger unseen forces at work. I feel that I am just an instrument of the ultimate destiny and that guiding hands appeared at the right time and at the right place to show me my path.

How I got involved in teaching and subsequently started the Ahmedabad School of Architecture is also an equally fascinating series of coincidences. I first met Dr Buckminster (Bucky) Fuller from the US—famous for his invention of the geodesic dome and the design of the Dymaxion car—in the Calico Textile Mill's office at Ahmedabad when I was about to leave for the US. I had actually gone there to speak to Dr Vikram Sarabhai, the space scientist, about my forthcoming trip and Bucky just happened to be there.

Also present there were Leo Lionni and his wife Nora. Leo was then the art director of New York-based *Fortune* magazine and loved India, its arts and philosophy. Bucky inquired as to when I was travelling, and if I was planning to visit Chicago. I told him I had not travelled to the US before, that it would be my first time, and had no idea about all places I might visit once there.

He then asked if I would like to teach at Washington University, St Louis, located some distance south of Chicago while I was there. I said, 'I have never taught.' To this, he said: 'It does not matter, there is always a first time.' We left it at that and parted ways.

In the next few days, before I left Ahmedabad, I received a letter from Dean Joseph R. Passonneau of Washington University wanting to know if I would like to go there and teach for three weeks. Taking Bucky's advice, I accepted. That is how I ventured into teaching, which eventually became an important part of my life and career.

When I reached the US, Nora and Leo Lionni were kind enough to meet me at the JFK airport. I stayed with them for a few days to familiarize myself with the local ways, which were quite different from those I was familiar with in Europe. While there, I also met architect Philip Johnson, sculptor Alexander Calder and Ignazio Gardella, an architect from Milan.

Just like the chain of events that lead to the Graham Foundation Fellowship, in this case too, how did all these places, people come together at the right time and right place? Who made this happen and why? Perhaps this is explained by what Bucky mentioned to me years later. He had said, 'Every being has a pouch hidden deep within them, a homing device like some birds, which directs them to their destinations.'

Even my partnership with architects Joseph Allen Stein and J.R. Bhalla, who were already practising together, is another such story.

I first met Stein in 1954 at the Indian embassy in Paris. I was awaiting my turn while he was talking to the person at the visa counter. His conversation with the officer, which I could overhear in that small office, went something like this:

He said, 'I want to go to India.'

'Why are you going?'

'I am going to teach in a college near Calcutta known as Bengal Engineering College.'

'And what would you be teaching?'

'I will be teaching architecture. Currently, I am an architect practising in the west coast area of the US.'

The officer then asked him to wait and he came and sat near me. I said to him, 'I believe you are an architect.'

'Yes, I am, and you?'

'I am also an architect and I am here working with Le Corbusier.'

'Oh, it is always good to work with a master, I worked with Richard Neutra myself for a while,' he said.

We started talking, and later went out and had a beer. He then went his way and I came to Ahmedabad. Eventually, in 1974—almost 20 years later—I joined the firm of J.A. Stein and J.R. Bhalla (an architect from New Delhi and Stein's long-time partner) as a partner. Thus, it happened once again. I sometimes wonder, what brought us together at Paris with no inkling of what was to happen much later in India?

The formation of the partnership Stein, Doshi and Bhalla—SDB—came into being due to a fortuitous opportunity. The International Crop Research Institute in Semi-Arid Tropics, ICRISAT, happened to invite Vastu-Shilpa (my architecture practice) and Joseph Allen Stein and Associates separately to present our works as contenders for this significant international project to come up in Hyderabad, India.

Bhalla, a long-time associate of Stein's, instead suggested that our firms jointly solicit the project as equal partners. That is how SDB happened. The ICRISAT project lasted for about four years and the way in which our offices worked together encouraged formalizing our partnership with some unique organizational features.

We set up a holding company with a mandate to promote the talents and expertise, and two subsidiary companies: SDB Delhi under Stein's leadership, and SDB Ahmedabad under me. Thus organized, we were a formidable talent in the field of architecture and planning in India. As a result, several important projects were assigned to us, jointly as well as separately. These provided us a unique opportunity to deliberate on the approach and develop new ways to conceive and execute projects.

Then again, this partnership led to a rather momentous step that I took soon after. We had decided to name our partnership as Stein, Doshi and Bhalla. This meant that I had to close my own practice, known as Vastu-Shilpa since 1957. I was very reluctant to erase the memories of my own practice, and thought of recasting Vastu-Shilpa into what the School of Architecture was not, or could not be, in those days.

I was teaching, I was practising, so I thought now we must undertake research as the next logical act. That is why I set up Vastu-Shilpa Foundation for Studies and Research in Environmental Design in 1976 and formally registered it as a non-profit organization in 1978, under the chairmanship of Shrenikbhai, our family guide and Kasturbhai Lalbhai's son.

I may add here that the Foundation has been completely focused on the conditions of Indian habitats, and especially carries out research aimed at developing norms and practices appropriate to Indian contexts.

For a long time, the Vastu-Shilpa Foundation was the only organization of its kind in India, and has undertaken outstanding pioneering work to its credit. Here again, if it was not for the formation of SDB and my keen desire to keep the name of my firm alive, such an organization would never have seen the light of the day. Was that a destiny or an accident? I will never know!

How I went first to Bombay, then to London, from there to Paris, and finally came to settle in Ahmedabad is again an unusual chain of events. How these events fell into place puzzles me even now.

Hari Kanhere, four years senior to me at J.J. School of Architecture and a good friend, was then preparing to go to London. Since both of us stayed at Sardar Gruha boarding house very close to our School, we would often talk for long hours. When I met him a few days before he left, he invited me to stay with him in London if I ever considered moving there.

After he had settled down in London, he once wrote to me asking if I was interested in coming there and said that his offer to host me was still on. Almost immediately, I went to Pune and told Vallabh, my brother, 'I want to go to London and continue my studies there.'

Now that really came as a surprise to him and others in the family. I was expected to become an architect, go back to Pune, join the family business, marry a girl chosen by the family and raise my family as part of the extended family as was the tradition.

Eventually, as we talked more about it, I believe he understood my personal need to seek more from life as an individual and explore the opportunities that the newly independent India offered. So, he accepted my change of plans even though he did not fully like the idea.

There was, of course, the problem of money but my brother graciously decided to pay me the equivalent of my share in the ancestral property. Although that was just enough to cover and take care of my expenses for travel and some time to settle down, I was ready to sail the uncharted waters of the world.

That is it. I left Pune and the world I had known since birth—everything about it—and went. I realized only later that I never came back on a visit nor did I regularly correspond with my family—the centre of my life until then—during those five years that I was away. I believe that the strange new world I was reaching out to must have challenged and occupied me completely in all manners, so as to shut out my life until then.

Travel was not a simple matter in those days as it is today. For the journey to Paris, I first boarded the *Batory*, a ship operated by an Italian liner that was sailing to Genoa from Bombay. From Genoa, I was to continue further by train crossing into France and up north to Paris. To my ill luck, I was literally at sea in more ways than one. I was very seasick throughout the entire journey and that ruined what might have been an exciting journey. I went hungry all the way, as I just kept throwing up and never even made it to the dining hall.

In London, I initially stayed with Hari Mukund Kanhere and his wife for a while, before moving to a small breakfast and dinner pension run by one Sonapure family at Hampstead Heath. In time, I met many more J.J. School alumni working in London and started to feel at ease in the new environment.

Travelling by bus to the RIBA library and reading books and studying drawings became my daily routine in the months to come. The RIBA library was truly a treasure house. Every day, I spent about six hours in one of those cubicles, surrounded by books. Without any guide or any background, I was like a child in a curio shop, constantly exploring. Looking back, I wonder if I would have learnt what I did with conventional tutoring.

One day at the library, Warren Fuller, a student from the Northern Polytechnic, approached me to join him for a cup of tea at the RIBA cafeteria. Having tea and sympathy, we talked and later I also joined him at the Polytechnic for an evening course. This allowed us to continue meeting and talk at length about architecture and our countries. He was my first British friend and I learned a lot from him about England, its history and its ways. This also helped me to understand better the differences between Indian cities and London; be they of chaotic and orderly traffic, nature of buildings in extremely cold climate, notions of privacy or, most importantly, relations between the individual and the community.

Sense of History –
Tradition of Pluralism – not to be bound as with anyone thought

— Jugendstil – (Otto Wagner)

Memory of Renaissance brought to Vienna by Wagner

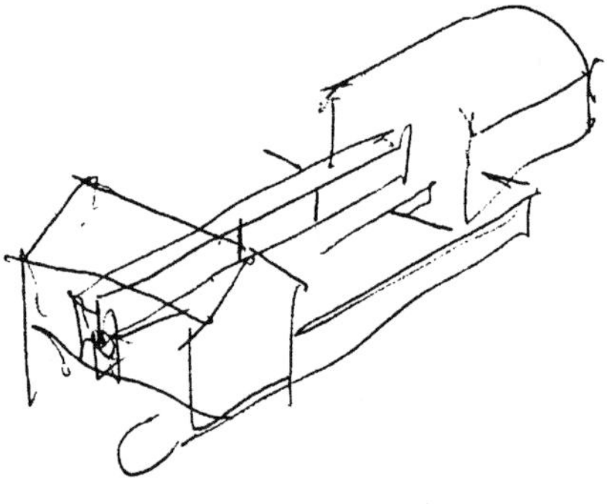

Just when I thought I had settled down and felt comfortable with my studies for the RIBA examination—unknown to me—a small event was about to change my life in a big way. Madhukar Yashvant Thackeray, a fellow student from J.J. School who was then working for London County Council, was also staying at the Sonapure pension. One day, he showed me an announcement of the Eighth Conference of the International Congress of Modern Architecture (CIAM), to be held in Hoddesdon. That was in 1951. The next day, I called Cadbury Brown, the Secretary of CIAM and pleaded with him to allow me to attend the Conference. He refused saying I was neither a member nor a full-time architecture student. However, driven by some strong inner urge, I persisted and managed to convince him in English that was still foreign to me. He relented and allowed me to join as an observer.

Even today, I often wonder about this rather bold act of calling him up, considering that I was quite shy and could not converse properly in English. What unknown force made me push my luck?

At the Conference, since I knew so little about the international goings on in architecture, I was blissfully unaware of the significance of the event itself. Once there, I hesitantly entered the vast exhibition area hoping to see projects and learn about the current trends.

After a while in there, to my surprise, I saw a man striding purposefully towards me. When he was close enough, he asked me, 'Are you an Indian?' After hearing my response, he introduced himself, 'I am German Samper from Bogota, Colombia, and I am currently working for Mons. Corbusier in Paris on the master plan for Chandigarh, the new capital for Punjab. Do you know anything about it?' Continuing without waiting for my answer, he asked, 'What does Chandigarh mean?'

I answered him and we started talking. After a few minutes, while he was explaining proposals for Chandigarh through sketches and plans, I ventured to ask him if he would like to see my portfolio. I then showed him my work, which was obviously and greatly influenced by the work of Brazilian architect Oscar Niemeyer, who was the only modern architect I had known of while in Mumbai, and whose work had impressed me. Much later, it came as no surprise to me that Le Corbusier's work had indeed influenced Niemeyer.

I was very curious about the Chandigarh project, so we met again the next day and we talked about Chandigarh and Le Corbusier's practice at length. During that meeting, at one point, without much thought, I asked him if I could work with Le Corbusier though I knew almost nothing about him, nor did I yet possess a professional degree. It seemed to me that he welcomed my query and readily suggested that I apply to Le Corbusier, in my own handwriting.

Now, I did not know how to write a formal letter or an application. Therefore, I approached Professor S.L. Solanki—my teacher at J.J. School, who was then studying for a postgraduate degree in planning and staying at the same boarding house—for help. Samper had told me that the application had to be handwritten, and I had to rewrite it six times to get it right without a mistake.

I was anxious but not sure if I would hear from Le Corbusier and thought of it more like taking a chance. However, I received a reply immediately, in French, which I had to have translated. His offer was, 'You will not be paid for eight months. If you want to come, come.'

I did not know what to do. I had some money, but it was not sufficient for the months I would not be paid. At the same time, I knew it was a once in a lifetime opportunity and I had to take my chances. So, trusting that something would eventually work out, I left for Paris on a boat from Dover to Calais with whatever savings I had.

Concerned about getting around once I reached France and then the onward journey to Paris, I was drawn to a man dressed in a tweed jacket and wearing glasses. I hesitatingly approached him simply because he seemed liked a helpful person. It turned out that he was an Iranian living in France and knew the country and city very well. I said to him, 'I do not speak French nor know anything about France or Paris, but I must go there,' and showed him the letter from Le Corbusier.

He said, 'Do not worry, I am also going to Paris and I will help you to reach this office.' Upon reaching Paris in the evening, we shared a hotel room and a frugal meal. Next day in the morning, he hired a taxi and was kind enough to drop me across the road in front of 35 Rue de Sevres.

I profusely thanked him, put the bag on my head, Indian style, and darted across the road bringing traffic to a screeching halt. As I reached up to the Atelier climbing a wide wooden stair, Madame Jeanne, secretary to Le Corbusier, met me. 'Mr Doshi?' she asked me in English, shook hands, and informed German Samper about my arrival. In some time, I could see Samper come towards me along a passage in a long and narrow studio with tables on either side.

I had not informed him of the details of my arrival, and he seemed a bit surprised. 'Welcome,' he said. 'If you had informed me of your travel plan, I would have gladly picked you up. Come, let me introduce you to everyone here and then I will find you a hotel room. You must be exhausted.'

Once inside the studio, I saw very large, adjustable drafting boards, drawings and scores of working models all over. The entrance wall served as a large black board and a large painting hung on the rear wall. Introducing me to everyone along the entire length of the studio, Samper finally led me to his own drafting board at the end.

We stood there for some time, while he spoke of the work he was doing. He then accompanied me to a small hotel where I would stay. I guess, as a Colombian, Samper understood that I must feel like being in an alien land, so just before leaving he said, 'Don't worry. Now that you are here, it will all work out. It is Friday today, so good that you came today. You will have the whole weekend to rest. I will see you on Monday, and here is my number if you need it.'

Thus, I began yet another chapter in my life, in yet another strange city, just as in Mumbai and London earlier. Here again, the first few weeks were tough. Time flew while at the office, but at six in the evening, everyone else went home and I would be all alone.

I had no acquaintance outside of the office and worse, did not know the language. I was quite used to the English ways, but French ways and manners were so different. All stressed out, I kept asking myself what I was doing there and why had I come? Lonely, exhausted and nervous, I would go to the hotel, drink some milk and cry.

The language barrier was the toughest part initially. Knowledge of English was a bit of a problem in London too but there were so many J.J. School alumni to help me. But here, how do I ask for something as simple and basic as a sandwich or something to drink, except by pointing?

I believe what kept me going was the advice Dada had given me. He often told me. **'Bal, don't leave anything halfway because, if you do, you will repent it all your life, think of it as a failure and chances are you will never again take another risk. Determination to go on is very crucial for excellence and success.'**

He would remind me of the slogan inscribed in the symbol of my school—Nutan High School, in Pune—which in Marathi read, '*haati ghyaal te tadis nyaa*', meaning always complete the task you have undertaken. I also recalled what my father often said with regard to my future. He used to say that he would prefer to be better known as my father than have me be known as his son. That was his way of suggesting that I should work harder and do better in life than him. Slowly, I acquired the confidence to deal with my new life in the belief that there was a reason for all this to happen, just that I did not know what it was, but I must go on and do my best.

At the office, I had to muster a lot of determination and even courage to get going. I was assigned to work on the High Court at Chandigarh, the sections were already firmed up, I had to detail them and reflect that in the plan. Strangely nobody asked if I could do such work because it was assumed that I was a trained architect whereas I was not.

I still can recall how nervous I was on the first day at the office. It was not so much about being an Indian, however, since there were architects from so many nationalities. It was about my skills and understanding of architecture, especially Corbusier's ways. Everybody else seemed well acquainted with the Master's way of working and they were all busy preparing drawing, making models and such.

Yet, they were all as different as possible, hailing from different countries and cultures. There was a Greek engineer-architect and an avant-garde musician Iannis Xenakis, who later became a very close friend; Acevedo Tobito, a Venezuelan; Rogelio Salmona, a Colombian architect; Jacque Michel, a French architect and André Maisonnier, a rather senior member of the Atelier's team.

I was, of course, the first Indian to work with Le Corbusier, also the youngest in both age and work experience at the office. Not knowing French was a major handicap. For weeks, I did not know what they were discussing with each other. Being a strict vegetarian and having limited funds, I avoided joining them for lunch and took to eating olives, cheese and bread with Sachinidis, a Greek draughtsman who could only speak Greek and French.

Although our day at the Atelier began at nine in the morning, I would arrive even earlier. I would generally start the day by going around the studio to see what the others were doing. Since I had never read Le Corbusier's writings, nor seen drawings and photographs of his designs; this habit helped me to become familiar with his way of thinking.

What fascinated me at the office was something I saw in everyone's eyes, expressions and gestures. There was a deep sense of camaraderie, a sense of freedom, affection for each other and most importantly, the way they approached their work. It was like everybody there was very conscious of the significance of the work they were doing.

My learning in the Atelier began with André Maisonnier. On my starting work, he gave me a large tracing showing several sections and elevations of the portico walls in the high court entrance. Now André could not speak English and I could not speak French, so Samper would come to our rescue now and then and explain what André wanted me to do.

Seeing those tracings of the High Court, I wondered what should I draw or where I should even begin. I asked myself as to what hidden solutions I was expected to discover in the thick portico walls. Therefore, to help understand the sections, I began to trace them.

I was actually jittery when I began to trace because I had never before used a bow pen, which was commonly used there. All I had ever used were soft pencils. Therefore, my ink lines came out uneven and I spent a lot of time trying to scratch them out with a razor blade, smooth the surface with my thumbnail, and redraw.

For me it was disheartening to see Maisonnier, Jacque Michel, Sachinidis and Samper develop designs from Corbusier's sketches and produce beautiful drawings all the time and so effortlessly. That made me more nervous and I did not know whom to ask for help.

Samper, sitting right behind me, must have realized my predicament. One day, he came over and guided me about developing design from sketches and drawing with a bow pen. He also assured me saying, 'Doshi, don't you worry. When Monsieur comes, he will show you how and what to design. I too have gone through this.' Some way to learn architecture, I thought! Will I be able to satisfy Le Corbusier? That was my greatest concern.

Corbusier came to the Atelier a few days after I had started working there. He first attended to some routine matters and after that came and stood across my table. I looked up at him and greeted him sheepishly, he looked at me, and then at the drawing on my table. It was obvious that he realized the state I was in, smiled and speaking slowly in cryptic English, as if to a child, he gestured to me to move, came over to my side and sat down on my stool.

'Show me all the drawings,' he said. He then took the sheet full of sections and elevations and placed a piece from the yellow tracing roll over it. With pencils, he started drawing and explaining to me what he was doing and why, like he was a teacher in a classroom and I was a student.

Drawing the outline of the inclined roof, he drew three human figures standing at the base of the section. 'This is how you measure scale of the building. Do you now see how large this volume is? Remember the reality is always measured by how and what we perceive. It depends on our perceptions.'

He then drew a round cornered rectangle at the base. 'Notice this; I am making an opening in the wall. This way we can now see across, towards another wall,' he said. Once again, he drew a human figure near the opening but now it was a seated figure.

Then, placing another tracing paper he again copied the outline, drew another rectangle, but slightly shifted, saying, 'Notice how two openings create transparency and make the wall porous. Connectivity, movement is what makes architecture. Remember, animating the walls starts a dialogue and thus they become active elements of architecture. Always bring life to all static elements and connect buildings to the cosmos. Give each element an identity by making it face its own self.'

Then he added, 'If you stagger the openings, views change, the change compels the eyes and body to move. Never allow only one experience of the same kind in a space.'

Taking another sheet, he drew two thin lines made of concrete at the end of the ramp and drew a standing figure. He increased the height of the parapets to the figure's chest height and said, 'See how the change of heights directs movements. When one moves between the side wall of the ramp and the parapet, one must feel as if sandwiched.' To help me understand better he drew another section of the ramp with the parapet height reduced.

'Never make such low parapets when you want people to see only in a particular direction. While walking, compel a person to feel the tight space and appreciate the tunnel-like space.' Drawing shadows on the elevation of a wall, he said, 'Notice how the High Court orientation is expressed. See its reflection in the water pool below.'

This was my first lesson on how to judge scale, create dynamic walls and make people move in the direction one wants. Transforming static elements into dynamic elements, creating varied scales and establishing connections with surroundings is the most essential part of architecture, I thought.

I had never before dealt with such large buildings and high volumes, nor did any of my teachers ask us to draw sections and plans concurrently or explain their significance in the design process. 'They are the generators, and, without them, architecture does not materialize,' Maisonnier explained in his broken English one day.

Thus, I learnt to draw, to see architecture in three dimensions using sections and plans, and tried to compensate for my lack of education by doing all kinds of exercises on my own when alone. I had acquired this habit in childhood when I would pick up wooden pieces and shavings from the family's furniture workshop, carry them upstairs to the third-floor landing, assemble them in many different ways and observe the resulting forms in silence.

At the Atelier, I had been noticing drawings with regulating lines drawn all over them, superimposed, and had been very curious about them for quite some time. I asked around and learnt that the office checked all the plans, sections and elevations for proportions using sequential dimensions from the Modular developed by Le Corbusier himself based on the Golden Section.

The atmosphere in the studio itself was a great experience for me. There were drawings and study models all over the place. There were drawings of Maison Jaoul in Paris pinned right next to those of Villa Sarabhai in Ahmedabad. Those of the High Court building hung next to those of the Secretariat in Chandigarh. It was all very instructive; about not only architecture but also how varied functions and varied scales offer choices to discover different ways to experience architecture and how design progresses from an idea to final design.

That is how I finally began to learn architecture after travelling across the continents. I often think of those four years spent at Corbusier's Atelier like the fabled journeys taken by Hindu scholars who, in ancient times, went to Varanasi and the Himalayas to find a guru and seek knowledge.

As they say, everything in life has its own price. My perseverance as well as hard work must have impressed Corbusier, because he started paying me a salary from the sixth month itself despite his letter mentioning that he would not pay me for the first eight months. That was a big relief, for now I could enjoy the small pleasures of Paris instead of living on olive and bread, which had been my staple food for the past six months.

I now realize that all the events that significantly influenced my life—which I had thought were accidents—were actually destined to happen. These occurred when I was not aware, not conscious of my ego or of being logical, and always caught me by surprise. However, these were scenarios, situations, which I had subconsciously visualized and forgotten; situations drew me towards them.

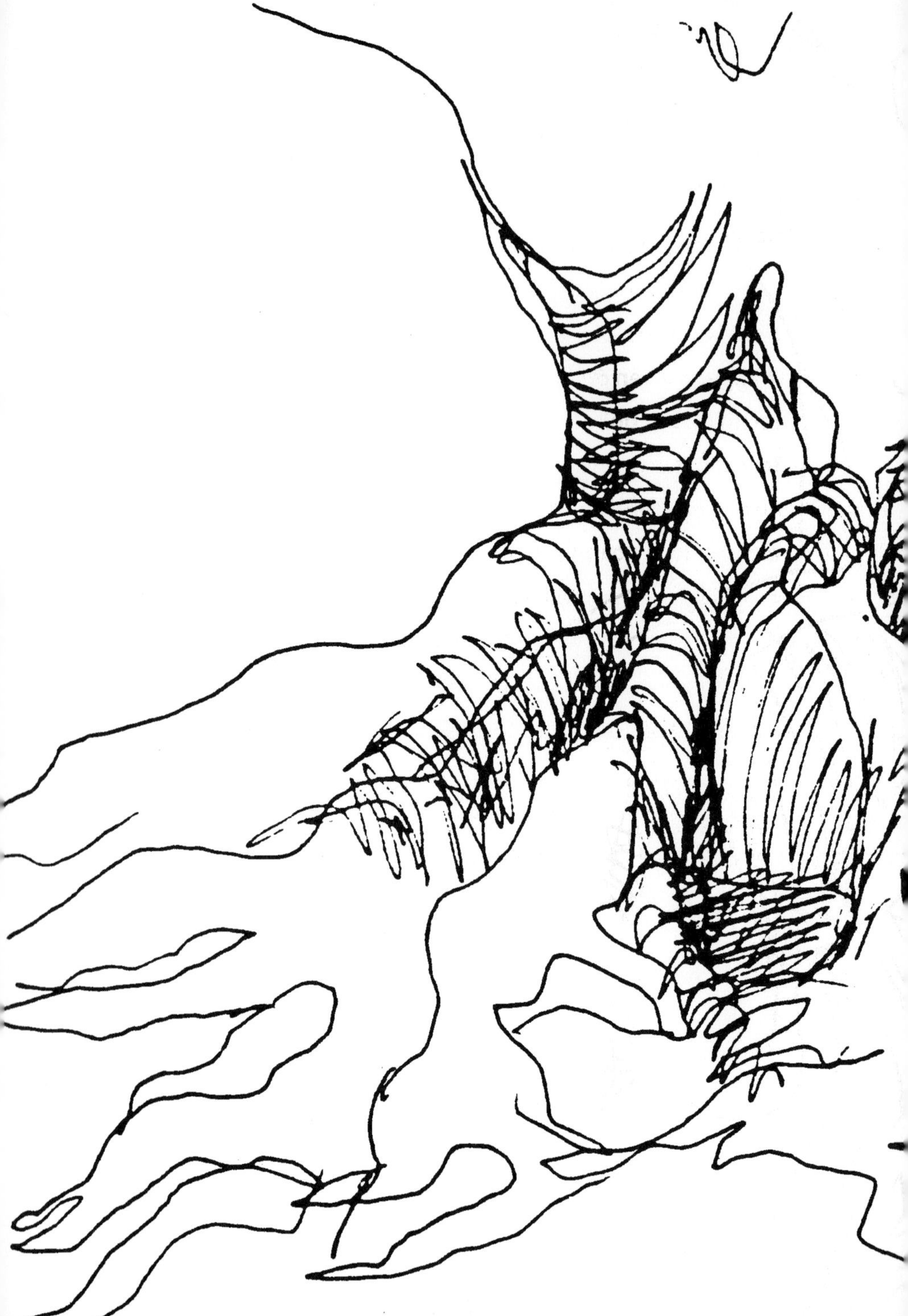

I have observed that growth and survival are an integral part of nature. A small seed hides within it the potential of becoming either a big banyan tree or a modest flowering plant. Only the seed knows what transforms it to become any of those. This means one can go back to one's seed potential. That happens when one meditates. Over the years, I have learnt this technique of going within by practising yoga.

To establish roots, one should create one's own mythology and establish one's own contexts. Without this framing, architecture cannot become valid. Climate, technology, function and economy are normal ways of establishing the context of architecture. However, they would not necessarily touch the psyche, which links the past, the present and the future.

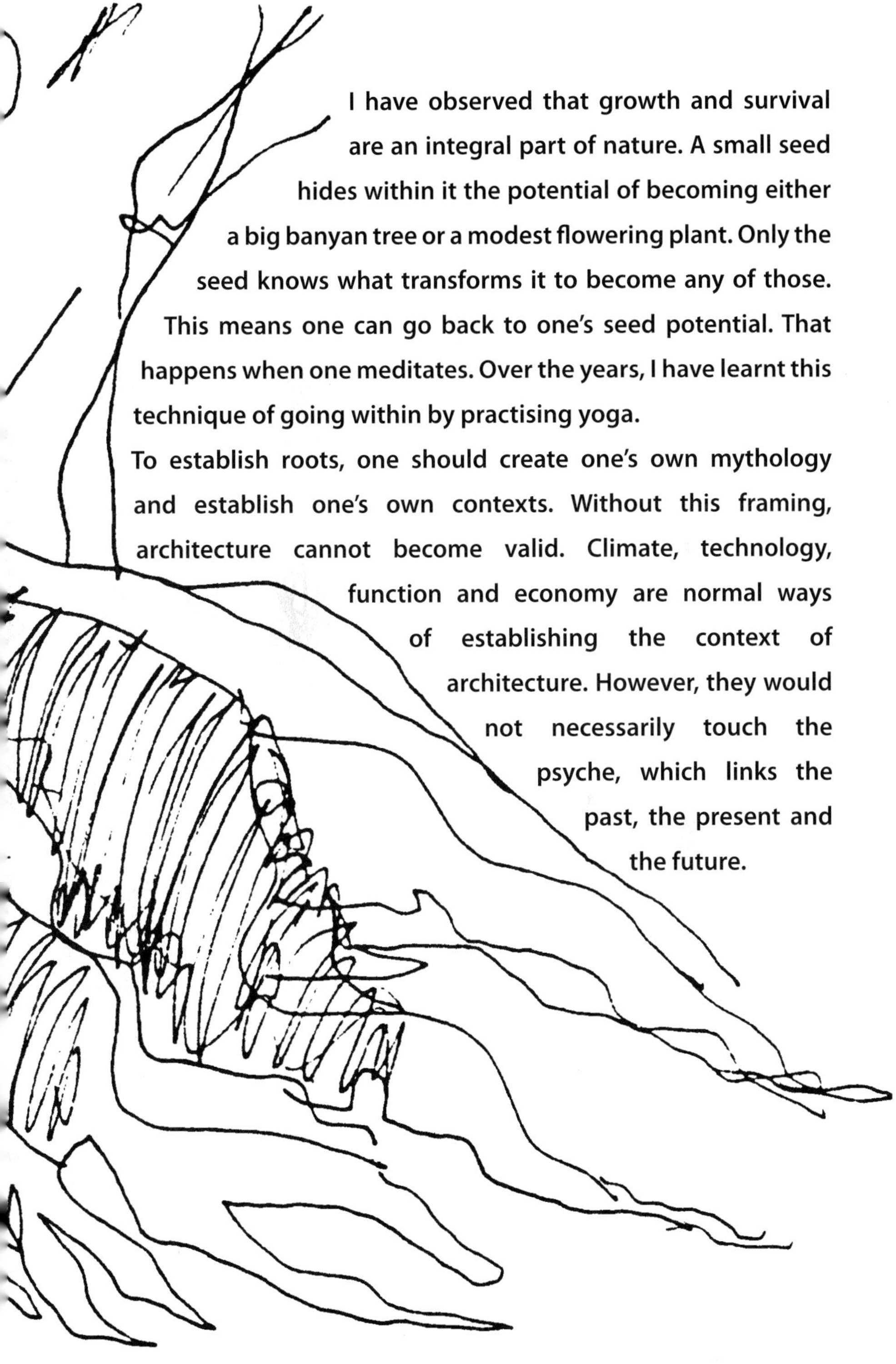

Some of
the strongest
memories and
images in my life include
going to a temple, offering
prayers, attending enactment
of stories from the epics such as
Mahabharata and Ramayana, recitation
of sacred hymns in and around Pune.
I was born and brought up in a very traditional,
middle-class family and, yet, my life has turned so
differently! It puzzles me no end.

After I had completed high school, I joined a painting class at the Institute of Modern Art run by Venkatesh Patil. Diwakar Dengle, my neighbour and classmate, introduced me to the place. I spent two years at the institute going to villages for drawing landscapes, traditional houses, small temples, rural folks, animals, etc., and quite enjoyed the company of the new friends I made at the Institute. With all that exposure I had at the Institute, I began to discover myself.

'Why don't you join J.J. School of Architecture?' Patil asked me one day. 'You are good in maths and science and draw very well. What else would you do after graduating in science? Join your family's business, making furniture?' His question opened a new door for me. Now, that question had never occurred to me before. Put differently it was, 'Would I carry on my ancestral legacy, or would I take an untravelled path?' My attempts to answer this question excited me as well as scared me.

In those days, moving to a big city at that young an age—especially for someone with my background—was almost unthinkable. However, my elder brother Vallabh came to my rescue and agreed to let me go. So, I went to Bombay and joined the J.J School of Architecture. Bombay was such a different world from the one at Pune. I was suddenly amidst a very cosmopolitan group of students comprising Parsis, Christians, and others from all over India. Almost all of them were very urbane in their ways and conversed fluently in English. For a while, I was clueless.

I was used to living in the sheltered comfort of the extended family in our Pune home whereas, here, I was sharing a room with strangers at a boarding house near the college. Except for me, the four other occupants were often travellers coming to Mumbai on business.

Every day, at least one of the other occupants would ask me as to

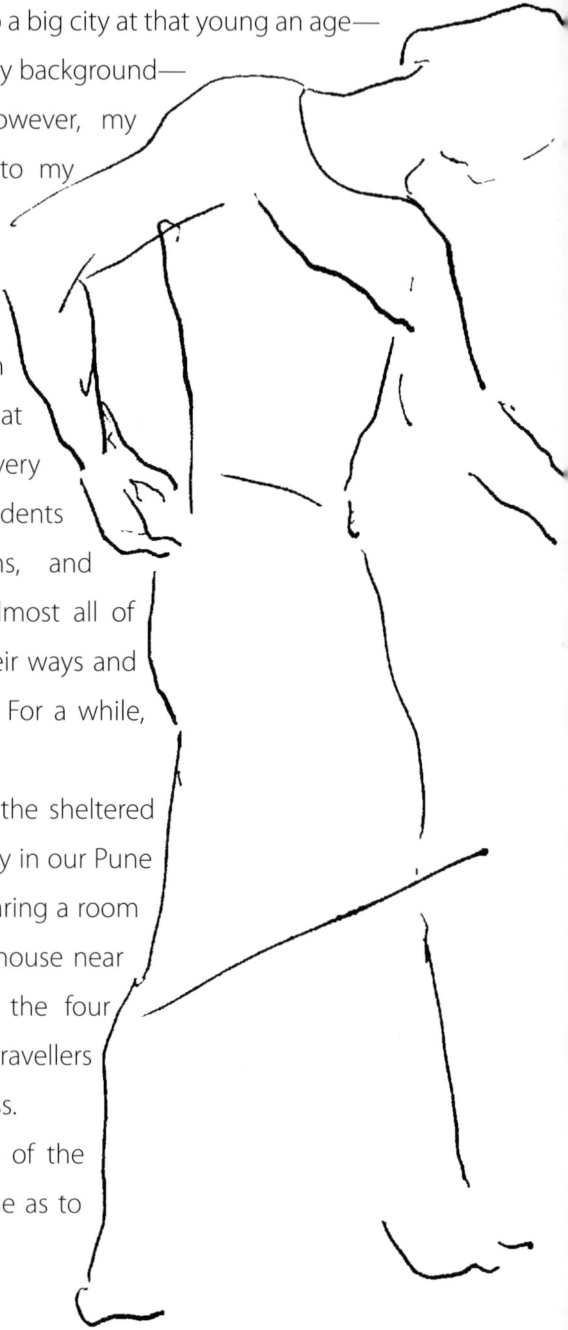

what architecture was and why I wanted to be an architect. While it got repetitive and boring over time, it was a good experience. It offered me glimpses into life in the different regions from where they came. It also made me aware of the place of architecture in common person's life as I tried to answer their questions.

The boarding house experiences often remind me of my time at Atelier Le Corbusier. The Atelier was, in some ways, a place of pilgrimage for all those interested in modern architecture. So, there were many visitors from all over the world, and this offered glimpses into the different countries, ethnic groups, cultures, and yet, universal aspirations of people everywhere.

It was there I met international architects like Ernesto Rogers from Milan, Dr Sigfried Giedion and Alfred Roth from Zurich, Pier Luigi Nervi, the engineer from Rome, Serge Chermayeff, Jose Louis Sert from the US, Lucio Costa from Brazil, Jacqueline Tyrwhitt from England and many others from the CIAM group.

The studio was constantly buzzing with discussions in several languages about architecture and life in our home countries. Once I started receiving a pay, we would go to bookshops, lunch in the various bistros that dotted Paris and attend events at galleries, concerts and theatres. It was, I must say, a great place and time to learn about architecture and life.

I also attended lectures on sociology and arts with German Samper, Rogelio Salmona and others at Sorbonne University. I started seeing French films, which helped me to learn French rather quickly. Soon, I spoke French without any accent and lived like a Frenchman; including going hitchhiking all over Europe, as was the custom then.

However, that happened after what seemed like a long time. In the first few months of being in Paris, with no one to converse with, I would often walk alone before reaching my hotel room. I would hesitantly ask for milk and a cheese sandwich at the cheapest bistro I could find and would eat by myself in the hotel room while looking out from a narrow vertical window.

When I did not wish to walk, I rode the bus rather than the underground metro so I could see the streetscapes, the displays in the shop fronts, and large buildings with several stories lining the streets of massive stone walls, carvings on building facades. These seemed many times larger than those in Bombay. The richness of the city had a great impact on me in the initial days. Grand open spaces, large public buildings embellished with statues of lions, men and women standing tall against dozens of kiosks, and hundreds of billboards announcing cinema shows, or theatrical or musical events offered fascinating sights.

Owing to Xenakis's interest in modern music and his close friendship with avant-garde composers such as Edgard Varèse and Olivier Messiaen, I became aware about Western classical and modern music. Together, we spent many evenings at the concert halls in Paris, visited museums, went camping in the summer and spent time in the small towns around.

I learnt so much else about societal issues, politics—especially Leftist politics—and concerns of the have-nots. For the first time, I became conscious of the poorer segments of the society everywhere and not just in Pune or India—these I was aware of already. I believe this phase of my life has had the greatest and longest-lasting impact on my work and world view. Frugal living, making most of available resources, economies in architecture from the choice of building materials to appropriate construction techniques, emphasis on multiple use of spaces; these have been important concerns all my life since then.

Paris being Paris, there were plenty of opportunities to meet artists from India such as S.H. Raza, F.N. Souza, Akbar Padamsee and Paritosh Sen in bistros near Cité Universitaire. I also lived for a while in a room at Maison du Japon and, luckily, my room faced the Swiss Pavilion. That building, like the icon of a deity in a temple, became the object of my daily morning darshan.

When finally I talked about leaving, Le Corbusier was not willing to let me return to India; but he knew about my chronic colitis and reluctantly agreed.

A few days before my departure, he invited me to his home at Rue Nungesser et Coli for lunch, which was a rare treat for anyone. Even now, I vividly remember that visit.

The most striking element of his apartment was the spiral staircase with one vertical pipe that served as a railing: so sculptural, reaching the glass-enclosed terrace cabin. That apartment offers a supreme lesson in an incredible flow of spaces. Each room there flows into another with his characteristically large full-height pivoted doors. Its plan and spaces conveyed everything that one could also see in his Purist paintings of the 1930s.

He had also designed the furniture. I well remember the dining table: I felt the exquisitely chiselled edge of the white marble top with only two steel pipes for support. Then, there was the leather sofa, sliding shutters on cupboards, a selectively displayed painting of his and other objects of art. The place felt very intimate.

After the meal, Corbusier took me to his personal study and then, pointing his finger at a stack of sketches and drawings on a table, he said, 'Choose one.' I hesitated but then picked one—a 1942 gouache of four women. He said, 'You have good taste. Pick another.' I picked another. 'I am happy you chose that,' he said. He then picked one himself and gave it to me saying, 'Here is another one for you.'

He then signed them all and said, 'How about a certificate? You will need it in India. People will ask.' He picked another, wrote in French 'Excellent Architect' and signed it 'Le Corbusier'. 'This will do you good,' he said. At that moment, I felt like I was in India and here was my guru, blessing me. Even now, I feel his presence every day.

Corbusier did not want me to leave until the Indian projects were close to completion. Mme Jeanne, his secretary, however, began to pass on the correspondence about the Indian projects to me even though Samper and Jacque Michael were actually handling the projects.

In the meanwhile, P.L. Varma—the secretary and chief engineer of the Chandigarh Capitol project—realizing the need to expedite the execution of Governor's Palace, wanted me at the Chandigarh site office immediately. So, he created a special post for me and asked Corbusier to relieve me at the earliest.

It was now clear that I was going back to India. Leaving Paris was not easy in the least. This was the place where I truly learnt architecture. This was the place where I learnt all about the achievements of Western civilization and lived a life so different from my upbringing and yet, so very fulfilling.

Would I ever live these times again? Sadness appeared between the plans of departure and the enigma of arrival. Would I come back to these places? In the 1950s, travel was not as simple as it has now become and even as I was happy to come back, I was sad to leave. Just in case things did not work out again, I decided to travel to various places in Europe celebrated by architects of all time before I set sail for India.

I decided to go to Brindisi on the southern coast of Italy, Priene in Greece, and then to Alexandria in Egypt as main destinations in those countries. In Alexandria, I would board a ship sailing to Bombay. There was to be no fixed schedule except the departure from Alexandria and I would spend as much time as I wanted at all other significant places along the route.

I had planned to hitchhike all along. So, to travel light, I shipped ahead my books, one large wooden box for my newly purchased drafting board similar to the one in Le Corbusier's studio and an oil painting presented to me by S.H. Raza. That painting was a complete surprise. One day, as I was preparing to leave Paris, Raza just came over to my room and presented his most recent work as a parting gift. What a gesture of friendship!

Soon, I began what I then regarded as my last chance to see achievements of other cultures in Europe, especially in the field of visual arts. My time in Paris and journeys to other parts of France had exposed me well to the developments in general, but I wanted to see some of these first-hand. I had already taken my chances, moving from J.J. School in Bombay to Corbusier's famed Atelier in Paris via London, and did not really know if I would do such a thing again.

So, a few days later, I was in the office of Vittorio Gregotti, where I saw the plan of Rome drawn by 17th century Italian architect Piranesi. With criss-crossing arches, staircases and plans of varied building types, this drawing really fascinated me. Structural elements supporting large, deep vaults, openings allowing indirect light with their varied configurations of spaces and scales navigated multiple stories in this drawing. In his plan for Rome, I saw how weights, plans, structure, rhythm, configuration created infinite volumes and both inside and outside.

Prints of many such drawings hang on the walls of my studio at Sangath because they are a link to many phases and events of my life. In them are hidden my childhood, my school days, my professional life, my family life and inspirational sources which have guided me all along.

I also went to Ernesto Roger's office in Milan, having met him earlier at the Atelier in Paris. He introduced me to two other guests at his office, Brian Richards from London, and an architect from the US whose name I now forget. They were also visiting Milan as part of their European travel and we decided to go around the city together.

I want to recall this because of a rather unusual incident. Remember, in those days the world was not as well connected as it is now. There were not so many tourists from different countries and races criss-crossing the world, or so much exposure to different cultures afforded by today's digital media.

As we moved around the city, at one point, the three of us happened to be in this magnificent but modest church, appreciating its interiors. Suddenly four old women dressed in black came close to all three of us.

First, one lady touched me, then the other touched Brian, and a third one touched our architect friend from the US and pulled at his thick, curly hair, as if to check all of us were for real! Then they started to talk to one another excitedly pointing fingers at us now and then.

When eventually we did understand what all the excitement was about, it was a real surprise. Together, we were an unusual bunch: Brian was White, the other architect was African-American, and I was a brown man from India. Somehow, in that church, we reminded those women of the Magi—three wise men who appeared at the time of Christ's birth!

This encounter made me think about how associations and memories eliminate sense of time and space. Should not our work and activities contain such myths?

If Vallabh and *bhabhi*, my sister-in-law, had not agreed to support me, if I had not come to London, I would not have been in Paris or in Milan, on my way to Athens via Rome and Venice and finally Alexandria. Our ancestors have left behind so much by way of myths, history and heritage for us to help rediscover our origins and our purpose.

I do not know why but I tend to think and even dream like this. I do not like confinement and my dreams belong to me. Isn't this journey connecting centuries similar? Is there a hidden undercurrent in all this? Is there a binding thread that joins the real and the imagined? Have we forgotten our sense of wonder, the magic and mystery of light and shadow, appearance and disappearance of surfaces, silhouettes, sounds and greenery?

I remembered Le Corbusier's discussions on cities and my own experience as a child. Why did these people think so much about celebrating life all the time, and why do we not? Is something wrong in the way we move, gather; go around without a second glance?

Why are we always rushing from one place to another, from one event to another, and not walking? Why do we not have time for the finer things? Are not sculpture, colours, paintings, frescos, songs, dances part of our inner being? Le Corbusier always talked about his painting and sculpture; is this not an ancient tradition? There is so much art embodied in good buildings. What impact does it have on architecture?

Many of these questions were answered when I was next in Venice. What a magical city! So different from the others, with its people-friendly gondolas moving quietly in the canals, the numerous footbridges, friendly open spaces and the overpowering silence.

With its rather virtuous constraints, how could there be fast movement along some grand boulevards? Then again, what purpose would that serve? Are not intimacy, slow pace, and interaction and silence important ingredients of good city life?

When I reached Piazza San Marco, I recalled Corbusier describing it—and very aptly at that—as the biggest living room in the world. So many types of buildings existed in one place. It was like several centuries frozen in time. **Each one of those buildings spoke a different language, yet human aspirations had strung them together. Otherwise, how can one explain the differences between the facades of the library court, the Doge's Palace and St Mark's Basilica?**

I believe the doges asked architects to create the magical experience of the Eastern world in the design of the Basilica. In these buildings, I really understood the richness that good design development contributes to detailing: be it the mosaic floor, the domes, the frescos, the doors or the stained glass works.

How does one create a dream that one cannot even begin to describe? In a dream, we are mostly happy. In a dream, there is nothing to lose. Here, I am thinking of the Indraprastha palace mentioned in the epic Mahabharata. Created by *maya*, it is said to have had many illusionary experiences built in there.

For example, the regular floor in a passage might appear to be a pool of water; this would lead to many embarrassing situations for the occupants who would move about trying not to get their feet or clothes wet. That illusion was indeed intended. Perhaps architecture has the power to create such illusions, but we have lost those skills.

What an experience it was to see gondolas right on one edge of the San Marco plaza floor! Until I went there, I had not realized the wonder of not having any steps or level difference between water and the floor that was the norm in India.

On some days, I learnt to my surprise, water does cover the entire piazza and people traverse on temporary raised wooden paths. Such a gesture expresses people's love for life. That despite a few seasonal inconveniences, celebrations and joys offered by a place must be cherished and life must go on.

Equally memorable is the visit to the Acropolis. I had heard and read glowing descriptions of it. It took me a while to connect to the place and achievements of the individual and the whole group of buildings. Eventually, observing from the buildings located on the edge overlooking the amphitheatre and their connection to the vast horizon really impressed me.

Wandering on the periphery of the Parthenon, I discovered a different view of the surrounding landscape. Some distance away, caryatids were holding up part of another temple, that of Erechtheion. Was it an ancient practice to use human beings to support buildings, I wondered.

Thinking of the site of Acropolis itself, I was reminded of our temple sites. These too are always located on high spots in the landscape, visible from far away. They are somewhat physically isolated to make it difficult to reach, yet visible enough to attract the devout.

All is in the mind
give up EGO
Separation, identity
become "That"
become everything
It's only a
notion an Experience

Temple is not
a temple
nor is the statue
a statue
or the Samatgam
a Sangagrum

Walk-see-feel the connectedness
These are all walls – create one
space, one room, one notion

Rest is all shadow

Overall, it was a very educative and joyous trip—made even more so by working long hours in an office for four years in Paris. I could see important milestones in the development of architecture and the cities in Europe. It also offered me ample time and opportunities to reflect on my own past and the future that awaited me at the end of the trip.

Travelling to places off the beaten path means that public transport is not available. This meant that I often sought rides from motorists. Waiting on the roadside watching cars zoom past can be fun provided one is not seeking a ride. For a ride, one must be patient and persevere—sometimes for hours—especially in desolate areas.

I remember once, having waited long for a ride, I was puzzled to see a truck full of melons pass by and then reverse some distance. The driver asked us what we were doing in that desolate place and learning that we had been waiting long hours for a ride, he offered to take us to a place close enough to Brindisi.

It was still a long ride that passed closely by his own village. So, he asked us, 'Would you like to sleep in my house tonight? I am sure you will enjoy our dinner and of course, the melons. Please do not hesitate.' Camaraderie among strangers is often instantaneous, despite the language barrier.

So, a friend and I spent the night at his home, had our breakfast with him and, for most of the morning, became a focus of this small village. We were introduced to almost all the residents and drank several cups of coffee with them. It was such joy to experience simple acts of humanity in strange lands and places.

This is so different from the life in cities. I wonder sometimes if it is our own doing that we live a routine, mechanical life without the joys of simple pleasures such as I experienced that time on the way to Brindisi.

Finally, my first true vacation, or I should say a very educative tour, ended in Alexandria via Athens.

My return journey on the boat was a very pleasant experience as compared to my trip from Bombay to Genoa four years previously. I was able to enjoy my cabin, food, dance and drinks in the dining hall. It was fun.

It started right from the moment I was boarding the ship. I was asked to show my passport at the gate to verify my identity. When I asked later why, the official said it was because I held a first-class ticket but had turned up wearing clothes that looked like I had slept in them for several days. That was indeed true; I was hitchhiking, I told him, and we laughed.

The reality of leaving Paris hit me on the journey. Despite the troubles in the early stages, I had started to enjoy my work there as well as the quality of life it offered. I wondered if I would ever go back there or to any of other places that I had visited or wished to visit.

All kinds of thoughts flashed through my mind. A lot of them concerned the pros and cons of the two entirely different ways of living and viewing the world, relating to family members, friends, colleagues, and the larger community.

Not to forget adjusting back to the ways I had left behind four or five years ago. I had no savings, and I was returning home with only the experience of having worked with a great architect and travelled distant lands.

What little money I had on the boat, I spent on a rather expensive party I threw for some of my co-passengers whom I had befriended. I wanted to reach home with good memories and so I called them, and ordered a large cake and lots of wine. My last franc disappeared with this gesture.

Many of my new friends had their future very well planned. One of them was returning to teach at Fergusson College in Pune, while another was joining the family business; as for me, I was not so sure.

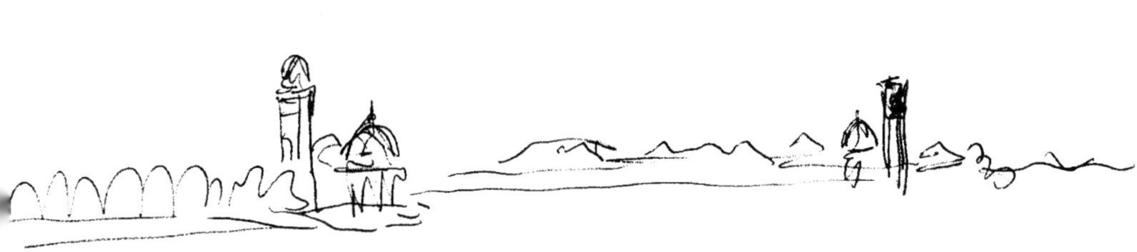

As the ship neared Bombay, I suddenly felt homesick and all the memories that lay dormant came rushing back. I remembered our house in Pune where I grew up, and all of the members of my extended family who meant so much to me.

Anxiety suddenly gripped me. I had not kept in touch with anyone of them and had no clue as to the state of affairs in the lives of my kith and kin. I did even not know whether my brother Vallabh would be there at the port when I landed.

Would he be happy to see me, or would he be angry for not writing to him more often? Besides the backpack, I had nothing, not even a rupee to buy gifts for anyone. What would I do?

I knew how much they all loved me but what would they be thinking, Vallabh and my *bhabhi*? Would they expect me to join the furniture business or allow me to leave them again to work in Chandigarh? I had written to them a short letter about my arrival a few weeks earlier.

But he was there as I disembarked. With joy and tears, and without a word, Vallabh embraced me. I felt at home. 'Would you lend me a thousand rupees?' I asked Vallabh almost immediately. 'You have not changed at all, Bal. I remember your habits very well,' he said as he handed me the money.

'We wondered if you would ever return, you did not write for months together. Were you angry because we did not send you any money? Were you all right there or you did not want us to know if you were not? How did you manage in Paris without money, not knowing the language? We missed you so much during Diwali, our New Year celebrations and all other festivals but we always prayed for you. Many a vow your *bhabhi* kept for your safety and return! Did you enjoy your work, make any friends?' he continued inquiring to make up for all the years that we had not communicated.

It was as if I had walked back into a situation that had been frozen for four years, full of affection. There was no talk about my work or personal progress, or even money. However, they were quite anxious to know more about the distant lands I had seen.

So, more questions followed: 'Is it true that the streets in Paris are made of glass because they say they are so clean and shiny? Is Paris a beautiful city? We hear that Prime Minister Nehru's clothes are sent to Paris for dry cleaning, is that true? And how has your health been all this time?'

The questions kept coming and I answered them as best as I could. However, when I mentioned about my plans for working in Chandigarh with Le Corbusier, for a moment, Vallabh was taken aback. Here I was again going off, if not abroad, elsewhere in India, he must have thought. So, he asked, 'Why do you want to go to Chandigarh? Don't you want to join our family workshop and practise architecture in Pune?'

He must have realized it was all too much too soon, because he finally said: 'Well, you have just arrived after so many years and we would like you to come and stay with us for at least two weeks. Besides, we want to show you a girl your *bhabhi* has chosen for you.'

'You used to know her, and I have made all the arrangements,' *bhabhi* added later while we were having dinner. Observing my indifference, *bhabhi* asked, 'Do you have any other girl in mind, here or in Paris?' Perhaps she wanted me to join Vallabh as a furniture manufacturer.

Suddenly, I felt like I did not belong there, to their world. Marriage was the last thing on my mind. There was so much exciting work to do, of building a very modern Indian capital city and all those Capitol buildings with one of the foremost architect-planners in the world. It was a project that was practically unique and a very rare opportunity for sure.

How could I have explained my priorities and my aspirations—now bolstered by my work during the last four years—to them? I did the best I could and finally assured them that I would take their consent before taking any decision about my marriage. Thus assured, they relented and let me leave for Chandigarh.

I still wonder, had I married then, would I be writing these notes today?

I very much enjoyed the few weeks I spent in Pune. Although I had hardly thought of the place and the people during the last few years, my stay reconnected me to both. I recalled my life before I left for Bombay, London, then Paris and this allowed me to revisit the nature of my association with the place.

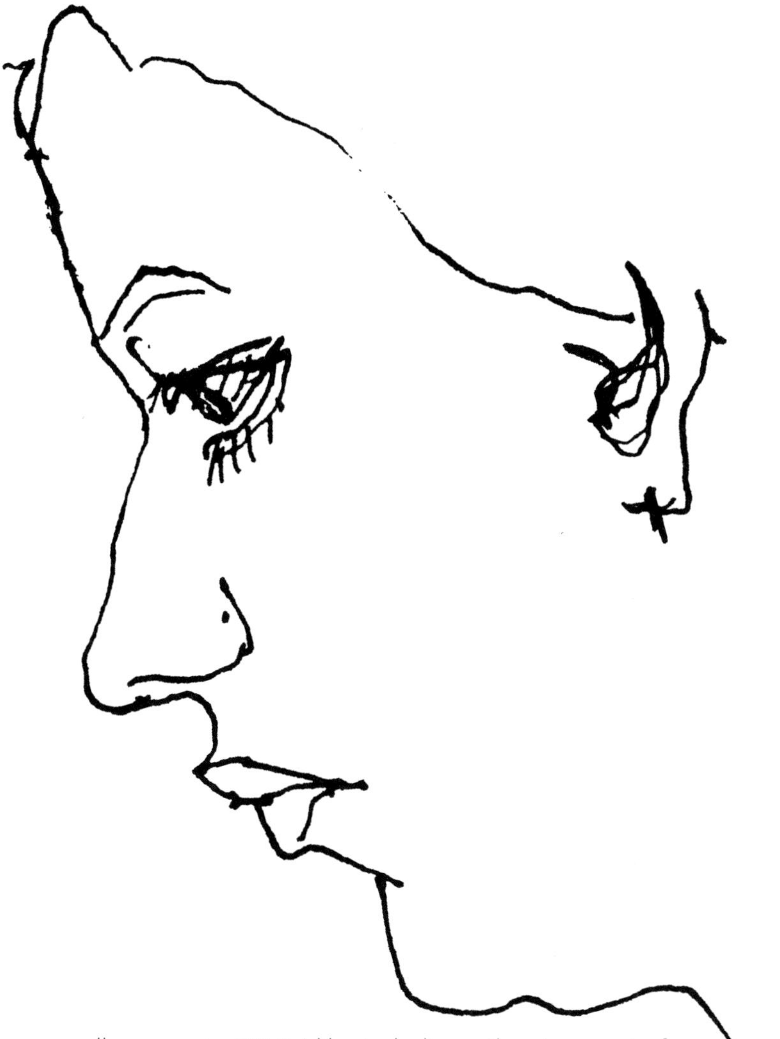

Then, as well as now in 2019, I like to believe, the strongest of my memories were those relating to my mother, my Dada and a rather serious accident I suffered as a young boy. I particularly recall the six months I spent in bed in one of the rooms after serious burn injuries on my leg. That I escaped amputation with only a slight limp is still a wonder to me. Was it the doctor? Was it the care? Or was it my mother whose presence I have felt on several occasions since then assuring me of protection and support?

There are times in life when one feels a vacuum. At such times, there is an inner calling, wanting to be all alone in isolation and silence. In my case, such has happened a few times but one of them is the most memorable. This happened when I was 11 years old. I burned my right leg, and it was my own fault. I had often watched with fascination the way in which my elder brother lit the kerosene stove. A part of it involved him inserting a burning prong in a bottle full of petrol. This would catch fire, and he would quickly douse it by putting the cap back on. It was like magic.

One day, careful not to be noticed by my aunts, I tried this trick but could not put the lid back quickly enough. Hence, the petrol in the bottle kept burning making the bottle hot. Scared, I let go of the bottle. That spilled the burning petrol on the floor and, as I had been sitting cross-legged on the floor, my shorts caught fire causing deep burns on my right leg. Luckily, my younger aunt heard all the commotion and rushed in, saw what had happened, fetched a blanket, covered my leg and doused the fire. Soon, all the other members of the family surrounded me. I could gather from their talk that it was a very serious burn injury. As far as I was concerned, it was a disaster and I felt so much pain, fear and shame for having done such a stupid thing.

Soon, I went blank. Much later, when I opened my eyes, I found myself all alone in the main room of the house with a bandage on the right leg. It was the same semi-dark space where I would play with my cousins all the time. Days, weeks, and months passed as I lay there with no one except for my aunt and my sisters to talk to most of the time. Of course, everyone passed through the room as they went about their daily activities but that was it.

After several weeks of dressing the wounds at home and trying home remedies, the elders realized that infection had set in and that it was very bad. Finally, Dr Vamanrao Apte, who had studied allopathic medicine, was called. As I lay there in my semiconscious state, I heard him speak softly, 'There is sepsis; the right leg is full of pus and he needs special medicines. Otherwise, we will have to amputate his leg to save his life.'

That was a particularly bad night, though not much worse than most others when I lay semiconscious and delirious from fever and pain. After everyone had retired for the night, there was silence, which was broken by someone playing popular songs of those days on a gramophone. One of them spoke of the singer's desire to build a unique bungalow for a joyous life and the other, like a lullaby, urged a princess to sleep well and peacefully. In my state, these songs began to haunt me.

I may have been dreaming of a joyous life and a good sleep, but they were not to be. Later, my pain grew unbearable, I could no more move nor cry, nor shout. Suddenly, I heard myself being called by my nickname, Balya. 'Balya, it is me, your mother,' the voice said. 'Do not worry, I am here with you. You will soon get well, and be just as good as you were before.'

I also felt as if she was gently stroking me, and patting me. She finally placed her hand on my infected wound with a healing touch. I felt as if the lullaby being played on the gramophone had come true and soon I went to sleep. Even today, I do not know for sure if it was the new medicines or my mother's healing touch, but I recovered very quickly after that night, albeit left with a slight limp.

Even today, I feel my mother's presence whenever I am lonely or desperate. Over the years, I have heard her voice many times through the utterances of my aunt while in a state of trance, the same aunt who had covered me with a blanket on the day of the accident. From what Dada told me later, my mother had asked her to look after us before she died. Perhaps her spirit was always present within my aunt, watching over and helping me all the time.

That night, I dreamt that my mother said to me: 'Do you know why your name is Bal, short for Balkrishna? You are to me the young Lord Krishna. Don't you want to be like him, always fully conscious of your duties? You have to remove poverty and bring prosperity. Don't you remember the story of Kaliya, the vicious cobra in Jamuna River? Krishna fought and vanquished him, and thus brought safety, peace, and prosperity in the region. I know you will be like him. With your work, you have to build a prosperous society, a paradise on earth. Remember no harm will ever come to you and I will always be there to guide you.'

Years later, Dr Pulin Garg, a renowned psychiatrist, told me about the significance of the *namadhikaran* ceremony—when a newborn is first given a name—on the 10th day.

He said that this ancient ritual is important because it moulds the person in the inherent spirit of his or her name; the name indeed influences the character of the person.

I can only hope that I have been true to my mother's wishes and my own name.

Among the other significant memories from my childhood is that of Dada's towering persona. Tall and well built, with a prominent Vaishnava tilak on his forehead, and dressed formally in the traditional manner with an elaborate turban or *pagadi*, he looked like a prince despite having lost his right eye. He was never religious in a dogmatic sense, but he was full of spiritual wisdom. Not only did he teach me much about religious ceremonies and rituals, he also explained their relevance and importance.

For example, every time we would sit down to eat, he would pick up very small portions from the varied preparations in the plate and set them aside. He would then sprinkle water near the food and silently pray. When we were old enough, he explained to us that he was offering the food and water to the spirits surrounding us; it is because of them that we have the food, and this was a way of thanking them.

He used to make me perform the rituals for Satyanarayan *katha* under his guidance. He would also ask me to go with him on his visits to the temples to meet scholars there. He commanded the respect of our community in Pune because of his success in the furniture business and because he was very worldly-wise. People came to our house to meet him and seek advice on all kinds of matters; they looked up to him like a family elder.

My most significant memory of him is of a time when he spoke to me about my mother. As I have mentioned earlier, my mother died when I was an infant so there is very little I remember or know of her first-hand.

One day, as I was passing by, he called me and said, 'Come here, I want to talk to you.' He then waved his hand and signalled me to sit down in front of him. 'I have never spoken to you about this before but today I want to. Of all the women in our household, it was Radha, your mother, whom I admired most. She was a very virtuous woman, cultured and gentle. She never said anything bad about any one. Even as others spoke negatively of her, she kept quiet and was actually forgiving of them. She was a very industrious woman, constantly working and looking after Vallabh, Gulab, Manek, Vithal, and all the rest of us.'

He continued after a pause, 'She was a very devout person, very religious, and every Monday she visited the Mahadev temple without fail. She used to have visions. One of her cherished desires was to help the poor, educate the uneducated, and help them in sickness. She was not educated but she could recite the entire Gita. She never missed an opportunity to meet the religious leaders who came to our home. She used to participate in all of the religious festivals we celebrated. I do not know from where she acquired the art of decorating the house but all the colours, fabrics, paintings that you see around here are her doing. Even after so many years since she passed away, we have not changed anything.'

Dada paused again and then continued, 'She loved Moti, your youngest aunt. She treated her like her own sister. I would say she was the most precious gem of the Gokuldas Narayandas Family. I miss her the most.' As he spoke the last sentence, he became overcome with emotion, and tears started rolling down his cheeks. He stopped for a few moments and then continued. 'Do you know how pious she was? Soon after she passed away, the drinking-water well behind the workshop that had served us for several generations suddenly dried up. I still do not understand that,' Dada said. 'I mean I know astrology and all that, but this is beyond my comprehension. When you were born, she insisted on calling you Balkrishna for reasons she must know. I believe in her visions, she knew more than I did.'

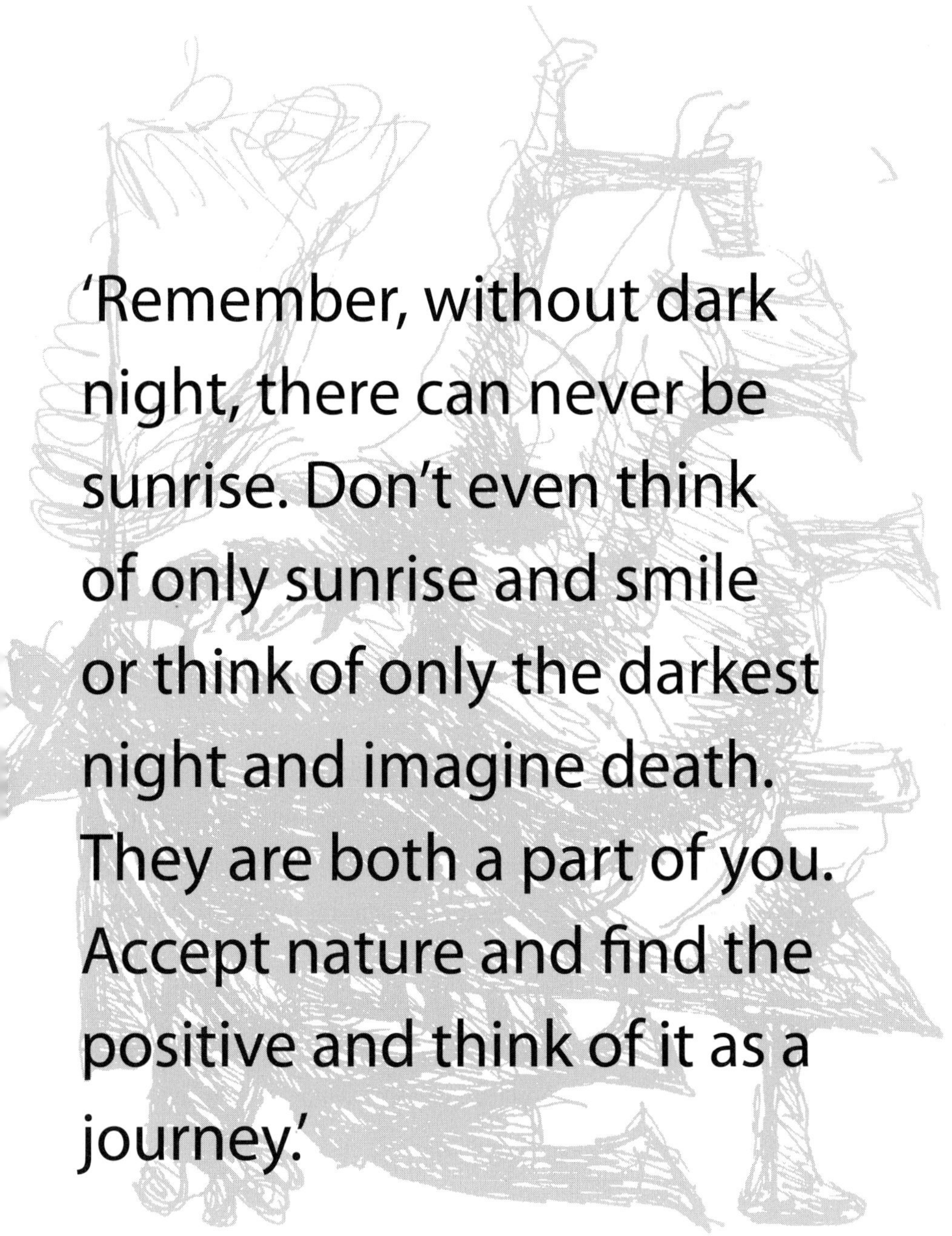

'Remember, without dark night, there can never be sunrise. Don't even think of only sunrise and smile or think of only the darkest night and imagine death. They are both a part of you. Accept nature and find the positive and think of it as a journey.'

Finally, with a gesture to convey that he was finished, he said, 'Bal, you have my blessings,' and he put his hands on my shoulders. Learning all that about my mother and for the first time, at that very moment I was kind of dumbfounded and not knowing what to do, I got up, touched Dada's feet and left the room. As I left, I was thinking of the water well, so slowly as if pulled by someone, I went to where the well was and asked a carpenter to open the cover. It was a very disturbing sight, an empty well. I noticed that the cover was something just pulled over, not a pukka, permanent one as if anticipating a miracle of some kind to recharge the well. I then wondered if my mother would help to rejuvenate it.

As I stood there having just come back from my years in Paris, I still felt the presence of my mattress laid on the floor and those painful six months. While I stood there, I again heard my mother's voice. 'Balya, it is me,' she said. 'You may not be aware but I was with you all along, during your travels, and your stay in Paris, too. I will always be with you doing my best to protect, guide and support you. Never lose heart, however daunting the task or future may seem. Remember, your name is Balkrishna.'

Slowly, childhood memories connected me again to the place. Somehow, after living in Paris with its broad avenues, Juni Bhaji Lane—where our home was located—appeared much narrower than I remembered. I noticed that nothing seemed to have changed; it was as if I had just left the previous day.

I remembered that the main door to our house was rarely closed. It was always left open, and especially at dawn and dusk, since it was believed that Laxmi—the Goddess of Wealth—visited homes at these hours and would go away if the door was closed, leaving the household poor. I like to believe that this gesture also made neighbours and guests feel welcome; they could just walk in.

However, I believe my most cherished memories are of the furniture workshop that Dada ran. This may be because, having chosen to become an architect, I have thought of the place and my experiences of it much more than the other aspects of my life there.

Our house in Juni Bhaji Lane had grown over the decades. It also suffered damage from two incidents of fire owing to the furniture workshop being located right next to it in a shed. However, it was rebuilt both times, wholly owing to Dada's perseverance. He never allowed mishaps to set him back but worked harder to overcome them. I have inherited that trait from him as well as from Corbusier, who was similarly inclined.

Every time I think of my home in Pune, I see a forest of staircases as this long narrow house grew over years to meet the needs of an expanding family over generations. As a child, I could never find its end, the very last room, or so I felt. There were indeed so many staircases, some very long, some very narrow, all connecting not only the floors within the house but also all the three floors of the workshop. So one could go around and up and down endlessly in an infinite loop.

I would often wander into the workshop, which was a large shed with a tin-sheet roof and a wooden mezzanine floor. The smell of fresh wood shavings, lacquer and spirit was all-pervasive there. I could see a huge variety of wooden members, sizes and stages of finish, finished, or raw with saw marks, and the patterns of grains shining through, once polished. There was also a huge stack of pieces in varied sizes piled up in certain ways and left for natural seasoning.

Here and there, I would see incomplete tables, chairs, beds or cupboards; and think about how something as large and grand as a tree could be transformed into something as small and useful as furniture. The smell of wood and polish and Dada's stories about his work were an endless source of fascination.

I also witnessed some important lessons about work. In my own practice, I often find myself reworking things often for a seemingly insignificant improvement. This exasperates my colleagues and assistants, but I just have to do it and cannot seem to help it. I have often thought about this and it occurs to me that this is a trait I have inherited from Dada. He was a stickler for perfection.

Thanks to Dada's keen eyes, our furniture was well known for its excellent workmanship. Dada could quickly spot the smallest of errors. I remember one day when he was reprimanding a carpenter for a tabletop even as he stood some 5–7m away. He called the carpenter and told him that it was a very shoddy work and that the tabletop was not level. However, the carpenter said, 'I don't think it's wrong.'

Therefore, Dada asked him to fetch a jug of water. He then poured some water on the tabletop and all the water quickly flowed to one side. Having proved his point, he went up to the man and slapped him. I was a bit taken aback by the incident. However, I learnt after a few days that, the morning after that incident, Dada had bought some sweets for the carpenter, had tea with him and talked about the importance of perfection in work. I like to believe that was his way of atonement for the hurt he must have caused.

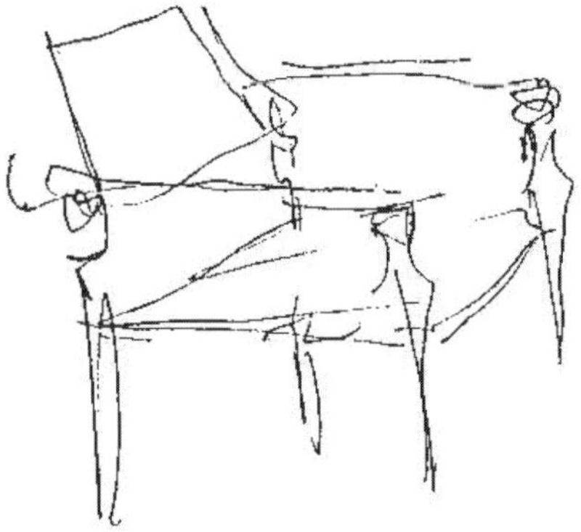

I remembered his saying another time that, **'God lies in perfection and we should seek perfection with as much passion as we seek God.'** It was a lesson I will never forget. Even now, when I see a new piece of furniture; I tend to check it the way Dada would have.

Among the other details I remember of Dada's house is that the windows were made from ready-made components, sometimes with two horizontal shutter divisions, which could be operated separately to control light and breeze and for privacy. Balconies had full-height doors-cum-windows along the entire facade of the house, and one could see right through the house from the home across the street.

Some of the houses in Juni Bhaji Lane had acquired an enigmatic character with additions and modifications. These expressed the constantly changing needs of the family as it grew. Standing in the balcony and conversing with cousins or relations across the street was a common practice. As I remember, there was never a silent moment in the houses or the street except at night.

At the street level, most of the houses had some form of commercial activity. These included selling incense sticks, perfumes, and household items. There was a goldsmith, a tailor and the house of our family doctor. It was like a total community with all the variety of activities and amenities required for daily life. It offered young ones like me growing up there the chance to learn and appreciate complex needs of the community and how mixed-uses within a neighbourhood make it easy to go about daily life.

Alas, this is in total contrast to a very recent visit when I saw many changes; there was much more traffic. It was very noisy, too. Unlike earlier, there were no children playing cricket there; nor were the elderly sitting out and discussing politics, a favourite pastime in India. It was bereft of the rich social life of the resident community that it supported earlier.

It was no more the Juni Bhaji Lane of my childhood. Tall concrete apartments with security grills all over them had replaced the modest houses with open verandas and balconies, which allowed neighbours to communicate with each other. Everyone was in their houses, in their own little worlds defined by soap operas on the television, I guess.

Even Ravivarpeth, the larger neighbourhood of which Juni Bhaji Lane is a part, is completely transformed. The workshops where artisans worked are converted to shops. There are no traces of families and friends I knew then, nor many others with whom I had a nodding acquaintance as I passed by their homes every day. The streets have now become roads with choking traffic, haphazard parking and are inhuman, to say the least.

I guess change is inevitable but, for me, the transformation of the area around my Pune home is the closest experience of what it entails. While I was there recently, on an impulse, I decided to go and sit down deep inside one of the shops selling plywood, close my eyes, and reconnect to my life 60 years ago.

I realized that however different the present reality may be, I can never efface my memories of the place, the people and their earlier lifestyle! Can we ever forget the sounds, smells, festivities, aroma and the fragrances of a place we have known intimately?

While at Corbusier's Atelier, André Maisonnier had once asked me about my habit—rather surprising to him—of holding a bunch of tiepins in my mouth as I stepped up on a stool for pinning up drawings. I then described to him how carpenters in India hold nails in their mouth to keep their hands free. This was so different from carrying tools and supplies in trouser pockets, tool belts, etc., which he was used to seeing. I then also explained to him that our carpenters always wore dhotis, so there was no question of pockets. That was because it was hot round the year. I also sketched for him people going around bare-chested. All of this delighted him to no end.

During that visit, climbing the steps to our house, I did notice some small changes that had happened since Dada had passed away. The room where he received visitors while seated on a thick mattress on the floor, which was covered in a white sheet, and where he read horoscopes for friends and told us stories now had a sofa set and chairs.

However, the same light blue paint chosen by my mother still covered the walls. The photographs hanging on the walls of the family members were the same as when I was there last. I recollected the smell of wood polish, sounds of carpentry in the workshop. Dada and his furniture workshop are so much a part of my being that I have never even once forgotten that I belong to a family of furniture manufacturers.

I was then very happy to meet all the members of my extended family there. Yet, this visit again made me very conscious about stagnancy that was all-pervasive in their homes and lives. The traditional ways of segregating duties and roles based on caste, class and gender were still practised very rigidly. In contrast, my own habits and views about these practices had changed dramatically.

That did create occasional conflicts but Kadam, our neighbour and Vallabh's childhood friend, came to my rescue asking everyone else to let me be. He said, 'Let Bal do things his way. His methods, I understand, are the way to live independently. Staying abroad, he has learned to live his life, without any domestic or such help. Let me also tell you that if he does not wish, please do not force him to join your furniture business. Whatever else he may do, I am sure that he will make us proud one day.' That seemed to settle a lot of conflicts and dilemmas building up for all of us.

Vallabh and I spent a lot of time recounting my time in Bombay, London, Paris and other places I had visited. I also enquired of what he had been up to since I left, and the state of family business and its future. I was feeling bad, if not outright guilty, about not joining him in the business but he understood my new calling in life and work.

He realized that given the places I had been to and the kind of work I had done, there was nothing in Pune that would interest me. I now clearly saw the environment there as a sheltered 'comfort zone', which was making people complacent and averse to change, without which there could be no growth.

However, I was quite willing to take risks and deal with new challenges, be they of new places, languages, food or work. A comfort zone of this kind would actually stifle me even as it suited my cousins. May be this is the reason why my cousins have never left their parental homes or the city.

When love dominates,
Emotions take wings,
Immediate surroundings
become the field.
But to reach the skies
One must hear
the call from the stars.
There indeed your dreams
wait for you.

Finally, after spending about a month in Pune, I left for Chandigarh via Mumbai and Delhi. In those days, it was a long journey. I was glad to be all by myself during the journey. It was a relief especially after being constantly in close contact with all the members of my extended family at Pune. It was so different from the life I had got used to in Paris.

Travelling by train is fun; one is in a crowd and yet alone. Other passengers were there but they had nothing to do with me. I again found myself thinking of architecture, all that I had learnt in Paris, and the opportunity to continue working with Le Corbusier on such important projects was exciting.

When the coach attendant woke me up and informed me that we had reached Chandigarh, it was three o'clock in the morning, and very cold. I got off with my backpack and a small bag on a practically deserted platform. From what I could see around at that dark hour, I told myself that some architects from Chandigarh city planning office must have designed the station!

When I approached a cycle rickshaw driver and told him where to go, his response was, 'Sir, I can take you to your friend in Sector 17, but it is too early to wake up your friend right now. How about having a hot glass of milk, or tea, as we wait for daybreak? We will be going through the new city and you can see all much better after the sunrise and enjoy the ride, I think.'

Though I was very sleepy, I saw his point but later asked him to take me to Sector 22 instead. Being actually in the place, after seeing all hundreds of sketches, drawings and models of it in Paris for years, I was quite awestruck by what I saw. As the rickshaw moved along various roads, I found myself recalling all the details of the V-7 system employed by Corbusier in the city.

'Is it busy? Do many people come to Sector 22?' I asked the rickshaw driver. 'Yes, they do, after all, it is the new city of the 20th century.' I was impressed that a rickshaw driver of the city was echoing Jawaharlal Nehru's description of the city, something that Le Corbusier himself quoted so often in Paris.

Corbusier used to come to Chandigarh twice a year, each time for a month. On one of his visits to Chandigarh after I started working there, we were once standing in front of the High Court. Pointing to the numerous mounds of excavated earth and the residential buildings rising beyond, he said, 'Doshi, you asked once why I have to do this. You know, actually I have nothing to do with this city now. I was supposed to prepare design guidelines and some details for sectors, but Maxwell Fry, Jane Drew and Pierre Jeanneret want me to concentrate only on the Capitol Complex. They do not realize the significance of what I want to express here in India, for Indians. Nor do they understand the character of the built form and the active use of open spaces required here, the importance of pedestrian mode and the nature of social life. The fact is that the conceptual sketches I have prepared for sectors and housing cluster plans have been set aside.'

I then ventured to ask him, ' Mons. Would you like to build the Unite here?' 'No, not at all,' he said forcefully, 'This is a place for Indian people; they love the ground and socializing. There has to be another way, suitable for India. In order to design a city for a free India and provide a vision for the 21st century, how can I follow my old theories? Will it be right to accept what was yesterday and what is suitable in the West? Is not this a great chance for me to be equally independent? Should I not refrain myself from the traditions of the past as well as the theories I have so far propounded?' He continued, 'Here, I have a chance to discover myself anew, freshly look at and learn from an ancient but alien civilization.'

I wonder sometimes if that is the reason, he reconsidered his design philosophies in the work that followed; rather than standing apart from nature to establish human identity, he chose to have a pact with nature—a philosophy that has stood the test of time in India.

Another incident I remember from that time is when Corbusier received a telegram informing him that he was being awarded the AIA (American Institute of Architects) gold medal, and asking if he would accept. 'Will this medal be as heavy as the Queens (Royal Institute of British architects) RIBA gold medal? What shall I answer? Should I accept?' he asked me, I am sure half in jest. When I answered in the affirmative, he replied 'OK, I will accept it.' 'Every morning I am born in the skin of a donkey – Thanks – I accept,' was his reply.

I thought about his reply. How wonderful! When one thinks that he is born a fool every day, he is free to act the way he chooses every day. There are no inhibitions, almost like an innocent child, with no baggage. Can I ever be free of my baggage? The choice is mine. It needs to efface all prejudices and welcome the morning rays.

On one of my subsequent visits to meet Le Corbusier at Chandigarh, when he was leaving in the evening for Paris via New Delhi, I asked him if I could travel with him up to Delhi. 'No,' he said. 'No one ever accompanies me, not even my secretary. I like to make the most of my time, which is why I always keep this notepad to write and sketch.'

I was shocked and felt dejected, and he must have noticed that so he said, 'OK, you can come, provided you are at the bus terminus sharp at seven in the morning.' Such was my guru, formal and informal, caring and detached, all in a single moment.

While we were in Delhi next day it was well past lunchtime so, Corbusier asked me,

'Doshi, are you hungry?'

'Yes,' I replied.

'Have you ever been to Moti Mahal? Tasted their tandoori chicken?'

I said, 'No.'

'Let's go then.'

After guiding the driver through endless meandering streets, he asked him to stop and announced: 'Yes, we are here.' He led me up a very narrow staircase, carefully avoiding the main dining hall and up to the terrace. It was very much like a roadside food joint, locally known as a *dhaba*, with steel and wood furniture, and ordered tandoori chicken.

As he began to eat, he said, 'Chicken from the mountains, mostly bones, very little meat on them but very tasty. Is not it, Doshi?' I was so surprised to see how 'native' Corbusier had become, relishing simple food at this rustic, rundown, and yet famous eatery in the whole of Delhi.

When we were finished, he looked at his watch, suddenly stood up and started walking to the stairs and I quickly followed him. We went down, walked to the Jeep and there he stopped and said, 'Au revoir, mon petit Doshi'. Saying that, he quickly turned around and walked away, I am sure, full of emotions and love.

Even as I was enjoying the work at Chandigarh, unknown to me, troubles were brewing in the office there. This was because of my position and the role I was able to play as an architect who best knew Corbusier's ideas and work expectations.

For all the independence and power that chief engineer P.L. Varma enjoyed in running the project office, with the growth in numbers, eventually some of the characteristics of a government organization did seep in. This included a strong sense of hierarchy based on qualifications and seniority.

At one point, it concerned me. The issue seemed to be, 'With four senior architects above him, how can Mr P.L. Varma appoint Doshi to a senior post created especially for him? He is not even qualified; not even an associate member of RIBA, just has experience of working in Corbusier's Paris Atelier. Who knows what role he actually played there?'

I came to know of all this one day when A.R. Prabhavalkar, a senior architect there, asked me, 'Doshi, how come you never got your Diploma from RIBA while you were in London?' 'Of course I have, who ever told you otherwise?' I asked back. He then told me that all the senior architects in the office believed that I had not completed my ARIBA studies, and therefore, I should not be appointed as an architect, let alone as a senior architect.

Of course, they did not challenge Varma about this, and both he and Prabhavalkar were much relieved that I was duly qualified for the post. I was, however, very uncomfortable from that moment in the office, and more so in continuing work with such colleagues. I knew that the sense of camaraderie, which is essential for the kind of work we were involved in, was lost forever. If that was the case, I did not wish to continue working there.

It had only been a few days ago that Corbusier had congratulated me for my ideas about the openings for the Governor's Palace. Corbusier's pat had made me euphoric but when I mentioned this to other colleagues during lunch, they did not respond. That was disheartening but indicative of the rivalry that was building up in the office.

I concluded that I never wanted to be in a place with people who did not value merit and talent as the only essential qualifications in pursuit of excellence. I also became aware of the rivalries that grow in a secure job, and how job security can cripple, leading to a sense of insecurity. Looking back, I think it was a good lesson as I embarked on my career in India.

Having decided to leave, I approached Varma and told him, 'Mr Varma, I am really thankful to you for granting me this special post and the opportunity to work on design of the Governor's Palace, but I would not like to continue working here. Please allow me to leave when we complete studies for the facades of the Governor's Palace.'

That took him by surprise and he asked me, 'What are you saying, Doshi? Has something happened? Has anybody insulted you?' He continued, 'I will sack whosoever is responsible, just tell me who it is.' I replied, 'No, please, no. I do not wish to make any one unhappy on my account. I would really like to leave quietly.'

When he asked me if I had options, I told him, 'Perhaps, I will go to Ahmedabad. From what I know, Jean-Louis Véret, who is looking after Corbusier's projects there, is leaving for his military service in a few weeks. I am sure Corbusier will be happy if I took charge of all the projects there. After all, those were among the Indian projects I worked on while in Paris.'

I left Chandigarh after a week. There I was, again, throwing away a secure job on a very prestigious project. I was also leaving a comfort zone very much like Pune, Bombay, London and Paris before, and heading to a completely new place and people.

During the journey from Chandigarh, I wondered if Ahmedabad was yet another stopover or if it would become my final destination. I told myself that—at least this time—culturally and in matters of food and language, I was going to settings that were less unfamiliar.

Of course, my visits to Chandigarh continued for quite some time subsequently, as long as the projects were going on and Corbusier kept coming for site visits. Most times, when he was to visit Chandigarh, I would also make it a point to go there and spend as much time with him as I could and show him my projects.

Among these trips, the one I most fondly remember is when I went there with Kamu soon after our marriage.

When I introduced Kamu to him, Corbusier was the perfect gracious guru. 'So this petite lady is your wife. Congratulations,' he said. Before we could say anything else, he said, 'Wait here for a few minutes,' and abruptly left us standing there. He went to his room in Pierre Jeanneret's house where he lived when in Chandigarh. Kamu and I waited, wondering as to what was in store for us.

After some time, we saw him coming back with a large sheet rolled up. When he reached us, he unrolled it to reveal a collage he seemed to have recently finished and showed it to us.

I did not know what to say and seeing no immediate reaction he said, 'Don't you like it?' 'It is good Mons. but...' I was still not sure of what was happening and what to say.

The same evening, just before dinner at Prabhavalkar's house, when Monsieur arrived, he gave us another drawing, again all rolled up. 'I hope, this time both of you like this one,' he said. As we unrolled it, an envelope fell to ground but we continued looking at the drawing. It was a beautiful coloured collage marked, 'With blessings for Doshi and his wife,' and signed by him.

Then we picked up the envelope, saw it was addressed to us and opened it. Inside we found five notes of hundred rupees each, and a note.

It said:

'Mme. Doshi and Doshi,

Here is a little grease to move the wheels of your happy married life. I hope you will have many occasions to break plates on each other's heads.

Yours with friendship,
Le Corbusier.'

Spontaneously, both of us bowed down and touched his feet. Even Prabhavalkar who was present there felt that Corbusier regarded me rather specially among all his disciples and said something to that effect.

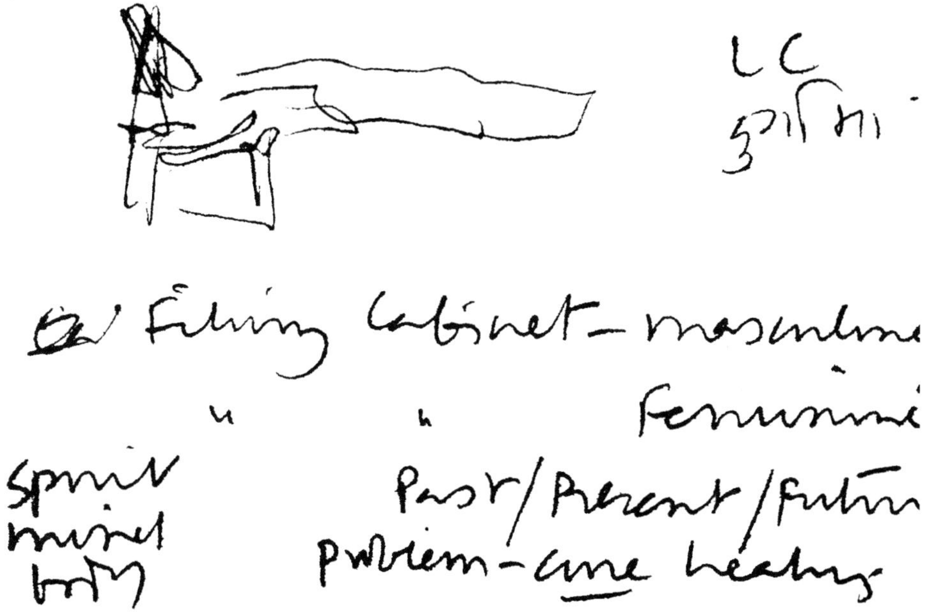

I think I have enjoyed Corbusier's affection all along the years that we had known each other and every now and then, there would be gestures indicating this. I remember one time when a large parcel arrived bringing yet another gift. This time it was more special, a copy of the limited-edition issue of 'Poem de la Angle Droit' marked for 'Balkrishna Doshi, Excellent architect and friend,' and signed 'Le Corbusier'.

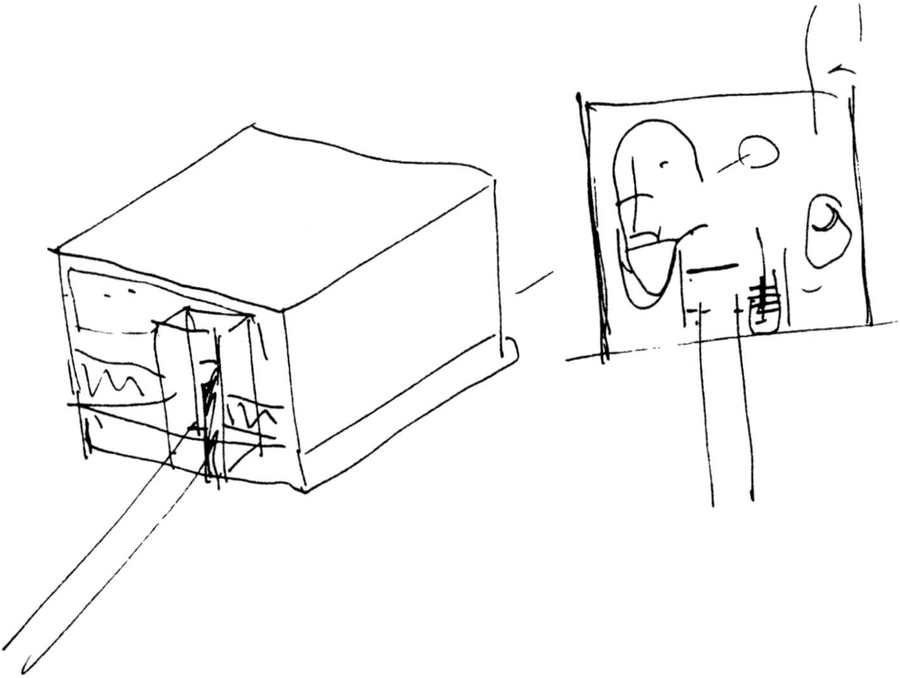

When I took over from Jean-Louis Véret, he had represented Le Corbusier in Ahmedabad for more than two years. Now it was my turn. Véret was very good in dealing with people and adapting to new places and cultures and therefore enjoyed a lot of goodwill. Maintaining the goodwill and adding to it was now my responsibility.

Before he left, Véret introduced me to Manorama Sarabhai whose home we were designing, and K.M. Kantawala, the chief engineer of the Ahmedabad Municipal Corporation, who was in charge of the museum project now known as Sanskar Kendra. He also introduced me to Harinarayan Acharya, secretary of the Ahmedabad Textile Mill-Owners' Association (ATMA), for whom we were designing an office and Shyamubhai Shodhan, who had purchased the design for a house originally prepared for Surottam Hutheesing, now known as Shodhan Villa.

Here I was, again, in an unknown city, and with the added responsibility of completing my guru's works to his utmost satisfaction. In many ways, I was reminded of the time I had started working in Corbusier's Paris office.

I often wondered why I allowed myself to get into such situations. Was this the last time ever? What gave me the courage to risk such challenges? Was it my mother's reassuring presence, maybe?

There were the initial troubles but I would then tell myself to just keep going; that, eventually, it would all work out. People here do not know you for now, but once they see you at work, they will appreciate what you are doing, just wait and watch. We face these situations every time we try something new, gradually they see its virtues.

As my luck would have it, I really needed a lot of courage right from the start. When I took over, the building contractor for ATMA had stopped work after preparing a sample for the end walls.

Surottam Hutheesing, then the President of ATMA, was not very happy about the unpolished Dholpur stone finish on the end walls. Therefore, he wanted Kasturbhai Lalbhai, the most senior and respected among the mill owners, to take the final decision.

I had not yet met Kasturbhai, but I had heard about his much-disciplined work habits, punctuality, efficiency and no-nonsense approach to dealing with people and decision-making. Therefore, I was a bit concerned about how the meeting might go. However, I knew that I must defend an architect's decision. After all, that was good for the building.

The next morning, precisely at 9.30, I saw Surottambhai approach my site office at the ATMA building accompanied by two men. One of them was a tall, impressive person clad in long coat of the kind that businesspersons wore, white dhoti and a white Gandhi cap. I guessed that must be Kasturbhai.

As they came close the tall person asked me, 'Doshi, aren't you a Gujarati?'

'Yes, I am, but from Pune.'

'Very good, so we can talk in Gujarati. However, you do speak with a Marathi accent. Now, tell me, what is the matter about the wall finish?'

I took them to where samples were prepared and said, 'This is a sample using unpolished Dholpur stone and Mons. Le Corbusier desires this. This looks right for this place; the rough surface of the stone will look even better when both the walls are fully covered.'

'You have other alternatives?'

'I don't think so,' I said, 'in the context of the dry bed of the Sabarmati River, this colour heightens the quality of this space.'

'If you think that is the right thing to do, then just go ahead.' He then left without saying another word.

After he left, a rather surprised Surottambhai asked me, 'How can you speak to him like this? Do you know who he is?'

'I don't know,' I replied.

So he said, 'That was Kasturbhai himself, textile baron, and chairman of several governmental committees and charitable organizations, and also my uncle.'

Acharya, who was there too added for my benefit, 'You know he has hired many architects and contractors to build several large campuses for institutions all over India,' perhaps to convey that ATMA building was just another project for Kasturbhai and that I was kind of a nobody.

In response, I said something to the effect that, for me, what is right for a building and architecture always comes first nothing else and nobody else matters.

Initially everyone in Ahmedabad was quite amused to hear of a Gujarati from Pune via Paris speaking Gujarati in a Marathi accent.

The fact was this was my first experience of executing a building, being on a construction site, and Corbusier's buildings required anything but standard construction techniques. Luckily, under Véret, Sarabhai Villa was almost completed and most of the civil work for ATMA building and Shodhan Villa too was done. The floor slabs for Sanskar Kendra had already been cast when I took over.

Although I had drawn many construction details in the office, I was not sure of my ability to supervise seeing them built. So I was very nervous, very similar to starting to work in Atelier in Paris. Here my knowledge of Gujarati, even with a Marathi accent, was a big advantage. At least I could communicate, explain the details I wanted and work with the construction workers, contractors, engineers and the clients.

Slowly, I mastered the construction process, managing the work on site, dealing with the contractors, the workers and the clients. In due course, I felt at ease in Ahmedabad, became well acquainted with many leading scholars, academicians, artists, merchants and industrialists. Eventually, I felt more at home in Ahmedabad than at Paris or even Pune.

When I left Chandigarh and moved to Ahmedabad to supervise Corbusier's local projects there, I had no further thoughts about a future or a career. I took it as it came, believing that something would always work out, as it had so far.

Setting up a practice is not easy for a young architect with little experience. It is even harder as an outsider. It takes patience, belief in one's self, readiness to starve, and a mentor. Initially, despite my best efforts to organize a like-minded group to discuss issues concerning arts and architecture, I felt lonely. So, after about a year, I felt like leaving Ahmedabad and joining Achyut Kanvinde's firm in Delhi. I had worked with him very briefly when I came back from Paris, so I knew enough about him and liked his work.

Instead, I decided to first speak to Kasturbhai about starting my practice in Ahmedabad. When I spoke to him, he simply asked, 'How much money do you need per month?' I said, 'Perhaps 500 rupees.' So, he said, 'If I provide you with enough work to earn that amount, would you stay?' 'Yes,' I said.

I did not realize it then, but that brief and to-the-point conversation became a major turning point in my life. That offer from Kasturbhai made me stay back here for good and finally changed the entire course of my professional and personal life.

Eventually, it was in Ahmedabad that I found the love of my life, Kamu, and it is here that we have raised a family, now spanning four generations. Looking back, I wonder sometimes if this was a hidden part of the design for Shodhan Villa that I worked upon while in Paris and later supervised its construction in Ahmedabad. Let me explain that.

In Paris, when Emilio Duhart from Chile left the office, Le Corbusier passed on this project to me rather than Maisonnier who had initiated work on it. After my arrival in Ahmedabad at the site of Shodhan Villa, I met Pramod Parikh, a friend of Shyamubhai who had agreed to manufacture the particular shades of paint Le Corbusier had chosen.

We met about that on several occasions and, one day, we got talking about life in Paris. So Pramod asked me if I missed it, and if I would like to join him for a meal sometime. He added that his wife Rosy was an American, and that they often prepared Western dishes at home.

I was then living by myself and the idea of a decent meal in good company was tempting. So, I accepted his offer, little realizing that this too was going to be a turning point in my life; it was at this meal that I first met Kamala, who I now know as Kamu, my wife. We took a liking to each other and continued to meet regularly at the Shodhan site. The rest, as they say, is history.

However, it was not smooth sailing for us. When I had come back from Paris and spent a few weeks in Pune, I had promised my brother and his wife that I would seek their opinion when I decided to marry and do so with their concurrence. Now that was not to be. Remember that this was the 1950s—a much more conservative time than now—and for my Vaishnavite family, my marriage to a Jain girl was just not acceptable.

However, as with most other decisions that I had taken, I held out. This meant that my own family boycotted the event. One of the strongest memories of my wedding is leaving the ATMA project, where I was supervising the terrace flooring work, on a rickety rickshaw to buy an inexpensive sari—all I could afford—and then going to Kamu's home for the marriage ceremony, all alone.

There was no boisterous crowd of friends or relatives accompanying me astride a horse with a band playing popular tunes. It was so private, almost like a hush-hush affair. However, I was very happy that the guests who did attend were very dear to me. These were Motabhai and his family, Manorama Sarabhai, Chinubhai Chimanlal, nephew of Kasturbhai and later a mayor of Ahmedabad, and Girishbhai Desai with his family, my host.

I must say that if it were not for Kamu, my confidence in us, and the support of her family, our marriage would not have been possible. My family finally accepted us, but that was many years later.

I still remember Vithalbhai, my father, visited us years later—after our family reconciliation. To everyone's surprise, he even prepared a garland to honour my success, came to Ahmedabad airport and garlanded me on my return from Delhi. I was touched, and it was our first embrace after many years.

Again, it is in this very city that I have matured as an architect, as a teacher and have lived very satisfying moments of professional joys and success. I surely believe that Ahmedabad was a special city of that time in all of India for reasons I shall discuss later in this memoir.

I must say Kasturbhai Lalbhai and Dr Vikram Sarabhai, whom I met later, were among the most enlightened clients I have known. Working with them as a young architect was a very educative experience too. Both of them emphasized the need to work in line with the local climate using local materials and skills. Kasturbhai also instructed me in business ethics and practices, as well as in Vastu Shastra, the Indian canon of building design that he himself strongly followed. Vikram Sarabhai often talked about science, technology, and their relevance to comfort conditions in architecture and planning.

While I grew up amid Hindu rituals and practices as a child, I acquired a mature understanding of the religious and spiritual dimensions of Hinduism from Rasikbhai Parikh, a renowned scholar and my uncle-in-law.

He opened my eyes to the wisdom of the ancients and the knowledge contained in our scriptures. He goaded me to look for the timeless ways of doing everything and we spent many hours discussing Vastu Shastra, Hindu traditions and culture.

From him, I learnt about scholars such as Hemchandra Acharya, about Indus Valley culture, India's freedom struggle, other religions, Gandhi's thoughts on development and Swaraj, and so on. I also met Jain saints such as Punyavijayji, Jinvijayji, Pandit Sukhlalji and others, while designing the building for the L.D. Institute of Indology in Ahmedabad.

After spending about five years in the UK and Europe, where I learnt about Western thoughts and practices, these years at Ahmedabad were my first serious education about India.

I must say I was very lucky to be among outstanding scholars in Ahmedabad who took the effort to educate me about my own heritage. This period also allowed me to learn all about the arts of India and their importance in better understanding the architecture of India.

I learnt nuances of Indian classical dance, rhythm, tonality and space manipulation from Mrinalini Sarabhai and Kumudini Lakhia. From the likes of M.F. Husain, K.G. Subramaniam, N.S. Bendre, Shankho Chaudhuri, Piraji Sagara and Jeram Patel, I learnt about the contemporary trends in visual arts.

Here, I have had opportunities to meet the best musicians of contemporary India, such as Kesarbai Kerkar, Bhimsen Joshi and Kumar Gandharva, Sharafat Hussain, Amjad Ali, and many more.

I have also spent many hours with the stalwarts of Gujarati theatre and literature such as Jaishankar Sundari, Jashwant Thakkar, and Dinaben Pathak.

I was also fortunate to have met distinguished persons from other disciplines such as Dr Kamala Chaudhury, a Ford Foundation consultant and an expert on behavioural sciences.

Nevertheless, as I have said earlier in this account of my life, a lot of that happened because of my personal urge to learn, to improve and to excel.

For example, I was very keen to learn about Indian music traditions before going to the US for the Graham Fellowship. I wanted to do that because I felt it was very necessary for being a good Indian architect. I also wanted to learn all that as I thought I would be acting as an ambassador of all things Indian.

Fortunately, Gita Sarabhai, Vikram Sarabhai's younger sister, was kind enough to help me and gave me lessons—if I may call our discussions lessons—on Indian classical music, the concept of ragas and time in Indian music. Eventually, this deepened my interest in classical music, which has now been a lifelong affair.

Looking back, I can say that I was learning so much about life, especially about Indian ways, past and present. And I was constantly seeking to bring all of it together, integrate all I was learning into some kind of unified view of India I might say, be they matters of the physical, creative or the spiritual worlds.

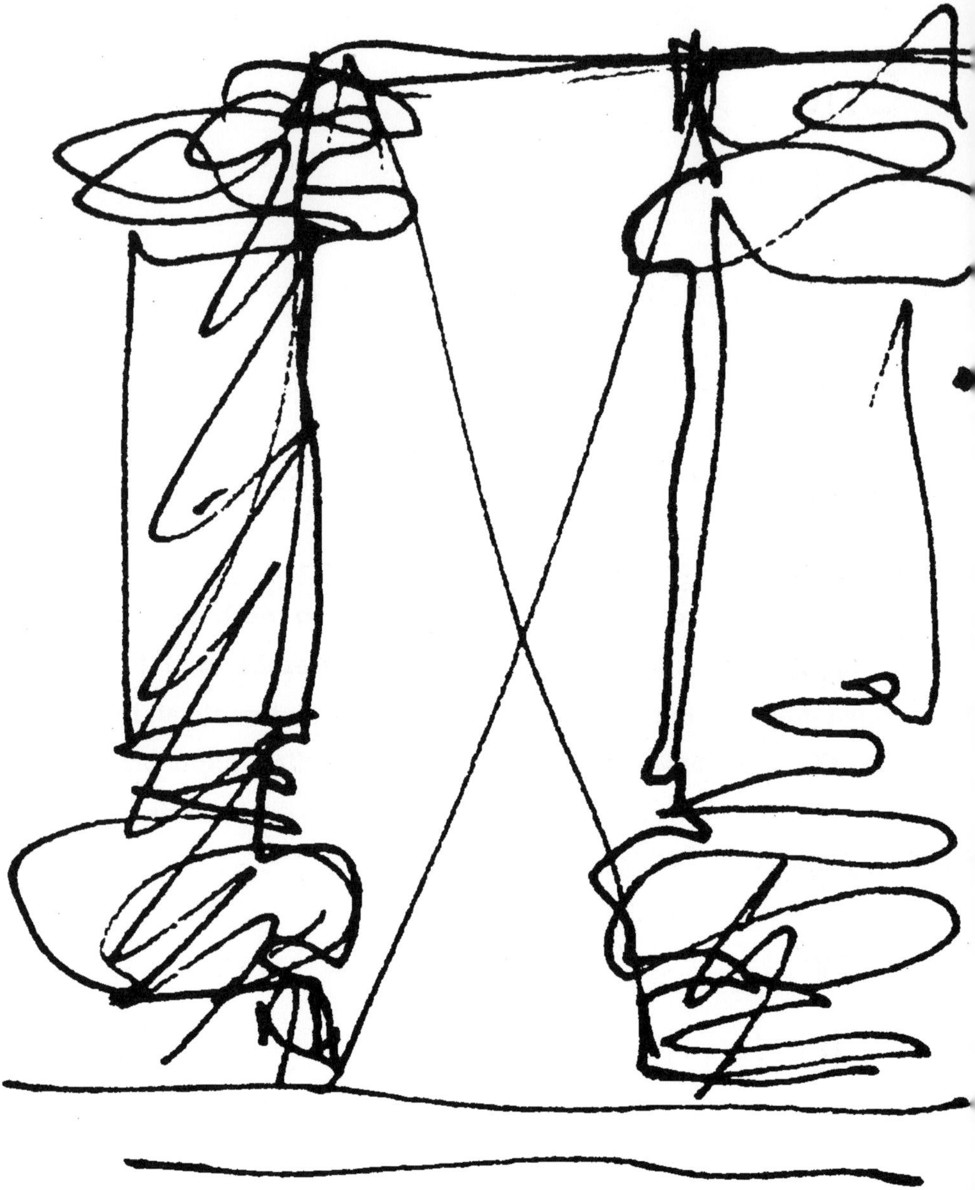

One cannot just be an architect, I thought to myself. The idea is to become a *sthapati* as described in the canonical texts. Stella Kramrisch, the much-respected scholar on Indian arts had mentioned to me once: 'An Indian *sthapati* has to be a yogi to feel the vibrations of every element in the cosmos, including the materials and users of that space.'

In one of the Vastu Shastras, namely Vishnudharmottara Purana, an exchange between King Vajra and Saint Markandeya clearly demonstrates how all art, architecture, sculpture, painting, dance, music, poetry and so on are interrelated in our traditions.

The exchange relates to the King's desire to make an image of the deity for which he seeks advice from the Saint. When I first read the dialogue, I was very inspired and it still fascinates me, so much so that I am reproducing it here.

King Vajra: O Sinless One, how should I make the forms of Gods so that the image made according to rules may always manifest (the deity)?

Saint Markandeya: He who does not know the canon of painting (*Chitra Sutram*) can never know the canon of image-making (*pratima laksanam*).

Vajra: O Scion of the Bhrigu Race, explain to me the canon of painting because one who knows the canon of painting knows the canon of image-making.

Markandeya: It is very difficult to know the canon of painting, without the canon of dance, because O King, in both, the world is to be imitated (or represented).

Vajra: Explain to me the canon of dance and then you will speak about the canon of painting because O Twice-born One, the one who knows the practice of the canon of dance, knows painting.

Markandeya: Dance is difficult to understand by one who is not acquainted with instrumental music (*atodya*). Dance can in no way be known without it.

Vajra: O Knower of Law, speak about instrumental music and then you will speak about the canon of dance, because O Excellent Bhargava, when instrumental music is properly understood, one understands dance.

Markandeya: O Achyut, without vocal music, it is not possible to know instrumental music. One who knows the practice of the canon of vocal music, knows everything according to rules.

Vajra: Explain to me the canon of vocal music, O Best of the Holder of Law, because someone who knows the canon of vocal music, is the best of men who knows everything.

Markandeya: Vocal music is two-fold, *Sanskrit* and *Prakrit*, and the third, *Apabhramsa*, however, is infinite.

O King, on account of the variety of local dialects, its limit cannot be determined in this world. Vocal music is to be understood as subject to recitation and recitation is done in two ways, prose and verse.

O Knower of Law, prose is as found in conversation while verse is as in metre. Metre is of many varieties.

The Saint then goes on to elaborate the entire process of image-making.

An architect is a being whose memory, associations and experiences dominate his life. Whatever he sees, dreams or an assignment he undertakes, begins by intermixing like a smorgasbord. From there, he filters some through a long process. After some time, by rejecting and adding, the overall structure emerges. A building is created out of memories, associations, sounds, forms, spaces and images and many other related and unrelated encounters. Through these, he reconstructs his image to connect to the world around.

In short, architecture, to borrow from Mao's idea, is not a dinner party, or writing an essay, or painting a picture, or doing embroidery; to be so leisurely and gently refined. It is temperate, kind, courteous, restrained and magnanimous to combine all classes of society.

So, here I was, understanding India with the help of some of the best scholars of that time when the Graham Fellowship came through. I may also mention here the long, winding journey that the letter followed to reach me, which again goes to show that my path was being guided strongly by unknown forces.

Since the Graham Foundation did not have my correct postal address, once the letter reached Ahmedabad, it was redirected to my site office at ATMA. From there it was again redirected to my house at Sharada Society. But I was then staying at the home of my brother-in-law, Pramod Parikh, because Kamu had just delivered Tejal, our eldest daughter, and was staying there as was the custom. So, the letter was redirected once again to Pramod's house!

The trip to Chicago in 1958 under the Fellowship was a very educative trip since I was travelling to the US for the first time. I met the luminaries of architecture such as Ludwig Mies van der Rohe, J.L. Sert, Charles Eames and Frederick Kiesler, and visited many of their works. I also met some distinguished persons such as the Spanish sculptor Eduardo Chillida, American painter José Guerrero, Japanese architect Fumihiko Maki, and Cuban artist Wifredo Lam, who are now as celebrated as our peers then.

The trip also exposed me to a world of new technologies and an aesthetic derived from technologies, not to forget the tremendous mobility among people, like a whole society on the move, which is still a characteristic of the US.

During my visit, I also met Eero Saarinen, who was on the jury for the Toronto City Hall. On describing my entry for the competition, he quickly drew the sketch of the elliptical sloping tower I had proposed with Dr. Yoshikatsu Tsuboi. While appreciating the cross-webbed structural system, he regretted the location of the main entrance. 'You just lost because of that,' he said.

From the US, I went to Japan via the West Coast and the tropical islands of Hawaii. It was a very educative experience in terms of the diversity of the people, places and their specific architectural expressions.

I would describe my four-month stay in Japan as one of the most unusual experiences at that stage in my life. Everything about it was different and fascinating: the food, clothing, manners and customs, just getting around the place, their work culture, obsession with precision, innovation and finally their pride.

Japanese architecture, both the traditional and contemporary, was a revelation. Of special interest was how Buddhism had influenced their architecture, way of life as well as their view on nature.

I could now begin to understand the evolution of religious thought from Hinduism to Jainism and finally to Buddhism. It is a fascinating journey ranging from *shringar* or opulence, to asceticism and finally to meditative practices!

During my four-month stay in Japan, while finalizing the design and structural drawings of Premabhai Hall with Prof. Tsuboi, I met almost all the architects who eventually became internationally famous. I also met members of the Metabolism Group that included Fumihiko Maki, Kenzo Tange, Yoshikatsu Tsuboi, Shegeru Aoki, Kiyonori Kikutake, Sori Yanagi and others.

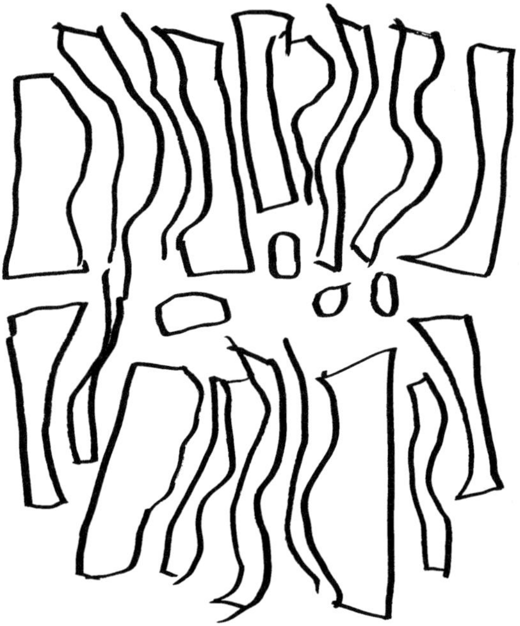

Despite their training with Modernist masters, the Japanese architects very well expressed their unique search, blending the West and the East in their designs. These early designs, even when executed in RCC, recalled their wooden traditions but slowly they developed their very own style.

To me, this raised a question: What would be the Indian way to seek such architecture? Is that a valid question to begin with? How do we become ourselves? Between 1960 and 1980, I attended several conferences in Japan and, each time, I raised this issue with the architects I met. Even today, I am preoccupied with questions about what is local and what is global about the architectural identity.

My design for the Institute of Indology, after several superimposed studies, now has the notion of an Indian building. All the elements one finds in Indian buildings are present there. I had studied a Jain *upashraya*, a home for monks, before I designed it. I had also met several Jain saints in the city to understand the traditional architecture for this building type.

I learnt there should be a high plinth; that the building should be not more than two storeys high, and it must have a full-length veranda, all around the upper floor. I had no hesitation and these very elements define my own design for the building.

I must add that here two concerns had preoccupied me. One was the characteristics of traditional architecture like plinth, veranda, etc., and the second one was saving energy. Since this building was to house fragile ancient manuscripts, maximizing indirect natural light, maintaining a constant temperature and controlling humidity were crucial.

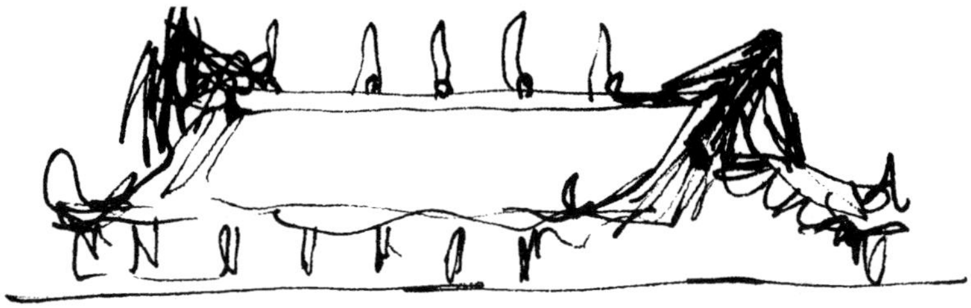

My visit to Japan and the buildings that made an impression on me did find a place here. I was certainly influenced by the Kurashiki Town Hall project by Kenzo Tange, especially with regard to integration of services and expression of the traditional architecture in RCC that I observed there.

If my coming to Ahmedabad to supervise Corbusier's projects exposed me to the matters of execution on the site, another happy coincidence made me understand and appreciate the role of a creative structural engineer in architecture.

In 1957, Kenzo Tange visited Ahmedabad, especially to see Corbusier's buildings, accompanied by Professor Yoshikatsu Tsuboi, a structural engineer. During the visit, Tange talked about his collaboration with Tsuboi for his Olympic Stadium in Tokyo. He particularly emphasized as to how that made the final design so much richer.

When I arranged for them to meet Kasturbhai, he readily invited Tsuboi to design factory buildings for Arvind Textile Mills owned by his company. I was then working on the design of Premabhai Hall located in the forecourt of the historic Bhadra citadel in Old Ahmedabad. So, I also asked Tsuboi if he would design the structure for the Hall and he accepted.

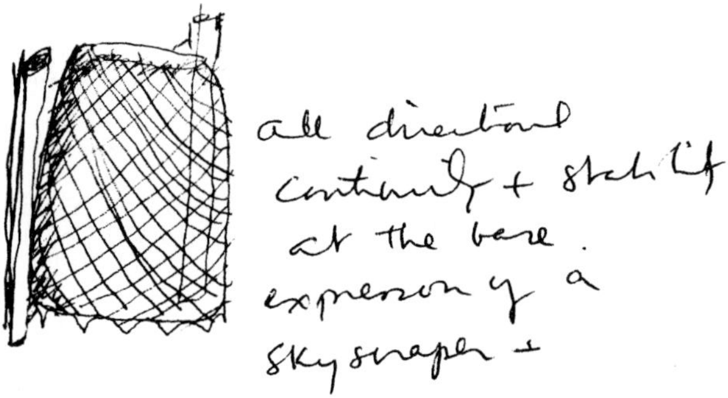

While we were working on that, I also decided to participate in an international competition for the design of the Toronto City Hall.

Upon my request, Prof. Tsuboi agreed to help design the structure for Toronto City Hall. Luckily, our design stood 15th in the international competition. The concept of the structure was based on the light-weight dumbbell-like cane structure used by hawkers as a stand.

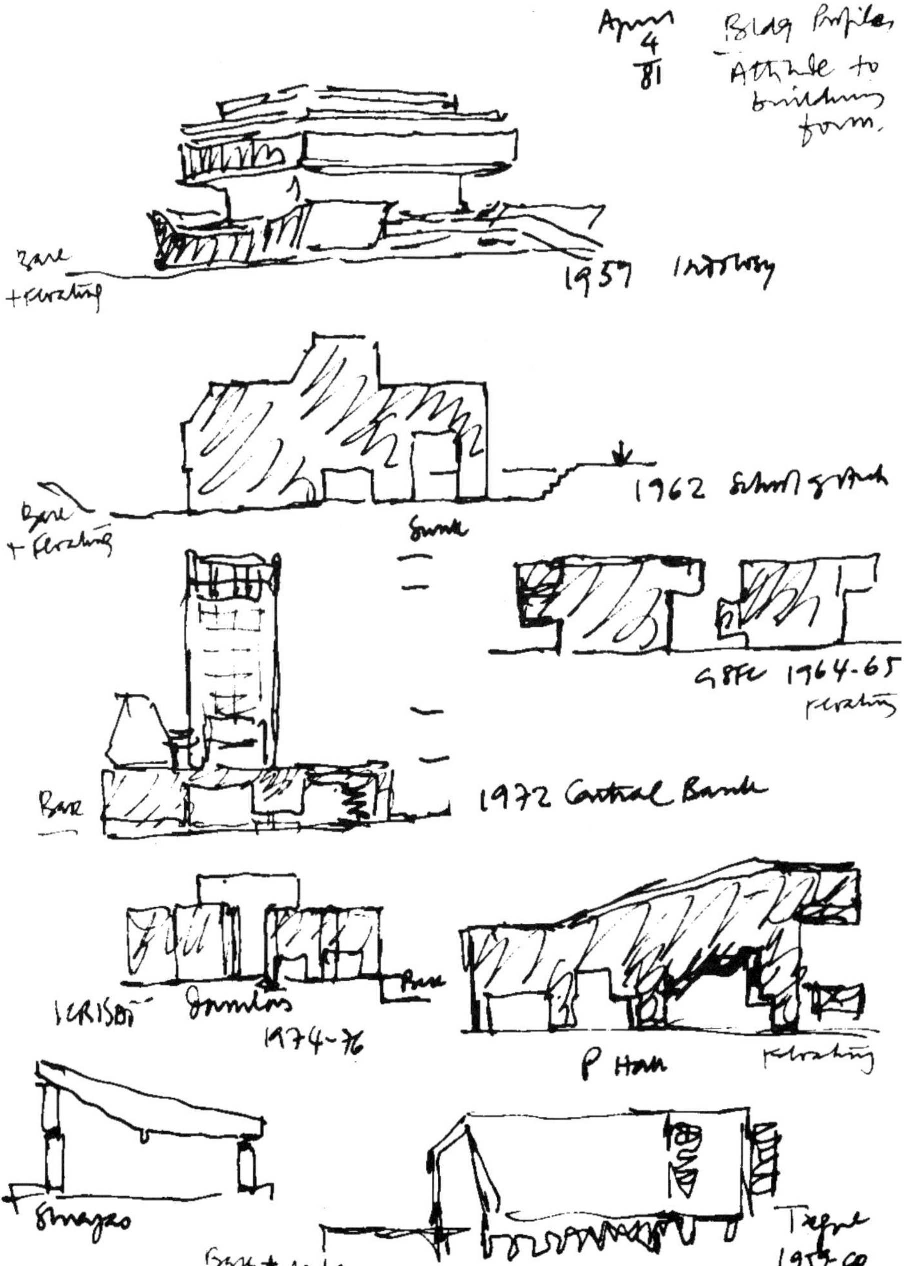
April 4 81
Bldg Profiles
Attitude to building form.
Base + floating
1957
Base + floating
1962
1964-65
floating
1972 Central Bank
Base
1974-76
P Hall
floating
Base + ends
1959-60

We spent about three weeks working together on the Toronto project. This collaboration in developing design revealed to me a new way of seeing the relationship between architecture and structural systems. It was for the first time that I had worked so closely with an engineer and Tsuboi's concepts and ideas transformed my understanding of architecture and structure. I believe that this was the most creative period of my life. At least, that is how I feel whenever I see the drawings and models we had prepared then.

On the day he was to leave for Tokyo, I joined Tsuboi for breakfast at Cama Hotel where he was staying. ATMA building is located right across the river and, from the dining area at the Cama Hotel, we could enjoy a beautiful view of its east facade in the soft morning light. While he looked at it, Tsuboi asked me, 'Doshi, do many people visit ATMA?' I said, 'Yes, the building receives a constant stream of visitors, not only architects from all over but also designers, artists, all kinds; it is like a place of pilgrimage.'

He then remarked, 'Doshi, always remember history and historic buildings. For example, the Grand Shrine at Ise in Japan is actually a very small structure and many centuries old, but the Japanese revere it immensely. To us, it exemplifies total integration of man and nature. That shrine is very much our measure of what great architecture should be. It is a symbol of perfection, not the size but quality matters.'

Soon after that, I was in Paris and went to meet Corbusier. I showed him our work on the Premabhai Hall project, mainly photographs of the model showing an eggshell building suspended in space, which we were then working on. He looked at the photos and said,

'My God, you think you can do this?'

'I am trying to design and build it.'

'Bravo, I can't have such an idea.'

Now, I do not know if he genuinely meant it or was sarcastic about the rather ambitious proposal I was showing him. Maybe it really was an ambitious, perhaps audacious, proposal. Nevertheless, I was very confident about it then. Though it was the beginning of my career, I had some of the best opportunities and recognition the world could then offer a young man hailing from the narrow lanes of Pune.

For example, in my paper for the Graham Fellowship, I had talked about a multi-disciplinary and multilevel approach to habitat ideas. I was involved in international teaching assignments, I had already met the who's who of international architects and I was ready for more. I guess it was at this point that I must have begun to acquire a separate identity with great confidence. So why would I not try something bold?

On one hand, I was getting to know India, its varied shades, hues and intricacies of not only architecture but its social, cultural and artistic aspects, too. The next day I could be in the US, meeting stalwarts like Philip Johnson, Louis Kahn, Buckminster Fuller, Eero Saarinen, Minoru Yamasaki, Paul Rudolf and Frank Gehry. I could also be in Europe and UK meeting Gian Carlo De Carlo, Peter Smithson, Aldo van Eyck, Herman Hertzberger, Jacob Bakema, or James Stirling.

At some stage or the other, most of these architects and designers I met abroad visited Ahmedabad. Their visits have helped them to understand the circumstances in which we work and share some insights. I remember when Stirling was visiting, our office was in a very hectic state, completing a project. He said it is good to be busy most times but then, very appropriately, spoke of the virtue of lean periods. He said he attributed his best work as resulting from reflecting on what had gone by and what he needed to do. The reflective periods allowed him to rediscover himself and improve his work.

Such experiences are the main threads of my life's fabric. This fabric now comprises hundreds of layers distilled from of all these experiences of the East and the West. I do not know which one dominates now. I do know that there are times when one clearly dominates the other. That is why I like to say there are many layers to my being. These layers have inevitably found their way, expressions, in my projects all along.

However, if I have to choose one single project as expressive of these complex layers and their interplay, I would choose Sangath in spite of many other subsequent projects of varied scales and functions. I believe images and experiences from all the multiple worlds I have inhabited are fused in Sangath. **In Gujarati, my mother tongue, *sangath* means 'moving together'.**

Sangath was conceived as an institution to encourage activities in the areas of fine and technological arts related to architecture and planning. The brief has evolved over the years mainly in terms of additional activities for educational courses and seminars, a professional architectural firm and an office for the Vastu-Shilpa Foundation.

Varied experiences and their layering in Sangath have come from my understanding of life and its associations. I am always attracted to architecture that has gone through mutations, and yet is within the order of its making.

That is why Sangath has this distinct, perhaps unique, character. I believe that is why everybody likes it. There is practically nothing about it that can be compared with any building anywhere. That perhaps makes it a very strikingly memorable experience.

Over time, I have acquired a habit of compartmentalizing my fleeting experiences to understand clearly their true meaning while in a different milieu. As a result, I am conscious of the other half, my true moorings, even though they constantly generate all kinds of difficulties and, sometimes, frustrations. However, after discovering the main thread, I am able to separate the layers and arrive at a new understanding and the compulsion to goad me. As a result, I cannot say this, this, or that is better in life.

I am conscious of the other self,
Which constantly creates difficulties,
frustrations and
Then bestows it with opportunity of the
unknown
And its compulsion to make me do things.

You cannot say that this or this or this is
better in life,
At any moment you think it is just right,
grab it and hold it.

But the next time you must ask the
question,
Was there a better way?

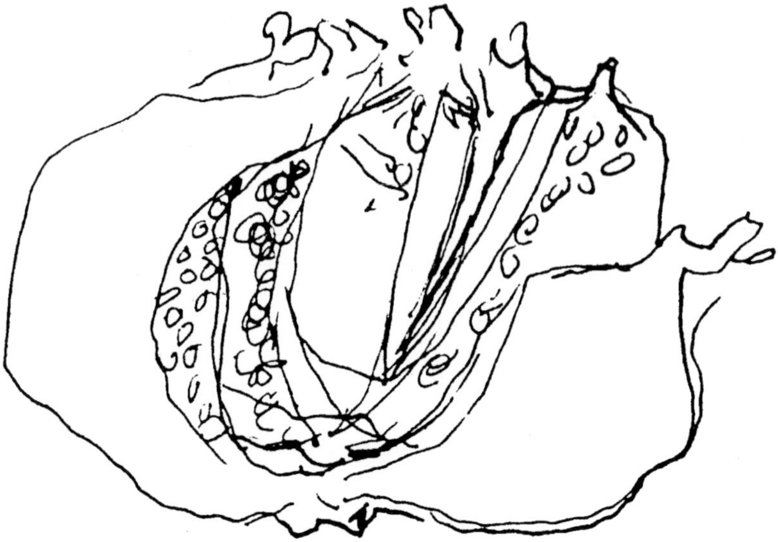

To be different just for the sake of it was never my intention, especially at Sangath. I always ask myself, 'How can I make something that I have not seen before?' There have been points in time when I know I have shut myself out, closed. But those are the times I hated myself. I knew that this was my capability, that I had reached my limits, and there could be no more. If—by then—I have failed, so be it, I have failed.

For me the struggle to do better is the most important aspect of work. How I constantly connect to my moorings, facing contradictions that tear my mind apart, resulting from happenings in past, present or future, and yet find appropriate and path-breaking solutions is a challenge I love.

I also know that, in each of my projects, I have failed on one or the other count, somewhere less, somewhere more. For example, I immensely enjoyed designing my own residence and its extension between 1960 and 1980. However, I am sure if I were to rework it, I would improve a few things.

For me, the reconsideration of all my beliefs and values in light of new learning is a continuous process. This can be about a project or some action I am contemplating. This is where my daily journal, notes and self-evaluation tools help to remind me of the lessons I have yet to learn, and my strengths and weaknesses.

Every time I am at a loss as to what to do next, especially when I am attempting something new, I keep pushing myself, knowing well that it will work out eventually.

THERE IS NO GREATER CRIME THAN CONVENTION

TRY TO DO YOUR OWN AND NEW

IF YOU TRY THERE IS NO SOLUTION WHICH IS IMPOSSIBLE

Sometimes, this resolution taken in Paris takes a long time to come and that can be a problem. I then begin to worry, even feel scared of failing and get upset during the period, but that is how I am.

While working on design projects, I spend a lot of time and often adopt circuitous and laborious working methods. Nevertheless, I seem to have taken a vow to only do things in a particular way. I would struggle, by trying several opposite ideas, often in circles, but then at some point all the circles change into a single helical spiral, converging onto a point, and then one day, the door opens to an unexpected solution.

Most often, the initial response is influenced by what I have seen recently, but unless I juxtapose it with what I had thought as the essential solution, it doesn't become what it should. To discover a new response, a new image, I must hang on to both the old (relevant) and the new (fleeting). In such contexts, I always recall the blotting papers widely used in my childhood, which, over time, acquired a unique patina from all the colours they absorbed.

I very well remember the day when Corbusier was copying a miniature painting depicting Krishna and Radha. It showed both of them so intertwined and together playing the flute as well as dancing as if the two of them were one being. This is an unusual concept conveying the singular presence, even though dual, which is the ultimate reality where there is no distinction between the two but a powerful presence of the whole.

Finally, when he showed me his modified version, a la Le Corbusier, I could realize what he meant by carefully looking and not just seeing. For him, creation was a demanding and patient search.

Years later, Piraji Sagara gifted me a similar interpretation of the Radha–Krishna union painted on glass. It hangs near our dining table, subtly reminding me about the distinction between duality and unity.

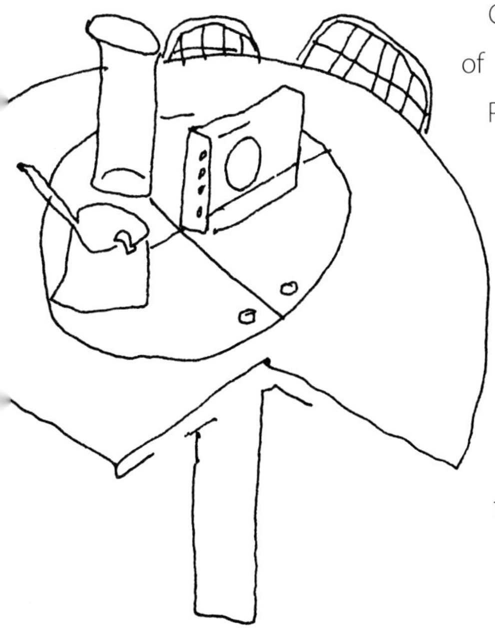

Corbusier's searches were like those of his friends Ferdinand Leger, Pablo Picasso, Jean Gris and others. They always picked up the most unusual images or objects from around. Then they would start copying and modifying their personal understanding in their own style, gradually resulting in a very different version, an unexpected transformation.

This reminds me of the day when Corbusier came to Samper's desk at the Atelier to look at the studies for the facade of the Chandigarh Secretariat he had prepared. There was a demand from P.L. Varma, the chief engineer, to provide additional supports for the extra-long cantilever provided in front of the ministers' offices.

Samper was finding it difficult to reach a satisfying solution. Corbusier took a good look at the studies drawn, spoke to Samper and Xenakis and then drew all the required columns on the elevation. He did this by fusing the elevation conceived earlier with additional supports. Then pointing at the sketch, he said, 'Here is the solution.' Being witness to such instances has been a very educative experience and it has helped me to quickly innovate and deal with all kinds of situations and needs.

The way he went about sketching and overlapping the old with the new was amazing and what we would now call 'out-of-the-box thinking'. Today, this is one of the most unconventional and yet, most admired facades that exist in the annals of contemporary architecture.

His approach for the design of Hutheesing House, which was eventually bought over by Shyamubhai Shodhan and built on another site near my uncle-in-law's house, is equally fascinating and indicative of his exceptional perceptual and observational skills. Knowing that the house was meant for Surottam Hutheesing, a rich, party-loving bachelor, he carefully studied the Indian miniatures depicting joyous, festive moments. He also studied the characteristics of the spaces of these activities. Then, he began with a cube and gradually hollowed out the volume leaving a set of playful facades and a range of terraces. These, he felt, allowed the life depicted in the miniatures to be lived in our times.

Corbusier's 'acrobatic abilities', as I would call them, were best experienced when we saw him working at the drawing board. He would ignore some of the services or even functions at times. Slowly, a plan would emerge but without certain essential elements that were deliberately left out. He would then superimpose, create a new plan and through this process a new discovery—a new vision—would emerge. It seems to me that one needs to ignore some of the existing facts and realities to seek new ways of doing things or new kinds of solutions.

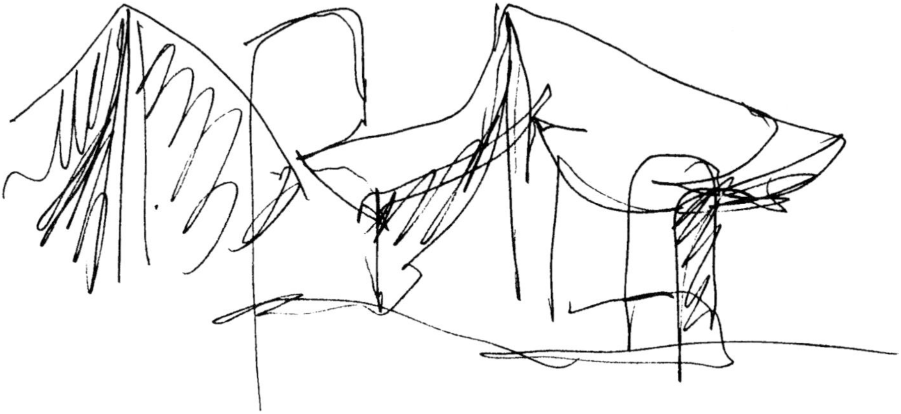

I have said earlier that I was fortunate to have made Ahmedabad my home. There is certainly something very special about the place. Throughout its history, right from 1411 when Ahmed Shah founded it, Ahmedabad has welcomed distinguished achievers in all fields and—among them—architects seem to have benefited the most for some reason. Be they medieval or modern, several architects have found opportunities and encouragement to experiment and innovate in this city.

It is because of this that Ahmedabad is home to historically unique Islamic-Hindu architecture as well as buildings by international masters like Corbusier and Kahn. It has much to do with the nature of patronage that has existed here all along. That again has much to do with its becoming the Manchester of India despite unfavourable conditions, and Mahatma Gandhi choosing it as his base for leading the Independence movement.

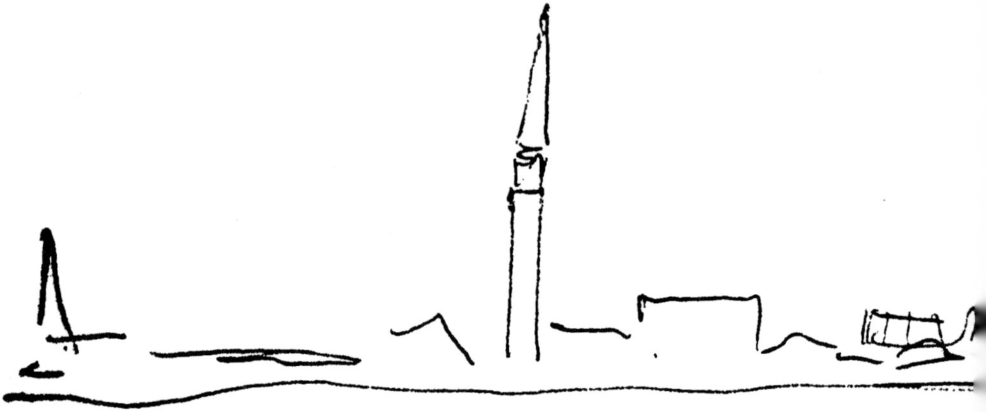

Finally, it was from Sabarmati Ashram here that he undertook the momentous Dandi March—often compared with *Mahabhinishkramana* of the Buddha—along with Sarojini Naidu, Sardar Patel, Jawaharlal Nehru, Maulana Azad and other stalwarts. Visits by all these persons and interactions with the local citizens have moulded the character of Ahmedabad significantly, not to forget that Sardar Patel has also served as the city's mayor.

The city was also home to persons such as Kasturbhai Lalbhai and Ambalal Sarabhai, who belonged to the nation's leading industrial families of the time. They were also at the helm of local guilds and built industrial empires, established an extensive network of charities, educational and research institutions.

Kasturbhai was well known for his vision, integrity and punctuality. He was frugal in his personal life but very generous in social service. For him, all assets belonged to society and he was just a trustee—a very Gandhian idea.

This was also the case with Vikram Ambalal Sarabhai. Together, they conceived the establishment of the Indian Institute of Management at Ahmedabad and the National Institute of Design. Even the establishment of the Ahmedabad School of Architecture, now under CEPT University, is owed to Kasturbhai and the Ahmedabad Education Society, which he led.

If one needs another reason to laud the quality of the leadership of the city, I would like to mention about Corbusier's four projects in the city. Not only were these awarded in a single day but also by the same family: that of Kasturbhai Lalbhai. These included three houses: one for Chinubhai Chimanlal as I have mentioned earlier, the second for Surottam Hutheesing, another of Kasturbhai's nephews, and the third for Manorama Sarabhai, his niece, married to a member of the Sarabhai family. The fourth was the museum for the city of Ahmedabad, where Chinubhai Chimanlal was the mayor.

All of them were extremely progressive, supportive of new trends in all fields, and connoisseurs of the arts.

I must say my continued contact with them for a range of activities has benefited me enormously as an architect and as a person. Visiting Kasturbhai, my chief mentor, if I may call him so, observing him at work at Arvind Textile Mills office and at his residence, I have learned a lot about charity, education and social service. He always set aside time, money and advice for the needs of the community. He was rooted in traditions but contemporary in attitude, in always welcoming new ways.

Even so, he was very meticulous in his ways, personal as well in business. One often found him switching off fans when it was not so hot, to save electricity.

He liked the best but also ensured that neither money nor resources were wasted. For example, while construction was going on at one of his earlier buildings, one would often find Kasturbhai at the project site taking stock of the materials brought in and checking their quality and quantity. That was also his way of setting working norms for his team to follow on a regular basis.

Whenever he was approached with a proposal to start a new educational institution that he liked, he would just say, 'Arrange for half of the funds you need, and we will contribute the rest.' He often said, 'We need to attract the best teachers to raise great institutions and provide them the best buildings we can.'

It was this quality about him, which eventually led a few of us to approach Kasturbhai with a proposal to set up the School of Architecture in 1962. Later, it was Kasturbhai who accepted my suggestion to invite Louis I. Kahn to design IIM at Ahmedabad.

I first met Kahn in 1960 with Leo Lionni's son, Manny Lionni. We had gone to see Kahn's Richards Medical Centre at Philadelphia. After that, we went to meet Kahn at his studio in the city. Once we reached there, I asked his receptionist to request a meeting and mention to him that I had worked with Corbusier—I thought that might help to make the meeting possible at such short notice!

We soon saw Lou come out from the studio to us. After greetings and small talk, he took us to the studio and showed us models and photographs of the Salk Institute that he was then designing.

After a while, hesitatingly I showed him pictures of my housing designs for Ahmedabad Textile Industries Research Association, ATIRA, as well as pictures of plans and model of my own residence, which was then under construction.

Looking at the images of my residence, he asked me 'How did you arrive at such a solution? What made you do a cross plan and such a section having low and high volumes?' Then he pulled out his proposals for an embassy in Luanda. 'Very similar to what I have in mind here,' he said, 'master spaces and servant spaces.' Since then I have often wondered if that coincidence might have greatly contributed to our friendship.

Talking to him, I felt a bit strange. I had never before met such a humble, friendly and encouraging person. It was a very memorable meeting. As we were leaving, he asked us to join him for dinner. I learnt later that he had asked his secretary to loan him some money to pay for that dinner, which again was so characteristic of him. After that first meeting, I frequently met Lou until his death in 1974; especially every time I was at the University of Pennsylvania to teach between 1961 and 1980.

This contact led me to suggest Lou for the IIM Ahmedabad project to Kasturbhai and Vikram Sarabhai. When during a meeting I suggested this to both of them, all Kasturbhai asked me was, 'Would you select him for your own project?' I told him I would, and that settled the decision to invite him.

I was keen to see another path-breaking project in India after Chandigarh, rather than do this project myself. Eventually, for practical reasons, I agreed to represent Kahn as an associate architect locally.

Over the years, my acquaintance with Lou grew stronger as an associate, my spiritual mentor and as a family friend. Lou was, by temperament, a Quaker. He believed in making do with the minimum, very austere.

He was always asking very fundamental questions about acts of living and working and basing his decisions on the answers he found. This was very similar to his famous question: 'What does the brick want to be?'

I would say Kahn was very committed to this project and was deeply involved. There was this rather strange incident once when I got a call from him saying, 'I am reaching Bombay tomorrow. Please arrange a plane ticket for Ahmedabad from there.' He reached Ahmedabad sometime around lunch. We met Kasturbhai and after a rather brief visit to the IIM site, he quietly said to me, 'Doshi, I need to leave tonight, please arrange for a railway or a plane ticket to Bombay. I must teach my class at Penn on Monday.'

I was somewhat shocked, but learnt later that he had come in from Tel Aviv and was on way to the US. I guess he must have been thinking of the project and, being in the region, wanted to see how the campus was shaping up; yet, he did not want to miss his meeting with his beloved students. For once, Kasturbhai was at loss of words when he heard about this turn of events!

Kahn loved spending time with students and loved to tell them stories including those from the Arabian Nights. He was a great teacher. I remember being at one of his classes where I saw him studying a rather bad project by a student. To everyone's surprise, Kahn focused on the area of the staircase there; slowly he expounded the virtues of this staircase, the movement, the journey of an old parent with his grandchild, vistas, railings, a seat on the landing and the formal destination. No sooner was his eloquent exploration over than all those present credited the student with having done a great job.

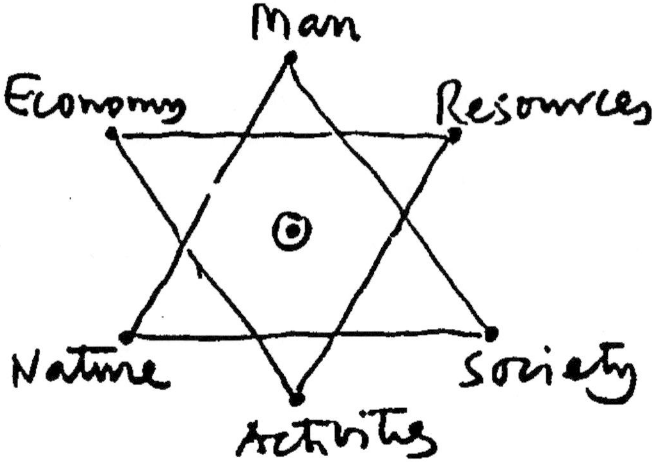

I happened to be with him once just after he had finished a meeting for an important private assignment in New York. He said to me, 'Today I was questioned by Eero Saarinen. He asked me how many colours I would use in a building. I told him maybe two—black and grey—and asked him the same question. His answer was, "Just one. I have tried this in the Central Broadcasting Corporation building."'

Lou was a very private person but for my family and me his house was always open. We might be among the very few lucky ones to have frequented his home so often. While at our home in Ahmedabad, Kahn would just go about as if he was a family member.

Sometimes when our youngest daughter Maneesha was painting, he would patiently sit with her, gently suggesting something or the other. Bringing encouragement and cheerfulness was his forte.

Once, Lou and I went out to buy a present for his wife, Esther. After rejecting dozens of shawls, he selected one. Then he asked the merchant if he had a similar one with minimal but thoughtfully placed embroidery. When—after a long search—he finally found one, he said, 'Minimalism expresses the true essence.' He often said, 'Go to the limit, and when there is nothing left, perhaps you will see the existence.' Truly Zen.

Vikram Sarabhai, although an industrialist, devoted most his life to science and technology in India and the development of rural areas through satellite-based communication as a part of India's space application programme with which he was deeply involved.

Despite his busy schedule, he was so amicable that there was no bar on anyone meeting him. He would spend time to make each visitor feel special. His encouragement and support significantly helped my career initially when I was commissioned to design housing for ATIRA and the Physical Research Laboratory in Ahmedabad.

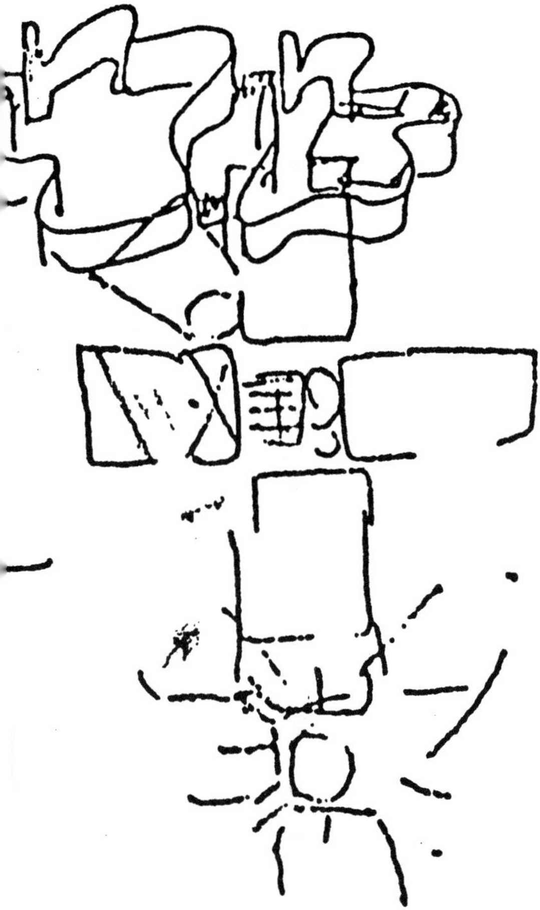

At a more personal level, I remember an incident involving him and his family. We had invited Vikrambhai, his wife Mrinalini and their daughter Mallika for lunch. My eldest daughter Tejal was then two years old. Seeing her, Mrinaliniben said, 'Vikram, we should send our newly born Siamese kittens for Tejal. She will enjoy playing with them.' It seemed like a good idea.

Later that very afternoon, their car brought two beautiful, brown Siamese kittens with blue eyes. Very lovely, but no sooner were they pulled out of the basket than they started crying. We tried all kinds of options, but nothing would stop them.

Thinking that they could be hungry, some milk was placed in a saucer for them. They would not accept that and kept on crying. In some time, Ba, my mother-in-law, Kamu and Tejal panicked.

Finally, I had to telephone Mrinaliniben to seek help about what to do. She said, 'No milk, they will only eat meat.' Now, I did not know how to deal with that. Ba was a strict follower of Jainism who would not even allow certain vegetables like potatoes or onions in the house.

Reluctantly I told Ba what we needed to do. After some thought she said, 'Okay, ask our servants to get some meat from the market and feed them outside our house. Don't bring it in.' However, even that did not work and that was a very troubled night for all of us.

We decided early in the morning to put them in a basket, went to Mrinaliniben, and with much regret returned the kittens. Even now, we wonder if there was something we could have done to keep them. It may well be that the kittens just wanted to be back where they were born. May be they felt that was their home?

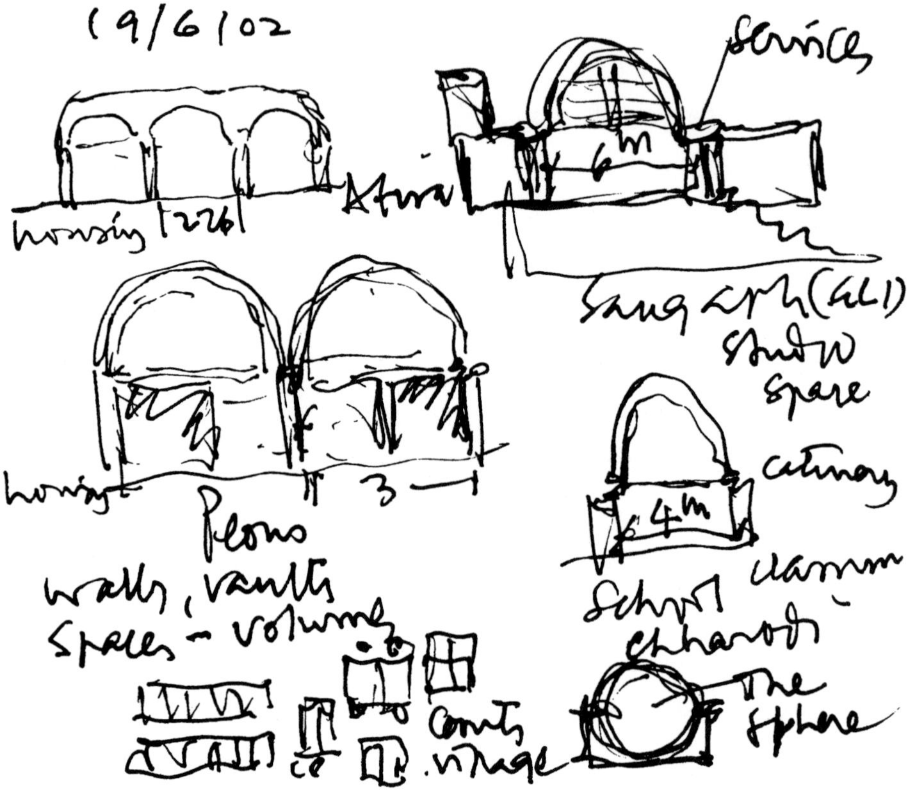
19/6/02
Services
housing
Atria
studio
space
catenary
classroom
School
walls, vaults
spaces – volumes
courts
village
The
sphere

Housing design for ATIRA was my first major assignment in many ways. I did not know where and how to begin working on it. Therefore, I decided to do something that I knew about and explore some of the ideas I had learned from Corbusier. I chose to use bricks for load-bearing walls as well as a segmental brick vault as roof. I thought of this as an appropriate solution since both cement and steel were in short supply in those days, as also because a vaulted roof would lend a feeling of a large space for that otherwise modest house.

Unfortunately, to save costs, I had not provided the tie rods and the first vault collapsed. That was a serious matter for all concerned with the project except me who knew the why of it. Nonetheless, Vikrambhai was requested to visit the site and discuss the future course. When I explained to him about the need and cost of the tie rod, all he said was, 'There is no going back. Our task is to find an appropriate solution, correct and redo the way it should be,' which was very encouraging.

My design also could not be more expensive than the cost of similar buildings then. Therefore, I proposed plain cement flooring, known locally as Indian Patent Stone, and aluminium vertical louvers. I designed a minimalist house maximizing multiple use of space through sliding doors. Enraged, the faculty did not wish to move to these railway barrack-looking houses. They tried their best to find faults in the house. Finally, over time, they praised the spaciousness of the houses.

When Kahn saw these houses, he remarked, 'When basic nature of form is wilfully expressed, architecture happens.' So well put, as only he could.

Another project of low-cost housing for the so-called Class IV employees, now known as Peons' Quarters in Ahmedabad, was designed to be roofed using conical *guna* tubes inserted into each other to make an arch as the basis of a vault, like in a Nubian vault. *Guna* are conical clay cylinders made by a potter on a wheel which, when cut in to half, yield two of the traditional country tiles used in most parts of India for roofing.

If we used them as cylinders, they would also provide a hollow space within the vault that would act as good insulation and help keep the house cooler in Indian summers, we thought. Because these are conical, they readily slide into each other and can be adjusted to make an arch, so we were very hopeful about a vault made of these.

However, after building the first vault, it just collapsed when the supports were removed. The locally fired *guna* tubes were too weak to bear the load. I then opted to build vaults using regular bricks. I very much wanted the vaults to be hollow in the middle for insulation, but that did not happen until at Sangath years later.

The cluster plan of the Quarters was like a village with small community spaces interspersed randomly. Aldo van Eyck, whom I had accompanied on a visit to the project, had remarked that it was an 'ideal solution for contemporary Indian housing.'

Shreyas Comprehensive Educational Campus in Ahmedabad was designed during the same period I was a Graham Fellow. That was my very first large assignment, commissioned by Leenaben Mangaldas, née Sarabhai. She was an ardent follower of Maria Montessori's educational philosophy, and education at Shreyas was to be based on that.

I designed the campus as a cluster of independent classes with veranda but without a conventional connecting corridor. The scale of the classrooms related to different height groups, from the teacher at 165cm and children ranging from 90cm to 150cm. The intent was to offer both the scales, intimate and large, at the same time. Cross-ventilation was necessary to keep the spaces cool in Ahmedabad climate. This was further complemented by deep veranda and overhangs which keep the direct harsh sun away from the active spaces.

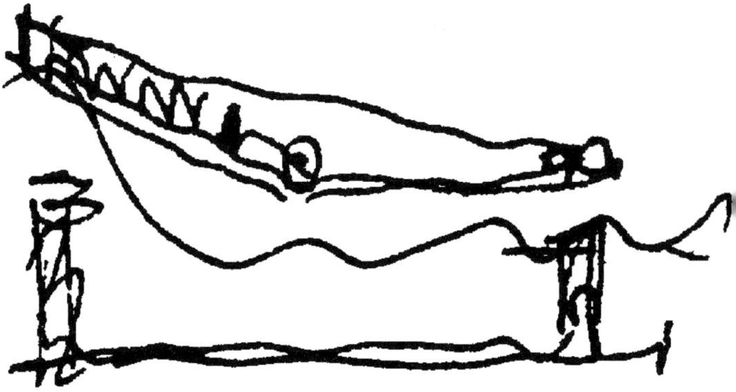

The questions we asked were: How does a child learn? What does a child learn? Where does a child learn? Education is not only what happens inside the classroom, but also outside, in the changing seasons. Every time you go out, you see trees blossoming, changes in the landscape, rhythm in nature, shadows, materials, volumes… the juxtaposition of all these become important in learning.

As a teacher, one goes about more like a gardener. When asked once, Sarala Devi Sarabhai, mother of Vikram Sarabhai, attributed the success of her children to right pruning, love, nourishment and care. She had added, **'Remember, never expect an apple tree to yield a mango. Allow it to excel at what its nature is.'**

As I said earlier, I was very lucky to have made Ahmedabad my home. I was so fortunate to have all these enlightened clients commission their projects. Here, the task was not just to raise another building, but search for spaces, an environment that would allow the pursuit of higher-level goals.

Such projects allowed me to learn, grow and mature not only as an architect but also as a human being. I must add, however, that it was not only the nature of projects but also the number that was very gratifying. It felt nice to be doing good work and in good numbers, which allowed me to learn quickly, rise in standing among my peers and also improve my material well-being.

I believe all of this was important for me because it made me feel settled, take roots and, in a way, taste success after years of moving from one city to another across continents, starting from modest beginnings in Pune.

Soon after the Shreyas Campus, I was designing laboratories for the Gujarat University in Ahmedabad. I felt the need to design a new prototype for laboratories where the need for future growth and flexibility in upgrading services would become primary elements. Akin to the natural growth of trees, I designed a structural module allowing expansion in both the vertical and the horizontal directions. Besides, the same module responded to climatic conditions and gave a unique character to the chemistry, botany and physics laboratories.

Then there was the cafeteria for the Saraspur Textile Mill, where I struggled hard to find a climate control device without using Le Corbusier's sun breakers or a glass curtain wall. In my mind I asked, 'What would Mies (van der Rohe) do if he had to create an insulating wall which is economical and needs minimum maintenance in the tropics?' I then thought of utilizing a brick cavity wall similar to the museum but adding depth to create random storage spaces, and recessing the windows to provide me a new curtain wall suitable to our context.

Here, for the first time, I built a wall with cavity in brick with vertical and horizontal supports, and windows staggered all over the wall. In the process I discovered—for myself at least—the meanings of load-bearing and non-load-bearing walls, structural and non-structural walls, cavity and solid walls, climatically controlled walls, economically built walls, etc. The key issues, I realized, were about the materials, technology and their expressions.

The period from 1960 to 1970 was indeed breathtaking and intense. There was an inner urge to consolidate my practice as an Indian *sthapati* as well as to be recognized for the work I was doing. I was trying to learn all the time; from projects, from my clients and my colleagues. Each time, the effort was to find an improved and more relevant solution to the tasks on hand.

I was working hard to search for expressions suitable to the Indian lifestyle and culture. A deep concern for the way traditional Indian houses harvested water, recycled waste, and dealt with climate and local lifestyle was a constant undercurrent in my work. Looking back, I really wonder how India came to dominate my attitude so soon after the global exposure. Maybe it was the beginning of a concern for a distinct identity.

For quite some time, my practice did not have a name. Perhaps I was happy to enjoy the anonymity like the traditional Indian architects; it may also be that I did not want the name to exclude anything I may want to do later.

Then one day when I was with Motabhai, we were talking about my projects and he suddenly asked me if I had named my practice, or what my firm was called. I told him I had not yet thought of naming it, nor did I like the idea of giving it my own name, which was in vogue then among architects. I also told him that I did not want the name to restrict my work to just architecture because, like Corbusier, I was keen to be involved in larger concerns such as planning, and urban and product design, including other arts.

I asked him if there was a name that could suggest that nothing was excluded. That was when he suggested that I name my firm Vastu-Shilpa. *Vastu*, he said, describes the total environment around us and *shilpa* means "to design", just the name that answered all my deeper concerns.

In those early days, I would often fall back on the lessons learnt at Paris to help me deal with work. To always view 'every problem as a virtue... and every problem as the mother of new ideas. In order to get into that position, I should create a problem.'

If you are making a square room, instead make it oblong or rectangular and see what happens. Set up for yourself constant challenges. The moment there is a challenge, you should be brave enough to face it and say, 'I will solve this.' That is what keeps you on the go. Setting up challenges like that, realizing one's inadequacies brought to notice directly or indirectly, must lead to new learning.

This reminds me of meeting the chief engineer of Chandigarh, P.L. Varma for the first time in Paris when he came to discuss the designs for the Governor's Palace at Chandigarh. Since Corbusier was at Cabanon, his summer house in the south of France, Varma asked me to show him around Paris for a day or so before accompanying him to join Corbusier at Cabanon.

Among the places we visited was Parc Montsouris. While we were there, he pointed at a tree and asked me, 'What is the name of this tree?' I said, 'I don't know.' He seemed surprised and shot back, 'How come you do not know? Don't you study horticulture in architecture?' I said, 'Sorry, but we don't.' 'Pity, how can architecture be complete without the knowledge of trees, plants, forests, gardens, land and the ecosystem?'

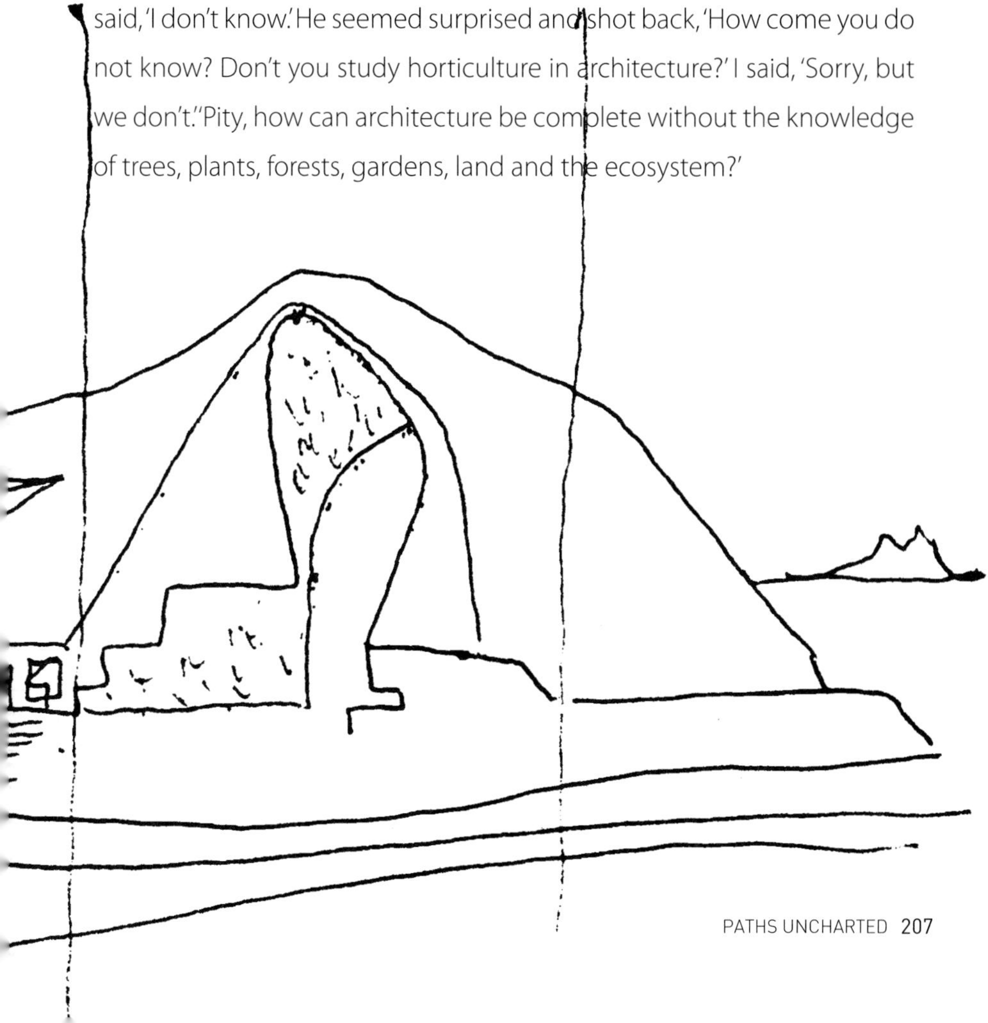

That set me thinking and, ever since I have never missed an opportunity to learn more about the elements of landscape. In fact, seeing our environment and its symbiotic relationship with the entire flora and fauna has been a fascinating preoccupation for me right from that moment in Parc Montsouris.

We then went to Cap Martin, where Corbusier had his Cabanon, just a one-room summer house. He often went there and immensely enjoyed living amid fishermen, most of whom were his good friends.

One day at the dining table, Corbusier suddenly spread a sheet of paper and said 'Varma, do you know what truth is?' Surprised, Varma nodded negatively.

Corbusier drew two parallel lines and said, 'These are two banks of the river.' Then drawing a meandering line between the parallel lines, he said, 'Truth never touches any of the river banks. It flows in the middle, sometimes more to the left, sometimes to the right, and eventually meets the ocean of greater truth. It never takes sides or is so definitive as to lose sight of the essential.'

When I once asked Motabhai what the essence of Hindu philosophy was, he wrote these four Sanskrit terms: *vikas*, meaning blossoming, *vistaar* meaning expansion, *kshobh*, meaning churning, and *drav*, meaning melting. He then said: 'The entire universe operates in this mode. Don't you remember reading in the Gita that transformation is the law of nature? Remember nothing stays constant, the only certainty is uncertainty.'

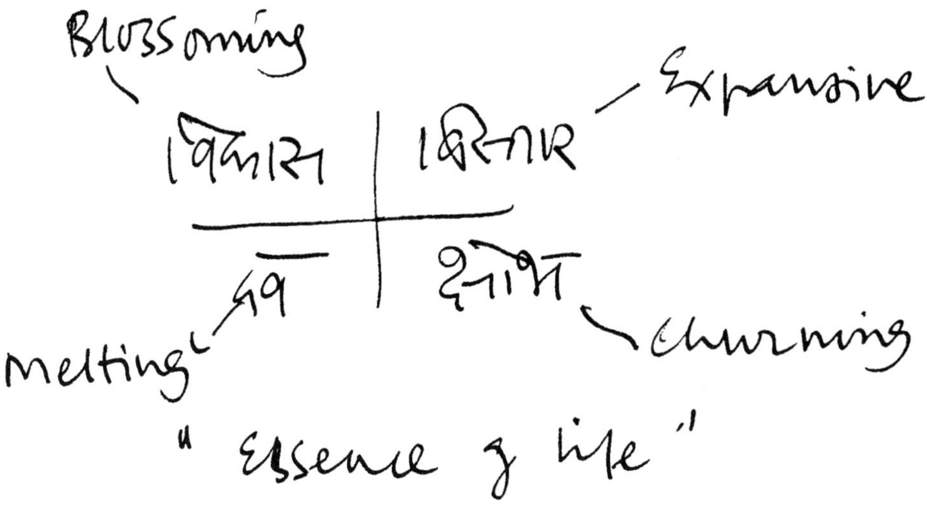

Time flows, so do thoughts, ideas and expressions. Their expansion is like clothing with added layers. What is constant is the churning, searching for the eternal truth—*sat-chit-anand*. To understand uncertainty as a constant, to search for the elusive divinity that is hidden in the spirit of internal harmony, openness, tolerance, compassion and forgiveness. In architecture, it is the essence of life that is memory, associations, the spaces, forms, light, colour, rhythm that make it happen.

You will always see an opportunity and potential to start all over again, however closed the situation may seem.

It is good to begin every morning as if it was the first morning of your life; as if you were born on that very morning, in that moment.

Corbusier visited Shodhan's house for the last time in 1957. Nearing the gate before leaving Shodhan Villa, he turned, looked back, said, 'I am Le Corbusier at 67 and let posterity match this.'

It was hard on me, and after my exposure in the US and seeing Kahn's work, I wondered how I could find a way to try my best to fulfil my guru's challenge. With the emergence of new India, with its independence and freedom, the challenges were obvious: to express Indian identity in its new avatar. I was haunted by the rock-cut temples and the traditional towns and wondered if they could give an inkling of our role now. I decided to invite Louis Kahn to take up this challenge so that I would learn to rediscover myself, and the architecture I needed to do in the process.

After the Institute of Indology, I had placed myself in a position the way our ancestors did during the earlier centuries through juxtapositions and by allowing different expressions and to create our own ways. For me, it was Lou on one side and Mons. Corbusier on the other.

Beginning with the School of Architecture, until now with Sangath and other projects, I am still searching for the semblance of roots that make India survive for centuries with changing definitions of styles and typologies while also understanding form, space, light, colour as well as technologies and plasticity and their multiple ways of transformed expressions and concerns for the ambiguous.

The flowing nature of Indian traditions and my personal vows of not imitating Le Corbusier or Kahn gave rise to a search for more appropriate expressions. India's enigmatic, mythical and rational way of looking at life as one continuum—sometimes hybrid yet open-ended, not necessarily fragmented yet not frozen in a particular form or style, sometimes porous yet not disconnected, but loose enough to combine various ways—gave rise to an experience of architecture as a loose object like Indian clothing, sometimes bare, sometimes multilayered, sometimes finite yet breaking. Sometimes prominent yet nondescript or hidden.

Mythical, not a house, nor a home nor an office nor a studio but just a place, a space; splendorous, yet conversing in quiet tones. A bag full of small anecdotes woven in an unending story as if ongoing; an expression very similar to our ambiguous ways of communication. A building built of components to perform its functions yet not rigid but bound and loose enough to serve, to delight, to give choices as if at home.

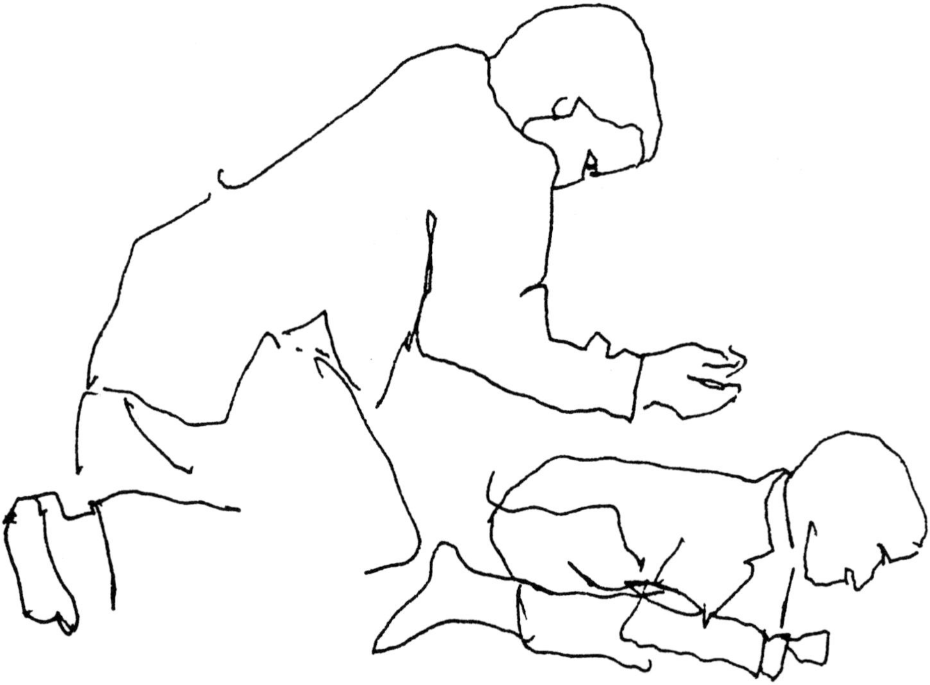

While in France, I was what the French would call a 'Leftist'. All of my close friends and most other colleagues were 'communist'. We were always talking about the 'revolution'. This outlook was so deeply ingrained in me that even after I had set up a practice in Ahmedabad, I would often think like, 'I don't want to buy any insurance, I don't believe in it; I don't want to own a house.'

All of these resolves disappeared without a trace when I once went to meet Rasikbhai. His colleagues were discussing buying land for their own homes, and he had often talked to me about buying a house.

Seeing me there, he again brought that up and added, 'If you want to starve to death then there is no problem. However, if you want to pursue a profession, design good buildings, and raise a family, you must have a small place where you can work and live, from where no proprietor can throw you out. Besides, you may actually grow some vegetables there and ward off starvation.'

I was still not too sure. One day, he again asked me if I would like to buy a plot and build a home. Slowly over the next few days, I found myself reflecting on his suggestion. I thought that it seemed like a good idea to own a house, but I had no money. So what do I do? However, the desire had taken roots, which indeed was a big change.

Then, I thought, I do not want to buy an average size plot measuring 300–400 square metres, which was the norm. If I do buy, I must buy a plot of about 900–1,000 square metres, because it should be big enough for a well-provided domestic life. Moreover, if I were going to beg and borrow to pay for the plot, why not beg and borrow like the king of beggars?

Seriously looking around, I thought I could try to borrow from Jayantilal Vora, an engineer and a friend I had first met while working on Sanskar Kendra. The same evening I asked him if he would loan me Rs 7,000 for buying the plot. He readily agreed. I took the money and went to Rasikbhai. He was indeed surprised and asked, 'How did you manage such a large amount so quickly?' He had purchased two plots of 400 square metre each for his two sons.

I told him that I had borrowed the money and that I would pay it back. That is how 14, Sadma Society—which I regard as one of my finest designs, and an inalienable part of my family's life and me—came into being. I must hasten to add that I borrowed again to pay for the actual construction of a home on the plot! This came in the form of a bank loan of Rs 15,000 through the cooperative set-up for our housing society with a bank guarantee provided by Shyamubhai Shodhan.

Earlier I had taken risks by moving to new cities in search of education and work, and now I was doing that differently in Ahmedabad but risking nonetheless. Sangath, my office, also owes its life to borrowed money. Somehow, I seem to have always borrowed for most such expenses.

The thought of not owning any material possessions has been with me for a long time. There is, I believe, a reason for this and it has to do with my childhood memories.

My mother died when I was just ten months old and my father remarried some years later. Vallabh, my brother, and I were very upset about it; I was then 15 years old. And for reasons that I have never been able to understand, in about a year's time, both of us brothers could not get along with our stepmother. For that reason, as well to express our displeasure at our father having remarried, one night we moved to an upper floor of the ancestral house and started living all by ourselves.

We must have felt so strongly that as soon as we could, in a few months, we moved to a rented house with very little resources. So much so that often our clothes were stitched from sheets that our youngest aunt spared for us. That was the time I took a vow not to possess any property nor anything else precious such as ornaments. I resolved to live my life like a wanderer. Ownership is not an issue with me. Even now, I do not own anything—neither my residence nor my office Sangath. I am happy about it.

I always think of Ba, my mother-in-law, as my own mother. She lived like a trustee of our home and our family, always giving and self-effacing. She would remember everyone's peculiar needs, even of all the guests who have been coming to the house since 1960.

Ba actually had no possessions to speak of, except a modest suitcase containing four sets of saris and blouses, all of them made from white fabric and hence interchangeable. The rest of us in the house have so many wardrobes and cupboards full of our clothes and other knick-knacks.

In many ways, that childhood resolve continues even today. I rarely base my decisions or accept conditions that threaten my material conditions. That is how I am.

Once, a person from Foundation Le Corbusier came to see me and asked,

'You had worked on the design of Shodhan House?'

'Yes.'

'You also worked on ATMA office, because I see your name there in records.'

'Yes.'

'But there are not many drawings in our records. There are only four to six drawings there. How come?'

'I don't know but I executed the whole building here. I made detailed drawings here; those drawings were also made by me while there.'

'There are no sections studying light and space.'

'I don't remember.'

'How is it possible? What is your background?'

'I have no background but whatever I learnt and felt, I drew.'

'Did you not study through school?'

'No, I was for a while at J.J. College in Bombay, but I left after the third year.'

'Then how have you managed all along?'

'I have no idea,' I said.

Then I drew for him a sketch of how the ATMA auditorium was designed, and I said, 'I will show you what I did. I used to draw like Corbusier and sign like him. One day, Corbusier saw a drawing of the project and asked me, "Doshi, have you drawn this?" I said, "Yes". He said, "You draw very well but you put too many people in there. You must have discretion". So I used to become like him. In Kahn's case, I was like Kahn.'

The visitor did not know what to say next and left abruptly.

Looking back, I can say that I had managed to grasp the spirit of Corbusier's architecture. He too had realized that and hence trusted me and allowed me to decide what was required for all of his local projects. When he came to Ahmedabad the next time, he would express his satisfaction on the decisions I had taken and endorse them.

I had designed the interiors of Shodhan Villa and the ATMA building entirely in his absence but during his last visit, he expressed his total satisfaction about the work. After a few years, for Shodhan Villa, I had sent him a proposal to modify the kitchen, with the addition of a bath near the swimming pool and servant quarters. His response to what I had proposed was so heartily approving and touching that I have kept it with me.

In his response, he had only suggested minor changes, but more importantly, argued as to how I could do this work much more quickly and independently as against months to prepare even a proposal at 35 Rue de Sevres. For some time, he had even pinned this handwritten letter on the wall there.

Another time I surprised myself was when I met Ludwig Mies van der Rohe at the Graham Foundation office. He was sitting next to me. Suddenly he turned to me and asked, 'Doshi, you have worked with Corbusier?' I said, 'Yes, sir.' Then he asked, 'How would Corbusier place his Ronchamp Chapel on the Madison Avenue in Manhattan?' Dumbfounded, I paused, then replied to him, 'Sir, how would you place your Chapel at IIT on that hill?' All he did was smile.

Sometimes, I feel that I am not overtly conscious of matters around me. Occasionally, I seem to blank out, and feel I am somewhere else. Strangely, I think this has helped me often. I can be in the office and not be there at the same time. I can take risks all the time. The truth may well be that every time I have taken a risk it was because I did not know what was in store for me.

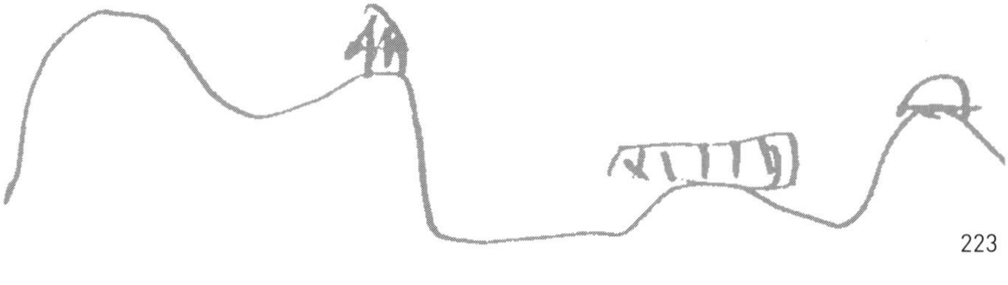

I have realized that when you constantly try to anticipate what will happen next, you are inhibited. Prejudices too can be inhibiting. I feel that our past knowledge constrains us from thinking freely.

A child is without such baggage, which is why a child is spontaneous and fearless. In the process, the child is able to discover and learn every living moment. As we grow up, we tend to anticipate the consequences and often not act spontaneously.

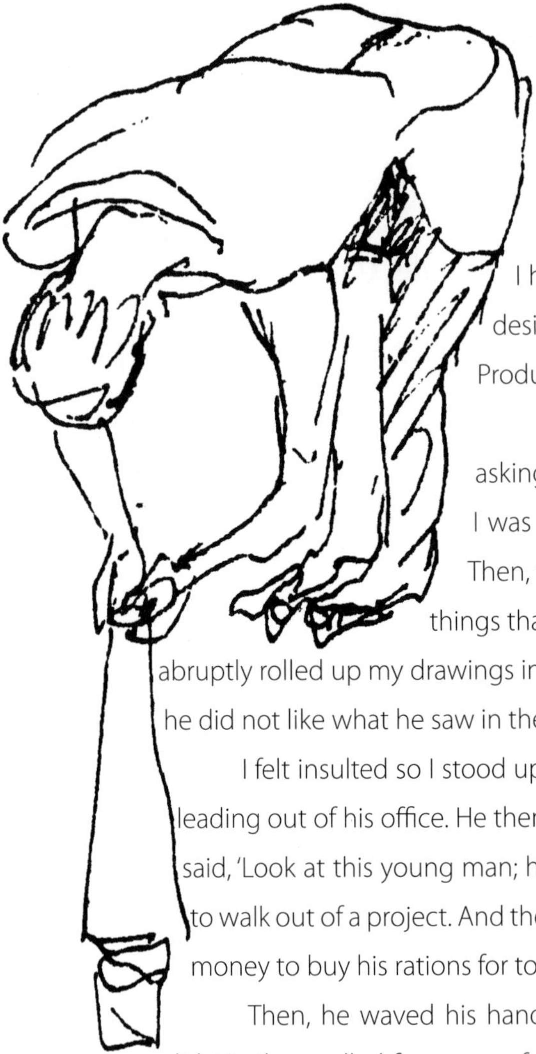

I well remember a rather spontaneous reaction on my part with Kasturbhai who otherwise meant so much to me. I had gone to discuss with him my design for a proposed office at Atul Products premises near Valsad.

He was looking at the drawings, asking me questions now and then and I was explaining to him all the details. Then, without any hint as to there were things that he did not like in my design, he abruptly rolled up my drawings in a manner clearly conveying that he did not like what he saw in the drawings. At least I thought so.

I felt insulted so I stood up and started walking to the door leading out of his office. He then glanced at his sister Lilaben and said, 'Look at this young man; he is so upset, and seems to want to walk out of a project. And the truth may well be that he has no money to buy his rations for tomorrow.'

Then, he waved his hand asking me to sit down which I did. He then called for a cup of tea and said, 'Doshi, why are you so impatient? There are times when two parties on a project may not agree, but that is not the end. We have gone through many such episodes and each time come closer and collaborate better.' He was truly my mentor and loved me like his son.

I have no fear of losing because actually there is nothing to lose. If you do not own anything, what is there to lose? My most prized possessions are not material ones. I have dreams. They are mine. Nobody can rob me of my dreams. My thoughts, my ideas; they are mine. However, I must find ways to use them; if I do not then I might as well lose them.

I would agree that I have a selective memory; I well remember the good times and quickly forget the bad events. I rarely get into arguments with people. It does not bother me if we do not agree. I have been shouted at, called names for many things but I do not mind. I know there is always another way to look at all situations. Therefore, you become more accepting of other views, like trees swaying in strong wind.

Often a student or a faculty member at the school, or one of my clients may accuse me of some wrongdoing based on hearsay but I reach out to them and eventually they become my close friends. This has made me a very different kind of a person—open, accessible and very hopeful, positive about the world and future.

Constant change and adaptation are obvious in my designs over the years. I still do not know what good aesthetics is. Is it an absolute manner of seeing things, as someone has said? I still do not understand what style is. I do not know what we can say, as being right. It seems to me that there are at least a thousand different ways to interpret things. That is also the view of the Hindu philosophy. It is necessary to forget the negatives and to search for potential solutions.

It was after my lecture at the RIBA in 1980 that an incident concerning Charles Jencks, the historian and a friend whom I had met during our travel in Italy, took place.

After the RIBA lecture he said to me, 'Doshi, you talked about Udaipur and Jaipur buildings and how the lifestyle of the people, their dresses, food and their habits, all come together in these cities. But how do you explain your own buildings and their architectural expressions in today's India?'

I have not forgotten this question and it keeps coming up all the time while I am planning and designing for clients who follow both traditional and Western lifestyles.

My work seems to draw on my childhood memories and the time I spent working and travelling in Europe. Strangely, the straightforward repetitive American scene has never attracted me; perhaps it is the subtle differences between scale, technology and the nature of issues.

Old European towns, with their easily accessible public spaces and amenities, always fascinate and inspire me. It may be the scales there and the cultural affinity, especially that of Italy and around. With Italy, Rajasthan, and Gujarat, my world expands. My expressions try to bring their relationships together. It is therefore natural that the current discussions on styles do not stir me.

When I left Paris, I had taken a vow that in my designs, I would not use sun breakers, nor would I use columns or the elements that my guru was popularly known for. I had also observed how he himself had put these elements aside and created a whole new language for his architecture such as that at Ronchamp. Even as I was conscious of this need in the beginning, most often I was falling back on the old and familiar ways.

Before I began to design my own home, I had designed two houses, one for K.C. Jhaveri and the other for Chinubhai Manibhai Sheth. I designed the Jhaveri House using a stilts frame structure, large pivoted doors and a brick-plastered curtain wall. At the Chinubhai House, I again used a frame structure, which was three storeys high, with small louvers and several projections. When I went to see the houses sometime after they were occupied, their designs actually shocked me since they did not at all represent what I was searching for.

Even so, a few months later, the first sketches of my house very much flowed from the ideas I had acquired in Paris. Sketches showed a concrete umbrella structure with peripheral walls of brick and glass and an interior space with double height in half of the volume and two floors in the other half. By then, I had realized the complete irrelevance of such ideas and their total alienation from what I was seeking in my designs. It was a struggle to get away from what I had learnt, and to be myself.

Often, when we have no springboard or when we don't look for simpler solutions, we can never get away from what we have learnt.

It was a chance event, as if godsend, during my visit to a brick kiln, which became the source of design for my home. Of course, inspiration for design is not a simple phenomenon. Chance encounters can flash images that can find their way in our designs. The real world seen mythically does shape the creative world.

That is what happened. Once visiting a brick kiln, I saw a woman descending a dusty, worn-out staircase in front of four columns. The whole scene was lit by thin shafts of sunlight streaming through punctures in the old tin roof, making it very memorable.

This is the image that generated the plan of my own house in 1958, with four brick columns in the centre with a cross plan enclosed by load-bearing peripheral walls. An open staircase placed between the central columns and the perimeter wall has become the most prominent and memorable element of the house.

Suitably modified 50 years later, the same plan has inspired two more homes that I designed for my daughters, Tejal and Maneesha. The columns and a staircase remain at the core of these homes, but I configured them differently in response to the plot and their lifestyles.

In the design of my home, the traditional temple 'S'-shaped s transformed themselves into vertical skylights within overhanging boxes. The quality of light and spaces came from Manorama Sarabhai's house. Finally, the experience of a traditional Pune house, with its narrow spaces and low height, shaped the spaces on the mezzanine floor. The addition of unusually narrow, low, long spaces for library and beds on the mezzanine floor gave an appearance of a one-storeyed house.

Like most other projects, my own home too underwent numerous changes and modifications even as it was being built. That is because I like to work as if what I am doing right now is the last project I will ever do and today is the very last day to make it right, and my best work. Therefore, whatever I want to modify or change, I must do so right now and not wait for the next project.

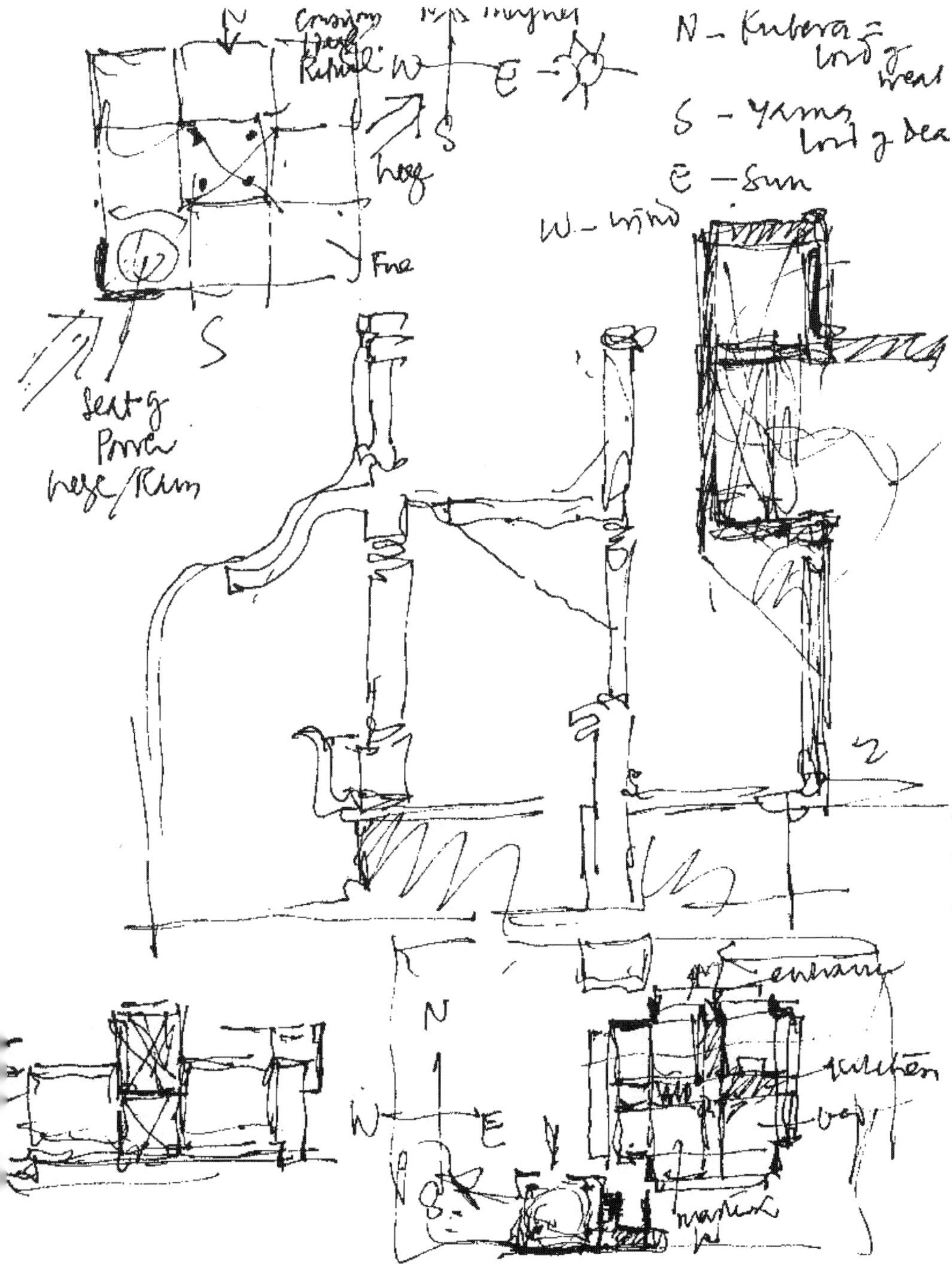
N – Kubera =
S – Yama
E – Sun
W – Wind
Fire
N
S
W
E
entrance
kitchen

LC – Parallel walls

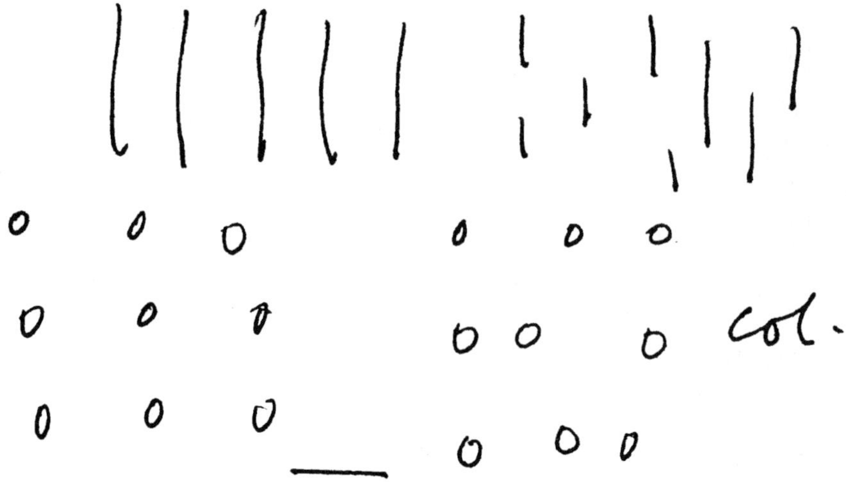

combinations
cube meandering
and cube + volumes

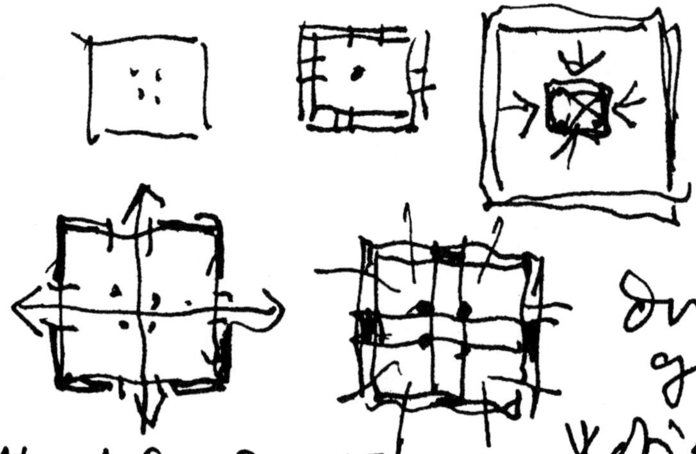

directions
of space
& objects in
space

attached objects
~~[illegible]~~ free objects

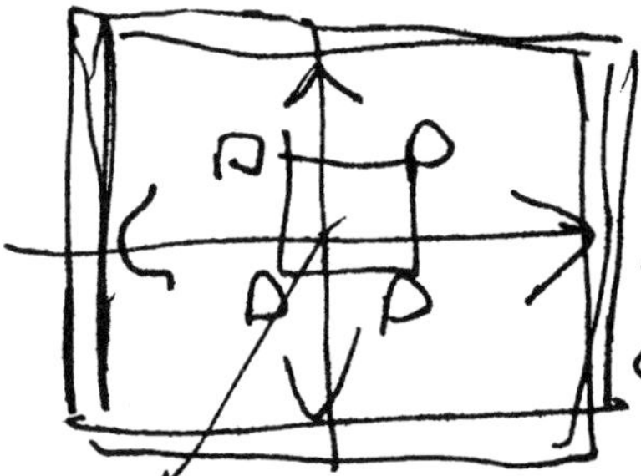

Static
Static
Central

Focus in the centre
Radiates towards
wall

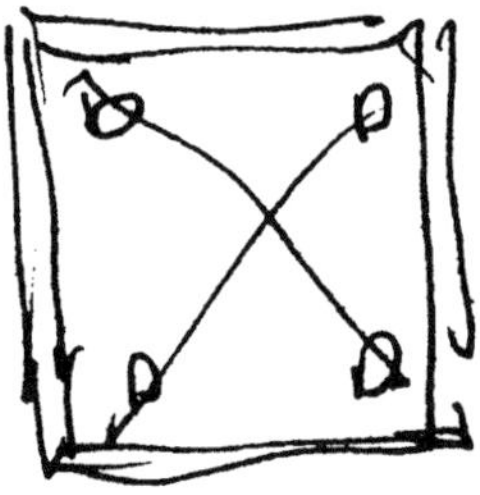

Static
but
larger

Contains space
and creates
Tensions between
walls + column

Quality of space
changes – directions
proportions become
different – In 3D the conquests
are few

Space suggest
another relationship
creates counter
points – movement
is dynamic

Inclined wall

Perhaps Amdavad Ni Gufa best expresses this spirit. Though the building seems to be finite, after a few years, when I organized its surrounding landscape and entrance, I tried to make it connected to the extended world. Similarly, the extension to Sangath in 2010, in order to accommodate the international studio and exhibition, is an extension in the most unexpected manner. This is also the case with the extensions for the Kanoria Centre and CEPT, which are ongoing projects. Here the issues of contemporariness and merging of the old and the new have been the focus of design.

I find that I have constantly followed the lessons learnt. I change my designs even during construction. Whether it is a large institutional project or modest homes, they are all modified several times in the course of design and execution to make them better.

Here, I recall another instance concerning Buckminster Fuller, from whom I picked up a good habit. Bucky reached Delhi in the morning and was to deliver the prestigious Nehru Memorial Lecture on the same day at 4.00 PM. Both Stein and I joined him for lunch and dropped him at the Ashoka Hotel at almost 3:00 PM. He was tired and yet he asked us to meet him in the lobby at 3:30 PM to reach the venue.

Stein and I thought we would give him a few more minutes of rest and decided not to call him from the lobby but go to his room on the fifth floor. No sooner were we close to his room than Bucky came out refreshed and ready for this rather important lecture. We were amazed. I ventured to ask him if he had rested at all. He said, 'Doshi, I thrive on catnaps. If you want to get full mileage from the day, learn to take catnaps.' I eventually learned to do that.

My career has gone through various phases. First, it was the discovery of India, and then the euphoric phase of Corbusier's work in India. Nevertheless, there was always a desire to innovate and do something, which was deeply rooted in Indian culture and lifestyles. The first two decades of practice were tough, full of challenges for survival and the search for an identity. I was struggling to discover an appropriate expression for Indian architecture.

From 1958 onwards, the opportunities under the Graham Fellowship allowed me to lecture at various US universities and meet all the top academicians and architects who then mattered. I would present at these lectures whatever I had discovered or designed. There would be questions, comments, discussions that would then inform my thoughts and my designs to come.

Knowing my interest in low-cost housing for the poor, Leo Lionni invited me to the Aspen Conference in the US on the theme of 'The Rest of Our Lives' in 1966. I led a group of Indians where Rajeev Sethi, now an internationally known designer and social activist, Adoor Gopalakrishnan, a world-renowned film-maker, and R.K. Joshi, a graphic designer, were the other members.

I had a chance to interact with Georges Candilis, Shadrach Woods, Aldo van Eyck, James Stirling, Giancarlo de Carlo and Jacob Bakema at the Urbino Conference of the Team 10. Team 10 was an offshoot of the CIAM I had mentioned earlier and meeting all these architects there was a rare opportunity for one's growth and development.

At the Conference, I had spoken on the subject of 'Time, Tolerance, Identity and Continuity'. There I had shown my proposals for a township for Electronic Corporation of India at Hyderabad where I had created a generic service core as the main structure to which one could add rooms as and when needed. I feel that all these concerns are still very valid for architects and planners in India.

Overall, I might say that 1960s was a very special decade in my life. I was lucky to be involved in the initial stages of formation of the National Institute of Design (NID), the Indian Institute of Management (IIM), the B.M. Institute of Occupational Health and of course, with the School of Architecture at Ahmedabad, founded in 1962.

I was also actively involved with preparation of the development plan for Ahmedabad city with the Ahmedabad Municipal Corporation. Moreover, I was just about in my mid-30s. Therefore, this was a great time for learning and facing new challenges for me.

As I mentioned earlier, it was in this period that Gautam Sarabhai and Gira Sarabhai worked hard to set up NID in Ahmedabad. This was a momentous happening for the city because it brought distinguished persons like Charles and Ray Eames, George Nakashima and Henri Cartier-Bresson to Ahmedabad. They spent several months in the city to develop the vision for NID and train faculty for the institute. That was a rare opportunity for a city in India.

Although both the School of Architecture and NID are based on the Bauhaus approach to design education, Charles and Ray Eames gave a twist to the vision of NID. They incorporated the wisdom of traditional, everyday Indian crafts and design for NID. The Eameses very much promoted the eternal validity of design of objects such as the humble *lota*, its variations across time and space and reasons for its survival as a design over centuries.

Besides, Ahmedabad's fame as a six-centuries-old living city with its historical monuments standing alongside Corbusier's four buildings made it an open book on modern architecture. Each building expressed several methods and techniques to trap the porosity in architecture. Inventive ways to harness light, breeze, views and creating diverse spatial experiences was a new experience in using singularly or combining varied materials, technologies and forms.

Kahn's IIM campus, on the other hand, demonstrated a different approach to using local materials, technologies and skills. These projects opened new ways of looking for practising architects all over India and abroad, a new avenue to create architecture suitable to its specific locale yet demonstrating alternatives besides the ones practised. As a result, Ahmedabad became an important stop for all interested in modern architecture. This brought visitors not only from India but also from all over the world to the city. Opportunities to interact with such persons from other countries, combined with my teaching assignments abroad, offered me many occasions to discuss and reflect on the nature of design in the local and global contexts.

One must simultaneously work on both small and large projects. A house is a grain, like a small sapling in the biodiverse wild forest. One needs to learn to focus on the smallest to the largest while also seeing them in isolation. Yet in both small and large, there are many common factors, except a particular emphasis at the time.

I met Charles Correa through my teacher Gore, who used to meet with young architects in Mumbai. Over time, we became close friends because of our interests in architecture, art and films. Our concerns for identity and appropriate architecture brought us together during his frequent visits to Ahmedabad to oversee the construction of Gandhi Ashram, one of his first and most significant works.

The common concern of rediscovering our identity made us debate on our works and the state of architectural education. This eventually culminated in developing close family friendship and professional association. One of the most memorable events in my life was when I had the privilege to be the best man at Charles and Monica's wedding.

Charles Correa and Achyut Kanvinde used to visit Ahmedabad to meet their clients and visit projects. Both house guests, we often discussed the virtues of Ahmedabad's clients and opportunities for experimentation. We frequently debated forming a group with younger architects to revitalize architectural education to give newer directions in India. Charles even suggested locating the proposed school of architecture in Mumbai.

I am glad that we had the opportunity to share our experiences with the students of architecture whenever possible.

I think it was natural that, inspired by all these happenings, I decided to initiate a School of Architecture at Ahmedabad. It was also natural that I approached Kasturbhai for help. Kasturbhai Lalbhai, Amrutlal Hargovandas, Rasikbhai Parikh, B.K. Majumdar and other members were then leading the most prominent and educational charity of the time, established in 1935, The Ahmedabad Education Society, or AES. At that juncture, AES was already running several high schools, teachers' training schools, and colleges in the arts, commerce, pharmacy and the sciences.

While most members of AES board liked the idea very much, there was some resistance from others. 'When we have so many civil engineering schools, why do we need a school of architecture?' argued Amrutlal Hargovandas, who was an important office bearer of the AES. However, Kasturbhai had a better understanding and appreciation of the new kind of architecture that India needed, emanating from his dealings with Le Corbusier. He convinced Amrutlal and all the other office bearers to approve of the idea.

I then approached other professionals, including engineers such as Dr Rasvihari N. Vakil, Sukumar M Parikh, Dr Mahendra Mehta, and Jeram Patel, an artist, with a request to join in the effort. Jeram Patel had studied arts in England, all the others had studied in the US, and were thus exposed to modern educational institutions. They readily agreed to participate, and we got going.

We were very fortunate that stalwarts like Kasturbhai Lalbhai, Dr Vikram Sarabhai, architect Achyut Kanvinde of Delhi, Dr K.R. Ramanathan of the Physical Research Laboratory, structural engineer Mahendra Raj from Delhi, Dr T.S. Subramanian of Ahmedabad Textile Industry's Research Association have been members of the Governing Council and the Advisory Committee of the school during its formative years. They very much helped to promote the unconventional ideas about education at the new school and helped develop the vision. I may add that they also helped us deal with the traditionalists in education!

Once the school got going, there was interest from many architects and artists from all over the country and beyond. For example, after one of my lectures at the University of Pennsylvania, Bernard Kohn who was then a student of Louis Kahn met me and decided to come over. All those visiting Ahmedabad for Corbusier and Kahn's projects made it a point to visit the school campus, later the CEPT University campus. Here—through their lectures and discussions with students and teachers—these visitors have enriched the educational and professional scene in the city. In turn, this has helped the whole country to keep abreast of the international developments in the field of architecture and planning.

I believe the school has benefited a lot from this kind of international exposure. There was something that bound us all together and that was the need to look at architectural education completely differently in India. We were questioning everything about it, sometimes naively too, given that we were all very young.

As an example, I might mention this incident. In July 1962, seeking to admit our first batch, we called for applications from students and set a date for interviews. While we were conducting interviews, Nagindas Shah, the Secretary of AES, came to us carrying a telegram from the office of the All India Council for Technical Education (AICTE) in New Delhi. It said that since our course was not approved beforehand, we could not admit students. In the circumstances, AICTE also objected to our announcement of offering a baccalaureate.

None of us involved in the effort then had any idea that such approval was necessary. We then stopped the interviews and quickly discussed our options. Seeking their approval meant that we would have to fall in line with a few other architecture colleges which were being run on ideas of education which were decades old. But we found that if we offered a diploma, then we could go on with what we had planned in terms of the course content and methods of teaching.

Therefore, we met the students and parents who had gathered and announced that at the end of their studies, the students will receive a diploma from the AES and they must decide if that was acceptable. I must say, the reputation that the AES enjoyed was so good that all of them accepted our proposal and we admitted 30 students from about 100 who had applied.

In 1962, in the absence of our premises, we requested H.L. College of Commerce and L.D. Arts College to allow us to use their rooms to conduct the initial courses. Subsequently, we moved to the badminton hall used by M.G. Science and L.D. Arts colleges. Thereafter, we added three tents to accommodate additional classes, electives and workshops. Our canteen was under the tree. Subsequently, owing to an intervention by the then Honourable Governor of Gujarat, Nityanand Kanungo, we began to formally award a Diploma certificate after two years. Eventually, the AICTE, New Delhi, recognized the new curriculum and the high standards we had achieved and granted its approval. This meant that our Diploma was now equivalent to a Bachelor's degree for the purpose of higher studies and government jobs, registration as an architect, etc. However, since we were not a university, we still could not call it a Bachelor's degree.

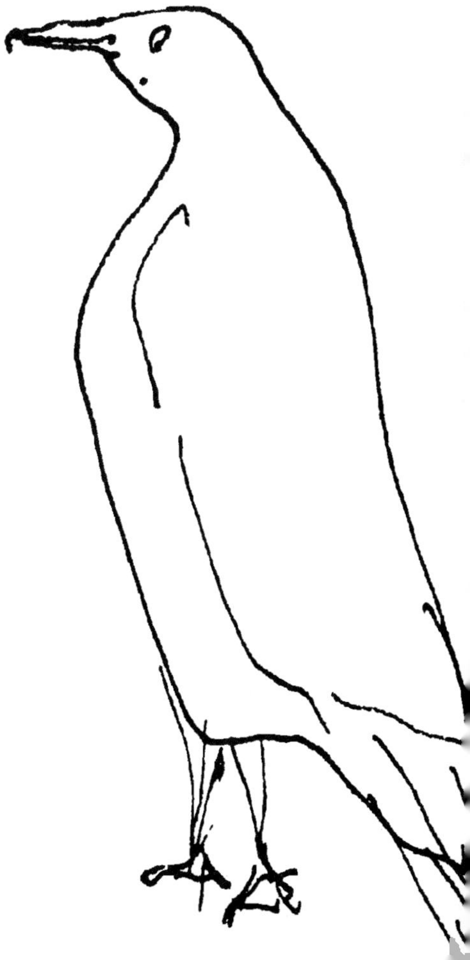

Distinguished architects, designers and artists continued to join us for long and short periods. Christopher Alexander, then more of a mathematician and a Harvard Fellow, conducted some of our early courses. When Jeram Patel decided to go back to Baroda, on his recommendation Piraji Sagara joined us. Around the same time, C.B. Shah joined us to teach engineering and technology courses.

In a few more years, Hasmukh Patel joined us after studying at Cornell University. Anant Raje and Kulbhushan Jain who had come back to India after working and studying with Louis Kahn in the US also joined us. With that kind of a team, we were well set on a path-breaking architectural education in India and, considering the standing the school enjoys in India and the world, it looks like we did things right.

We did incorporate many ideas hitherto unknown in the Indian educational institutions. We must have been the first in the country to introduce a semester system and offer elective courses. We did not subscribe to the idea of final examination as the supreme measure of a student's learning. We assigned highest importance to regular studies throughout the semester with better tutoring as crucial to learning.

Evaluation, we felt, need not be just a one-time pass or fail option. We thought of it as similar to developing an idea or project and presenting it to the clients, receiving a feedback on the idea and reworking it. The system of open juries for the design studios was a pioneering act in India and even now not many institutions practice it. This also encouraged students to develop visual and oral communication skills, which are very useful later in practice.

The studio spaces were open to students all the time and they could meet all the teachers without any hesitation. We used to have constant meetings and interactions among the faculty not just to discuss courses and curriculum but also the strengths and weaknesses of almost each student on the campus.

Here, I recall my meeting with Corbusier during the very early stages of setting up the school. I was travelling through Paris and I talked about our starting the school. He was kind of pleasantly surprised. 'You, starting a school, what would you teach?' he asked. Excitedly, I opened the brochure we had prepared for discussions and pointed out various courses in history, sociology, humanities, technology and the design studio.

'So you are going to teach all this? I did not know you know so much,' he said and looked at me rather questioningly. 'But what about this?' he said, waving the 30cm long wooden scale he had picked up from the drafting table. How true! Without a proper understanding of scale and proportions there cannot be good architecture.

How can we teach that? Are not these experiential and only to be felt? Can merely teaching to make flat plans help us to relate a building and its elements with each other and people? Even models cannot be matched with actual dimensions.

I have never forgotten the question that Corbusier asked me that day more than 50 years ago.

The other important milestone in the history of CEPT University emerged during discussions in the US with the faculty at Massachusetts Institute of Technology and University of Pennsylvania. That was when the programme for the School of Planning in 1972 took shape. Christopher Charles Benninger, then a visiting Fellow from Harvard University, joined me as a joint director and participated by developing the academic programme. The school has greatly benefited from eminent economists such as Dr B.N. Vishwanath, Prof. Jeevan Mittoo and Prof. Ganguly along with Dr Y.K. Alagh and Dr S.K. Subramaniam of the Sardar Patel Institute of Social and Economic Research. Over the years, this school too has made a mark in the country.

Then again, during an engineering conference at Ahmedabad in 1981, local real estate developers and building contractors such as Anil Bakeri, K.B. Mehta, H.S. Shah and other eminent contractors agreed to support setting up the School of Building Science and Technology to train a workforce for the building construction industry. That is how the first five-year full-time course for building engineers came up in India on the campus.

In 1991, Krishna Shastri, an alumna of School of Architecture, set up the School of Interior Design after studying and working in the US. She had observed first-hand the value of professional interior designers there, and felt the need for a formal education in interior design in India. That is how the first full-time five-year programme in India came into being under the Faculty of Design.

Thus, the sapling planted in 1962 is now a giant tree known as CEPT University with several faculties and dozens of programmes from the undergraduate to the doctoral level. It has not been an easy journey to reach here, for all of us involved in setting up and nurturing this institution, it has often been demanding. Like any other, we have had our share of conflicts among faculty members as well as students who have come here from across the country, from very diverse social and economic backgrounds. This was truer in the early years since we were trying out a model of education, which was unheard of in the country.

There were several conflicts, the passionate academic kind as well as more worldly. However, I think it was our ability to deal with conflicts based on our ideas about education and, more importantly, an environment for education, which saw us resolve the conflicts amicably and actually added to the strength of the place.

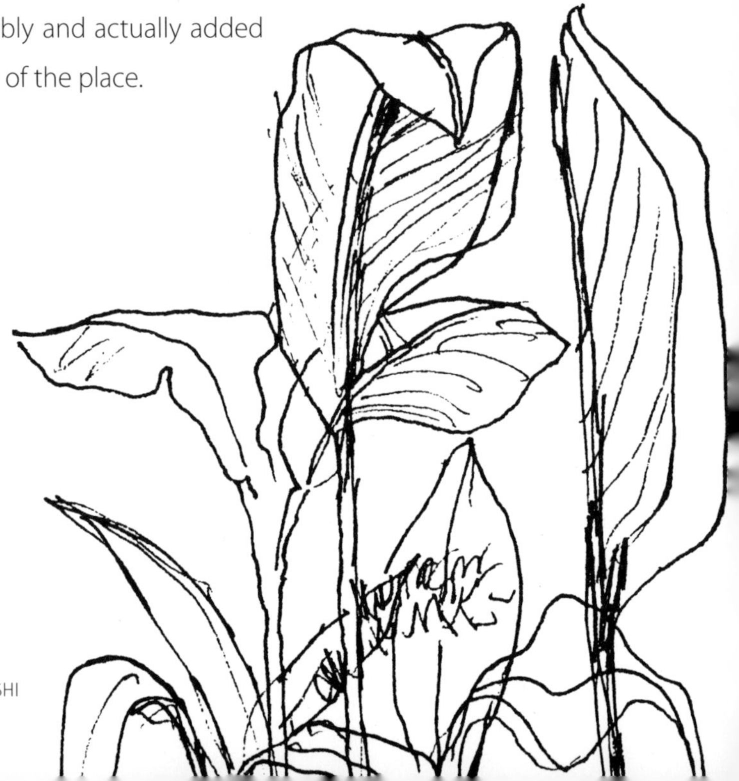

Sometimes, when I meet alumni of the School of Planning, together we recall the time when the first batch of students went on strike. At the root was a simple matter of the stipend paid to the students. It had been revised by the funding authority but we had no inkling of it. Nor had we received the additional funds to enable us to pay the revised stipend.

The matter had been brewing for a while, and the strike was called when I happened to be away. When I came back and went to the campus, I saw all the students lined up along the approach with placards, posters etc. There were slogans even on the long RCC beams in 30–40cm letters, announcing that the bell tolls for Doshi and such.

As I went towards the small cabin I used to occupy there, I saw that it was full of planning students who had occupied it, maybe in a gesture of takeover or such, I thought. However, as I got closer to my cabin door, for some reason all the students started to practically run away from there. Therefore, I went in there and first met with the faculty and administrative staff to learn what had happened while I was away.

Once I caught up with the developments until then, I asked the striking students to come and see me—against everybody's advice. However, I believed in facing all the conflicts squarely and resolving them satisfactorily. That was very necessary for the well-being of the students, teachers and the institution.

So, when all the students came in, I asked for tea for all of us present. Then I talked to them to convey that I was not at all upset, angry, or disturbed by their decision to strike; that they had a right to increased stipend, and I respected that. All I asked was for understanding that, given the shoestring budget on which we were operating, there was no way I could pay them the revised stipend until I got the additional funds from the funding authority.

I also added that if they felt that we were not doing enough in this case, or any other matter for that reason, I would be very happy to resign and let them handle the affairs. I like to believe this made the students realize that we were all on the same side. That was the end of the strike. Avoiding a confrontational approach was all it took to resolve the issue. I must say, such a response always works simply because both sides are usually right in a conflict; it is just the perception of the situation that has to be shared and appreciated by both. I believe a similar approach has helped the diverse growth of the campus.

The need to view life and education from a holistic perspective has all along guided the development of the campus with the establishment of several institutions. These institutions, with their focus on visual and performing arts, have added multiple dimensions to all programmes on the campus. Participation in the programmes offered by these institutions and interactions with the visiting artists has allowed students of all the programmes on the campus to appreciate other creative disciplines.

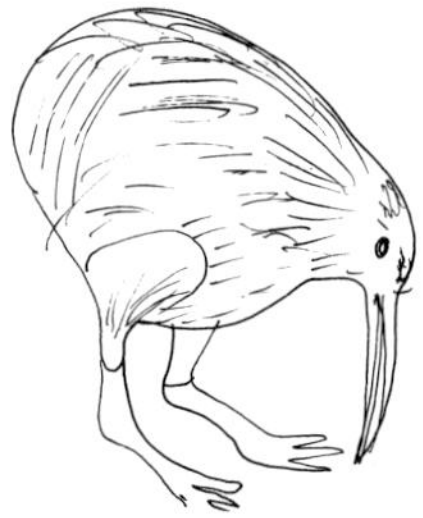

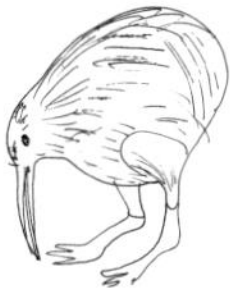

The first among these institutions was the L&P Hutheesing Visual Arts Centre. It came about in 1977, when I happened to meet Surottam Hutheesing on one of my Ahmedabad–Bombay train journeys. Shrimatiben Tagore and Sarojiniben Hutheesing, his sisters, endorsed the idea of holding art exhibitions, theatre workshops, music and film appreciation classes at the centre and provided a generous grant.

In yet another coincidence, the Kanoria Centre for Arts took shape during a chance meeting with Urmila Kanoria at our home during a dance performance by Kumudini Lakhia, which she had graciously agreed to do for Ba. The next day I met her on the Ahmedabad–New Delhi flight and firmed up the idea. Here, in consultation with well-known artists from all over India, we have facilitated young artists to pursue their careers by providing a studio space and allied amenities for a token fee. They work here until they have exhibited their works successfully and then make way for another group. Artists such as Ravindra Reddy, Walter D'Souza and Prithpal Singh Ladi were among the first such Fellows and office bearers of the centre.

All these developments have made this multidisciplinary campus unique in India. The underlying philosophy at CEPT campus has been: education without doors. It is like being in a bazaar where opportunities in several fields for learning are available without boundaries. Here, every aspect of education is discussed openly in frank and cordial settings because excellence is only achieved when you are free and relaxed.

The 22-acre piece of land allotted by the Ahmedabad Education Society for building the CEPT University campus used to be a brick kiln. Therefore, the topsoil had been dug up for making bricks leaving a deep, huge pit.

After several alternative studies, I designed a studio with partial double height to obtain northern light. This unusual staggered stacking of each studio, one on top of the other provided the much needed visual and physical interconnectivity, natural light and cross ventilation.

While laying the foundation stone away from the brick kiln, I realized the futility of the suspended floors and the load-bearing brick walls. Seeing the low-lying area around the brick kiln, I realized the virtue of pushing the building closer.

Overnight, while studying the sections, I discovered the most important element of how connecting different levels between the sloping grounds and flat surfaces creates unusual experiences.

Moving the building over the pit, I obtained a free ground-level space. Today I am glad to see everyone using this space for unlimited activities.

The quasi-basement space suspended between two thick brick walls appears as if shaking hands with the undulating green mounds and the higher level at the opposite end.

The most important component of architecture is the land on which you create. The site conditions will suggest to you the potentials that design must explore. As soon as I moved the building, the south-facing volumes changed, resulting in a double-height volume and a completely new section, encouraging constant multiple use of low and high spaces in the studio all through the year.

Visit the site often, give a patient ear to its murmurs, imagine the landscape, study the solar and wind movements. Buildings are walls of art to be experienced. Study the daily activities, then design.

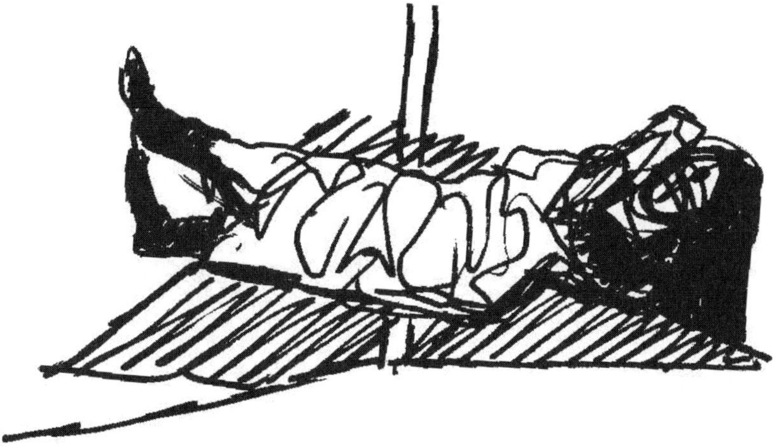

To achieve quality and to train craftsmen to adopt new technologies, it was essential to be at site more frequently. Such is the case even now.

Recently, in the course of designing my youngest daughter's house, I must have visited the site at least 30 times. For the Maharashtra state government's institute for senior officers' training, named YASHADA, at Pune, I must have made around 30 visits over three years to train the site staff and contractors in the use and execution of new materials with new technologies—almost the same as for the Amdavad Ni Gufa.

During the design for the Mahatma Gandhi Labour Institute in Ahmedabad, on one of my visits, I discovered the error of creating a very long vaulted tunnel without natural light. Luckily, it was yet to be cast. I had also specified certain finishes, which were not in the tender due to an oversight. I was wondering what could be done at that stage.

Fortuitously, just then the current director was transferred and a new one was appointed. During my next visit to acquaint him to the project, I also brought in the need for certain additions to the programme to make the institute better prepared for the proposed educational programmes. He accepted those, which then allowed me to rework parts of the design, rectifying all the previous errors, and an alternative proposal was finally approved.

Going to the site does not call for resolutions right there and then. It is the memories of the visit that will find a place in your design. The reason is that every time you go there, the land will tell you 'do this and not that'. It will speak to you of what it wants, likes done and not done.

Designing the campus for the Indian Institute of Management at Bangalore was a very different experience. No strong feature marked the site itself but the local environment, which in those days was far away from Bangalore, was quite distinct and isolated. It reminded me of vast plains in which one finds large precincts such as those of the temple cities.

When he first spoke to me about this project, the director, Prof. N.S. Ramaswamy had asked me, 'Doshi, how about conceiving a different model for teaching small-scale entrepreneurs?' So, while designing the campus, my emphasis was on inter-mixing of spaces of interactive dialogues rather than well-defined territories such that outdoor learning could take place all over the campus.

Given the larger contexts of the campus site, my references for this project were Madurai's Meenakshi Temple as a spiritual centre built using local stone, Jaisalmer—owing to the traditional neighbourhoods again built using local stone and, of course, the IIM Ahmedabad campus in red brick by Louis Kahn. I wanted to develop a system by which the buildings at IIM Bangalore disappear and spaces in between them dominate the experience of the place.

The question I asked was, what was important, was it the form of the building or the content, the space? That is the experience of moving through various spaces. I thought the most important things are the experience, the rasa, which is the subtle experience of the space that makes the space memorable. It extends the associations and enriches imagination.

The campus also draws inspiration from the Royal Complex at Fatehpur Sikri. Therefore, the corridors—like the streets—become the focus for the movement patterns. Since the 1980s, issues of nature, content and the container, which is the form, have made me study traditional forms and their interpretative expressions and experience.

While designing the Kanoria Centre for Arts, I was thinking about the relationship between the well-regulated administrative needs of the centre on one hand and the freedom for allowing the creativity of the artists and their relative organization, spatial and visual positioning in order to express the link between control and freedom. Here, the design attempted to express this conflicted relationship through a half-buried administrative block with a staircase from the terrace linked as a bridge to the terrace above the studios.

Recently, to incorporate the existing trees while designing additions to the Kanoria Centre building, I created an opening in the roof as if I had planted the building from above. Seeing this addition when complete, I realized once again the value of experiential architecture. Introducing a long and narrow crack along the ridge of the chamfered roof, I discovered the fragility of a solid stable structure.

In the two long parallel walls, I saw the strength of a long boat and in the openings placed strategically in the roof I saw how a building can be open and yet closed, transparent and solid at the same time. Finding a dry leaf, twisted and turned, without losing its centrality, I attempted an extension of the earlier one and, once again, found that forms, when twisted and turned, pressed and enlarged, give us a sense of freedom, even though we are within an enclosure.

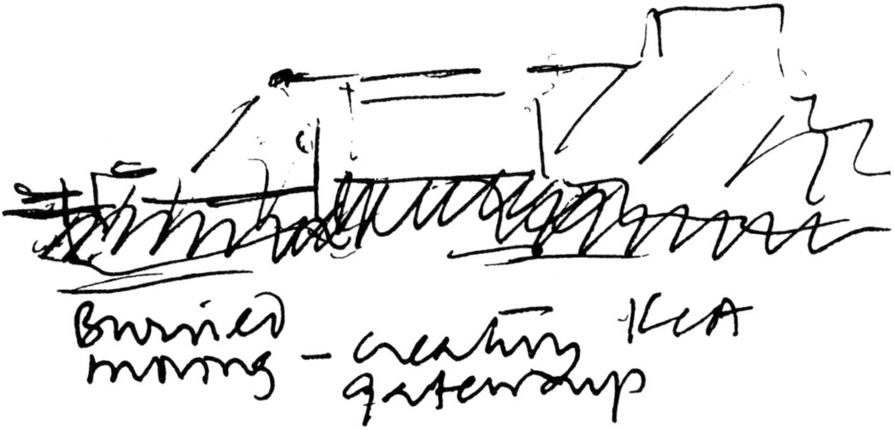

Some years ago, while on a trip to Sajjangarh Fort in Maharashtra, I had visited Swami Ramdas's samadhi, the place marking his departure from this world. He was a devotee of Lord Rama and spiritual guru to Shivaji Maharaj. While Swami's own samadhi was located in a semi-basement space, a temple dedicated to Lord Rama stood on the roof of Samadhi... how appropriate! This arrangement reaffirmed my faith in pursuing connotative values in architecture.

India is very fortunate to have a range of expressions in its religious architecture. Of these, I find the rock-cut complexes the most fascinating. I will never forget my first visit to the Kailash Temple at Ellora some 40 years ago. That is a completely breathtaking experience. Normally, you carve out a cave from a rock through the process of extraction.

However, to carve an entire multi-storeyed temple as a freestanding object from a living rock, and then create the space by extraction around its periphery as if it is built independently is a stunning accomplishment. Extraction is like the Hindu philosophy of '*neti, neti, neti*' meaning not this, not that, essentially defining by negation. So what could that mean or seek to convey? May be it is like saying: 'I am material and I want to do penance, to be ascetic. I want to shed what I have, what is visible and reveal what I stand for.'

As they say, Michelangelo did not create sculptures, he just revealed what was already there, hidden in the stone. To me, the Kailash Temple at Ellora similarly reveals what is within. Here the unfathomable has manifested. It is like when you look at a seed, you do not see a tree; but the tree is very much in there. One of the fundamental principles of Hindu philosophy is to find the universal through the personal microcosm.

Standing there, on the first-floor portico of the Kailash Temple, watching the sunset, I felt the whole place connect to the cosmic forces. I realized how thoughtfully the *sthapati* must have chosen the face of the living rock, orientation and movement of the sun. As I continued to stand there, I felt like I was on a celestial ride with a heightened consciousness of being amidst *chetna*, the life force that surrounds us all.

The most amazing thing about *chetna* is that one cannot see it, one cannot hold it, yet it is all-pervading. It is only when you see the leaves and branches of a tree sway that you become aware of the breeze,

chetna is like that. Complexes such as Ajanta Caves and rock-cut temples at Ellora beg other questions too, such as how long did it take for such a complex to be built? How many centuries are we talking about here, five or ten centuries?

If it were going to take that kind of time, what kind of organization would allow such high-quality work to be undertaken over centuries? That is several generations of *sthapati* and the artisans, so how do you instruct several generations? No one would know the final form it will take or which would be the very last icon to be carved on the wall of the deepest chamber to come. It is like recreating the unfathomable spatial universe, manifested as a temple. I believe only an accomplished yogi can visualize this.

Temple complexes are designed to be very accessible to all people at all levels; they become part of the family's daily life. They fulfil our day-to-day emotional and spiritual needs, and gradually lead us to the question, who am I? What is my purpose on earth?

For example, I saw—located at the entrance to Konark Temple—a rather unusual image. It depicted a grown-up lion astride a rather small, young elephant, a rather paradoxical representation. I sensed that this was intended as a playful gesture, like the rides offered by grandparents on their back for their grandchildren all the time, everywhere.

Similarly, at La Sagrada Familia, the most unusual church in Barcelona designed by Antoni Gaudi, there is a huge column supported by a tortoise, which is depicted as if trying to escape from the burden being imposed on it! I sensed in it a subtle message for us. That there is no burden ever so heavy which one cannot carry, if there is a will and faith.

I have noticed that in the structures at Ajanta and Ellora, some of the columns are not perfectly aligned vertically across all the floors. Nor are they of exact dimensions across all the floors, they are a bit thicker and thinner on different floors, not uniform. The lesson is one of dynamic balancing of the spiritual versus the intellectual as in nature, and not just a static transfer of load.

The lesson also is that there is no single theory or rule that we must follow, there exist exceptions and they too add richness to our world. A good structure follows principles of dynamic balancing, that is what Santiago Calatrava achieves in his designs, I might say.

That is what life is about. Life is not what you think it is. Life is about how you deal or play with it. It is like a river, which keeps flowing until it reaches the ocean, overcoming obstacles such as mountains, hills, rocks and even waterfalls. If it meets a lake, it silently pours into it, waits for it to overflow and then, by breaching the bank somewhere, it continues its journey to the ocean.

If you want to flow like a river, there should be no dualities. You have to meander like it in spite of apparent paradoxes; flow, dynamism and movement should be there. For example, a temple is a complete demonstration of life, like our body it incorporates its own entity and thus merges with the universal force.

I often wonder if designers of Kailash Temple had any reference to go by. If they were alive today, would they do what we are doing? Or would they do something unique because our definition of architecture comes either from the way we are taught or what we have read in the history books and learn what has happened in the history. Actually, there are no absolute definitions; these emerge from our daily life, from what you have experienced, what you have enjoyed.

To see or think of building as static, to think that it is made of inert materials, or materials that are temporary, and thinking that function is specific, unilateral, is a notion. In reality, it is a living organism like us, which primarily functions on its subtle energies with its own rhythm and pace. A great building is indeed a spiritual entity and to attain that in our designs, we must be free, we must be introspective and self-critical to rediscover ourselves.

We made some rules for ourselves and conditioned ourselves to follow them, thus we put ourselves in prisons of our own making. We have come to this because we are afraid. We are afraid because we constantly hanker for recognition by others, approval and endorsement of our work by others—all of these are props.

I believe the modest mud houses built by the villagers near Jaisalmer are as great as the structures at Ajanta and Ellora such as the Kailash Temple. What makes them great and unites them in their greatness, is that both have been created by designers—more appropriately the *sthapati* rooted in the local land—who only do what they enjoy doing.

A question that arises then is how should one work today? How do we shed our borrowed baggage that does not belong to our spiritual calling? I think the organizational structure employed in creating the structures at Ellora and Ajanta offers important lessons. This is to decide what is the main structure, what is the subsidiary one, and to allow everyone to excel in his or her own areas of excellence. This cannot be achieved without intense desire, devotion and faith.

After my first visit to Ajanta Caves, Christopher Alexander was visiting Ahmedabad. He and I wrote an article, titled *Main and Sub-structure*. It highlights the virtue of excellence and participation by surrendering to a larger goal. Similar organization exists even today in our society in the form of an extended family and communities to which we belong.

I have observed such systems and hierarchical structure in our traditional housing and planning projects, and they are relevant even today. These manifest in the hierarchy of spaces, use of technologies and materials, variations and control that one observes in our settlements. That is how I discovered the generic principles of planning of houses and streets of Jaisalmer, which gave me a clue to the main theme of architecture in India.

When the goal is for the larger, common good, the intention is to share the benefits or resources, the concern is universal. Function is beyond self. Power is to do good. Celebration is to share health, wealth and wisdom. Such design solutions transcend time and become valid and accessible to all ages, cultures, and economies. Complexes such as Fatehpur Sikri, Meenakshi Temple or the old city of Ahmedabad are good examples of this.

Although it was occupied only briefly, Fatehpur Sikri, the capital city built by the Mughal Emperor Akbar, still greatly impacts all visitors, be they scholars or laypersons. It is simple, well-proportioned in scale, form and relationship. It is easy to grasp. All of us can recognize the virtues of its open and enclosed areas, location of the main and the subsidiary buildings.

Prefabricated elements such as standard columns, *chhajja*s, and panels are brought together so harmoniously that you only notice the fluid, flowing spaces and the building envelope that defines them. What strikes you is the play of shadows, projections and courtyards and extended volumes.

The geometry here created by the play of shadows, projections and courtyards and extended volumes is perfect to get immersed in.

Its modest scales, low heights and vast courtyards are equally accessible to a very large crowd or just a single individual. Built centuries ago, it is still very contemporary. The complex is made from one colour, one material—red sandstone—and yet it is not monotonous. No frills, no emphasis, just gestures, it expresses its own identity. Fatehpur Sikri is truly timeless.

Power here does not corrupt as it is to do good. And absolute power here does not corrupt absolutely but does absolute good.

I was equally overwhelmed by the spatial experiences when I visited the Meenakshi Temple complex at Madurai, which is more than seven centuries old. To me, the formal and informal, controlled and loose, finite and infinite, closed and open spaces coexist at the Meenakshi Temple. Such a spatial organization continuously facilitates the pilgrims in performing the rituals and in experiencing the duality of life.

Here, one feels unstable, in a manner of speaking. The complex is like our traditional towns and villages, where the built forms and open spaces enrich private and public realms.

Corridors are of varied dimensions and scales to allow the pilgrim to recall our ancient history, as depicted on the elaborately carved and decorated columns and walls. The stories and myths depicted on these immediately connect us to other worlds. In doing so, they efface the present.

Feeling of
lightness/air/movement – mobility – Non Static

These experiences deeply enriched my thoughts about the purpose and nature of architecture. They linked my thinking to the eternal passage of the sun, the moon, and the ever-changing patterns of the stars in the sky, and the rhythms of seasons.

The many shrines and deities located in the niches on surrounding walls in the complex intercepted my movement. It was similar to the social context of our towns. Yet, they did not distract me from my intention to reach the inner sanctum. Instead, they connected me to the main deity and other shrines.

This vast complex became one wholesome experience. Noticing an image of Lord Ganesh, almost invisible in the corner of a dark room located off the main corridor, I somehow sensed the presence of Goddess Meenakshi located elsewhere at a good distance in the complex.

I could understand the purpose of layers that surrounded me. It was universal energy seeping through the dynamic relationship among solids and voids, built and unbuilt. After praying at the image of Goddess Meenakshi in the inner sanctum, when I came out in the open, I felt like there was nothing there except what I had experienced. Even now every time I begin work on a new project, I recall this experience.

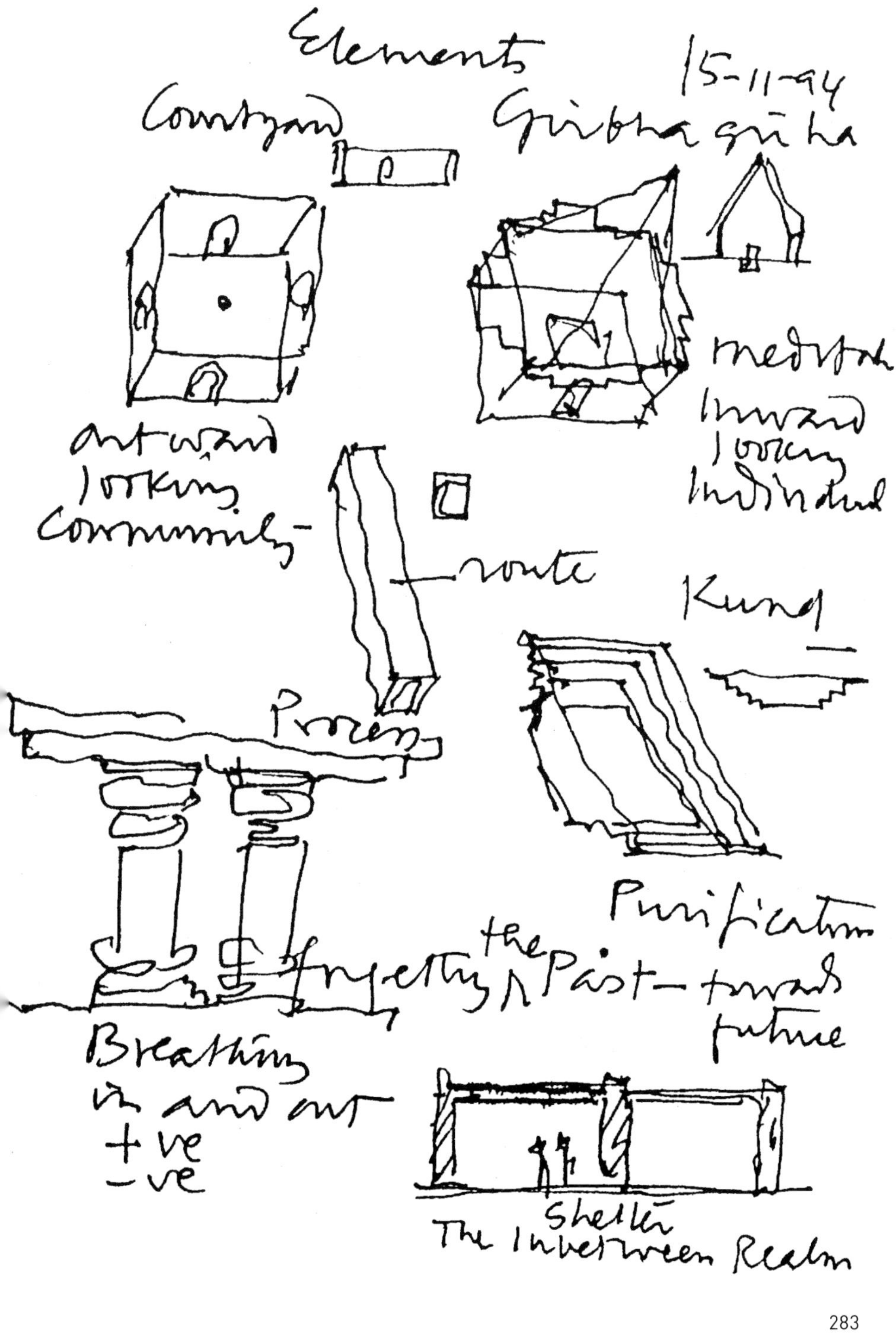
Elements
15-11-94
Courtyard
Garbha griha
meditation
inward
looking
individual
outward
looking
community
route
Kund
Process
Purification
forgetting the Past — toward
future
Breathing
in and out
+ ve
– ve
Shelter
The Inbetween Realm

One often hears of many well-planned cities but, for me, Jaipur is unique. It is here that I see a perfect fusion of East and West, of the traditional and the contemporary expressions. I see in Jaipur an orthogonal plan, which, in its details, combines the virtues of an Indian town grown organically. It is a city of many parts, ordered and loose.

When Maharaja Jai Singh, an astronomer, created this heaven on earth, he was concerned about the interplay of cosmic forces. The city was to be a physical expression of what he understood as celestial celebrations.

The plan for Jaipur is based on the principles of choice, flexibility, economic viability, and energy-saving lifestyles. It is fine-tuned to support daily life as well as the special events in the life of a family and the community. One can say that all the facets of our lives are brought together here in perfect harmony. Let me put it as follows.

To create a paradise on earth citizens must be happy
To be happy, they have to be healthy
To be healthy they must live well
To live the good life they must have well-provided surroundings
They must have opportunities to earn money
To do that they must have skills and knowledge of crafts
They should receive education of their choice
They must work cooperatively and market their products
To maintain all of these they must pay taxes
And to pay the taxes, they must be fruitfully employed

The diversity of cities and temple complexes, built over centuries in India, makes me realize that there is a common thread in their conceptions. This is the Hindu belief in transition and uncertainty; be it of seasons, resources and behaviour of people over generations.

I like to believe that cities and temples are created with people in mind, for fulfilling their material as well as spiritual needs. Architecture is its extension. Concepts have their roots in our philosophy: that of pursuing celebration of life by creating varied experiences and evoking memories and associations in our daily life.

For example, I was perhaps lucky that my mother guided me to create a place where all my memories, associations and visions of what one calls life and its relation to architecture would be fulfilled. This is what I have tried to recreate at Sangath. It is set back from the two roads abutting it and offers a very low profile, devoid of emphasis.

The approach to the building from the entrance gate, and its ambiguous route, starts to unsettle the visitor's perceptions of what an office building should be. This helps to change the mindset and question the unexpected. Time and pace change as if this is another world, unknown in many ways but felt psychically as a quiet, timeless and vast world within.

I wanted to create such an experience at Sangath because I feel that conventions imposed on us stop us from touching our real self. Why don't we take time to watch the world around us, the trees, the plants, the pebbles, the lotus, a bird, or us? Is there a need to be so definite? Slowly, I began to find what is correct for India, and it began to grow into something more specifically Indian. For me it was almost like a rebirth.

Sangath talks about one of the very important periods of my life. It was a period of searching for my identity. I had crossed the age of 50 when I conceived and started to build Sangath. I had become more aware about nature and had begun to observe it with much more attention. Looking at the way trees grow, I now realized that the way its branches twisted and turned was to seek most sunlight to grow and to avoid other branches in doing so.

If I were to reconsider my architecture, I wondered whether I could create such interactive spaces and manifest the glory of their own peculiarities. At Sangath, the unfolding of the freestanding thick wall near the entrance happened because of the presence of the row of tall eucalyptus trees nearby. The thickness served two purposes: one, to act as the reclining wall for the basement wall and, two, to withstand falling of trees if it ever came to it. An unknown gesture, but the enigma of the unforeseen and the accidental occurrence of the trees made me do what I did. This peculiar character created a hybrid rhythm with the well-ordered main structure. However, today I believe it has added another dimension to both the movement and the ordered structure.

I had begun to ask questions about my own identity and the purpose of my existence. I was looking back on my life until then. I think all the memorable events in my life, all the places where I have worked and dwelt have manifested here. To understand this phase, I spent six months with Motabhai, studying the Gita. I believe my struggles have borne fruits; Sangath makes me feel calm and peaceful.

Often we are confined and
influenced by the immediacy
Yet there are hidden layers
that need to be probed
To finally reach and reveal the memories
buried deep within us
They manifest in our work
at their chosen time and manner
Like the soil that nourishes a tree and makes it
specific, particular to a place,
memories play a similar role
That is rooting or identity, which is what you
treasure deep inside you
Eventually the roots break out
and manifest their character
That is your identity
There are no justifications required
because it is timeless

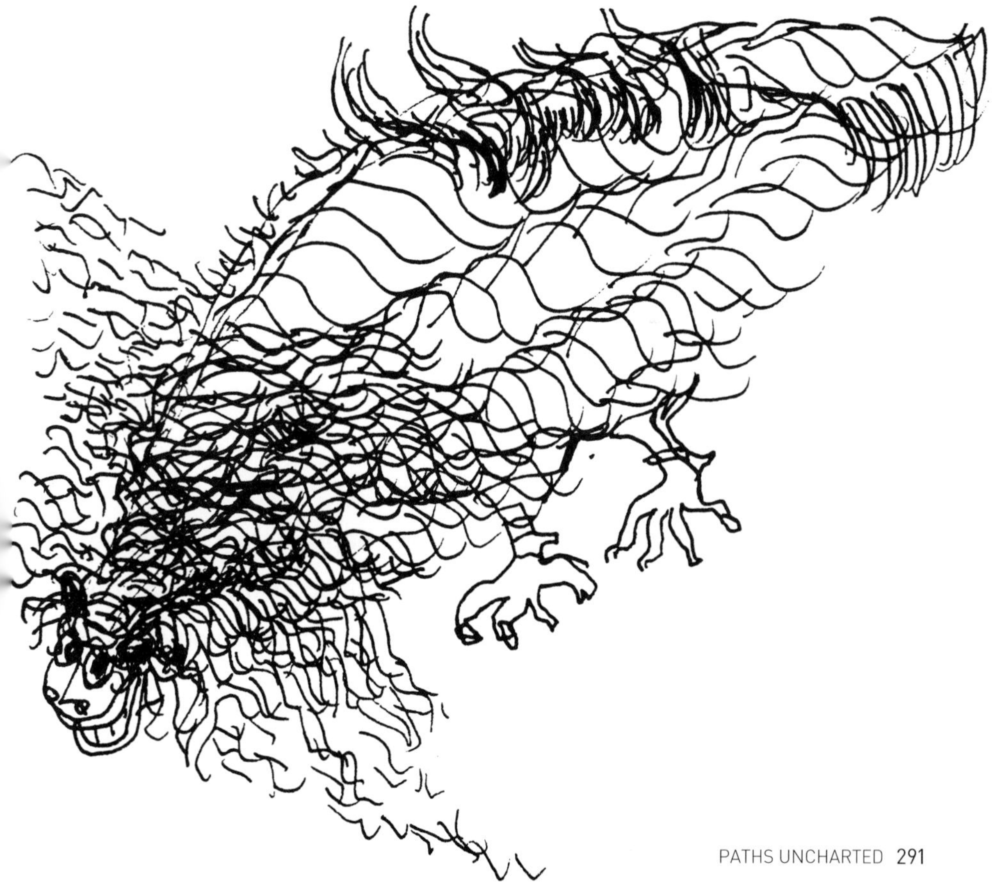

I remember once meeting Dr P.R. Pisharoty, then the Director of Ahmedabad's Physical Research Laboratory, at the airport. He was on his way to New Delhi to attend a conference. All he carried with him was a very small attaché case. Although well-known in the scientific community all over the world, he led a very simple life and always seemed in full control of himself and the surroundings—absolutely at peace.

Seated next to him I asked him, 'Doctor, tell me, how do you manage such composure? Don't you have conflicts? Aren't you ever in a state of hurry?' He said, 'Doshi, it's all in my mother's training when I was a child. You see, when I was around nine or ten years old, I realized that on my birthdays my relatives would bless me and give some gifts.

'However, my mother's guru, an old Brahmin, would sit there and call me names and abuse me after every guest had blessed me, given me a gift and left. So I asked my mother, "Why does your guru abuse me on my birthday, whereas everyone else blesses me and says nice words?"

'She said, "Son, you will always be happy when someone praises you, but remember in life there will be occasions when you will be abused. Learn to take abuses as well as you would take flattering words. This way you will be at peace." I will never forget this unique birthday lesson.'

The 1950s and the 1970s were very interesting times for me on several counts. Besides being part of all exciting new institutions in the city and the practice, things were moving well on the personal front, too. Soon after marriage, Kamu and I had moved to a rented two-room house at 72, Sharada Society, located a good kilometre from the pukka road.

There was no public transport and it would all be very muddy in the monsoon. In the beginning, I used to move around on a bicycle, which aggravated my colitis. So I borrowed money from my brother Vallabh and bought a German-make motorcycle, so it was easier to visit project sites. Due to colitis, I had to follow a strict diet, which meant plain boiled food. For almost four to five years, Kamu also ate boiled food.

However, with exciting developments all around that was the least of my trouble. Over time, Le Corbusier's clients, who were among the first people I knew in the city, became our family friends. Therefore, when we moved to our own home at 14, Sadma Society, in 1960, it was just the right time. It added a completely new dimension to our social life. We have hosted so many friends, colleagues and relatives for all kinds of reasons and occasions.

An unusual tradition was that of hosting students and faculty from the school. For many years, on special occasions such as Holi and on the first day of the new academic year, all faculty members and students of the School of Architecture—almost 200 of them—would come and spend a morning or an evening at our house. I am tempted to add here that the rather rash decision to buy a larger plot for our home has proved to be a blessing and allowed us to host such occasions to share joy and warmth.

A particularly joyous aspect of our home has been that we could host so many guests from India and abroad staying with us. Many of these have since become close family friends. We have enjoyed some exciting moments with them when we accompanied them to music concerts, art exhibitions, dance festivals and other events in and around the city.

I still remember the time around 1964, when Aldo van Eyck visited Ahmedabad with his wife Hannie. He spoke about how he works to lend his architecture that ethereal quality derived from his studies of life in villages, especially his studies of the Dogon villages in Africa and their collective ways of sustaining life in a very hostile environment.

We then took them to some villages near Ahmedabad during the Navratri festival. In those days, foreigners, especially of the Caucasian stock, were a rare sight. Therefore, the villagers at the festival venue practically mobbed both of them, much to our embarrassment. They came very close to take a good, long look at their fair skin, blue eyes and at times even touch to make certain that they were for real. Despite the embarrassment, this incident made Kamu and me aware of the socio-cultural aspects of life in our own villages.

We have been very fortunate to receive visitors and guests from all over India and abroad over the years. Owing to their varied backgrounds and training, we could share a lot about work and life and learn a lot from each other. Of special significance are the trips I have undertaken in the company of architects to places of architectural significance. These trips helped me to understand how a person from another background and culture sees our buildings and cities.

I specially remember a trip by Louis Kahn to see the temples at Dilwara and Ranakpur. When I asked him about it, he said, 'I prefer Ranakpur. It is clear, quite simple and extremely well ordered. Dilwara is too sweet and overworked, and lacks the strength of the Ranakpur Temple.'

I said, 'Lou, what you say is true, but there is the philosophy of spiritualizing the matter? For us Indians, when the material disappears, spirit manifests. Dilwara may not be architecturally understood but it is, overall, an experience of shedding the matter that we see.' Kahn then said, 'Perhaps, but I prefer Ranakpur.'

Thus, we have had the good fortune to be part of a fast-moving contemporary world on one hand and the slow-paced ways of the historic India at the same time. I would say I have learnt much from people around me and the way they acted in certain situations. I have often tried to look at things from others' point of view and that seems to have helped a lot.

It may not be an exaggeration to say that all of my memories including lessons from my gurus and observations from childhood are constantly manifested in my work. I do not know if it is good or bad, but I can adapt very well and be moulded very easily. It may be a gift or a curse, but that is how it is, and I humbly accept it.

Though at this stage I may not be associated much with public housing, it has in fact been a lifelong preoccupation for me. This is owing to my memories of poor people in Pune, their hardships as well as my exposure to socialist ideas while in Paris.

Since I was a regular visitor to our furniture workshop, I knew most of the workers, their families and friends rather well. This had exposed me to the lives of the low-income and poor sections of our society. I was also very well aware of the living conditions of these people because I had visited their homes as a child, and felt very strongly about doing something for them when I grew up.

This was so much so that in my fourth grade at school in Pune when we were asked to write an essay on a subject of our choice, I chose to write on making furniture and other household things cheaply so that the poor people can afford them and live life that is a little more comfortable.

As an architect, I have been actively involved in issues related to mass housing and especially housing for the urban poor. These have ranged from formulating housing policies, undertaking studies and research, as well as design of many housing projects.

Very early in my career, in the 1960s, I had planned several self-contained townships for the new industries that were being set up in India at the time. These ranged from about 500 dwellings to more than 2,000 in some of them, spread over 250 acres.

However, the industrial companies that built these townships owned and maintained them. The main purpose of these townships was to attract skilled technicians not available in those locations where the industries were being set up. Houses and facilities had to be better than what they would get in cities and at affordable costs that would be deducted from their salaries. But the transient ownership meant that residents would have less affinity with their homes and the larger community. This, as we know, is not healthy for a town and its character.

Nevertheless, there were very few projects like these happening in India then and it was an important phase in learning to develop and execute such townships in one go. Also of much interest was the search for appropriate forms of towns, transportation planning, provision and design of commercial, social and recreational amenities at such towns, developing standards and norms for all things that a self-sufficient town comprises. So, in many ways, these projects proved to be pioneers in modern India, and path-breaking too.

Among the first of these projects was the township for the Gujarat State Fertilizer Corporation near Baroda, spread over 75 acres of land and providing accommodation for 1,896 households. There was also provision for a complete range of all social and recreational amenities and shopping that a town of 10,000 people would require. That will give some idea about the scale of these projects. I remember I was quite fascinated with developing road junctions here to minimize vehicular accidents, and spent a lot of time developing the street pattern that actually determined the form of the town!

In another project for the design of housing for the Electronic Corporation of India in 1974 at Hyderabad, I had suggested water harvesting, as well as mixing various income groups and variations in the same category of housing in those days. The senior officials had strongly opposed the variations in the housing unit areas and the idea of integrating different classes of employees in my proposal. Luckily for me, Vikram Sarabhai was involved in the project as a scientist-advisor. He deplored the hierarchical, bureaucratic attitudes of the officials, and defended my proposals.

Yet another opportunity was planning a small township for 400 families proposed by the Indian Farmers' Fertilizer Cooperative Organization, in 1973, at Kalol, in north Gujarat. This project offered too many challenges. The funds were very limited but houses had to be very spacious. Since it was a cooperative, there was naturally greater interaction with the community in all decision-making which happily meant that the employees had a greater say in planning and design of the houses.

To obtain maximum space within the available funds, I remembered what I had observed in the rail coaches and ships. So I minimized the volume of each of the spaces by arriving at optimal dimensions, as if they were a bunch of separate boxes, meant to serve their specific purposes. Then I brought them together in their required relationships and added extra volume available to create another space. It is like buying fruits. If you want more numbers per kilogram, just choose smaller fruits. As a result, I created low-volume areas for kitchens and bathrooms, and normal ones for living rooms and bedrooms. Then, I added a pergola above the service core, which could be used for growing plants, outdoor sleeping in summer, etc.

However, one of my most favourite housing projects is the one I designed for the Life Insurance Corporation (LIC) at Ahmedabad. Unlike almost all others, these houses were to be owned by policyholders chosen through a lottery. Here, I knew that the houses would be occupied by several generations of the same family. That they would identify with it, that there will be a strong sense of belonging and that their needs will change, and they may modify parts of it.

Here, too, in spite of strong opposition by the LIC officials, I mixed and reversed the stacking order in a three-storeyed structure. There were to be three dwelling sizes under the project: a two-bedroom unit, a one-bedroom unit and then just a room-and-kitchen unit. I decided to place the largest unit on the ground floor, the medium size on the first floor and the smallest on the top, and made them all accessible by a common external staircase.

This has allowed the houses on upper floors to enjoy a terrace from Day One and convert them to rooms when needed. And if the family on the ground floor decided to add a room, they could still have their terrace. This community of 315 families have added and transformed their homes to suit their changing requirements. Its success is indicated by the fact that very few of the original households have moved out. When I walk down the streets there now, I see almost nothing of what it was on completion.

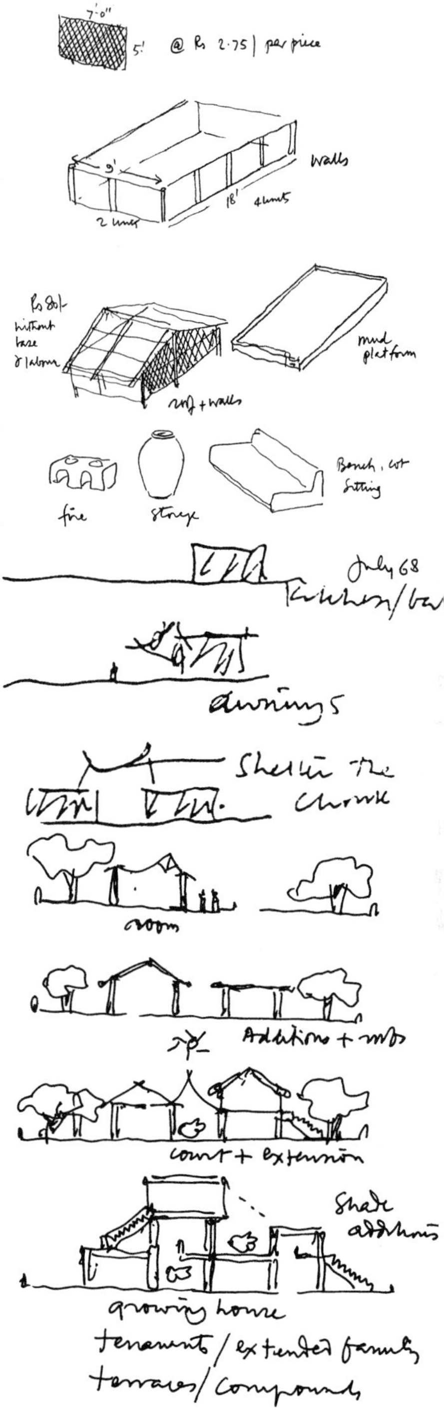

Having worked on so many housing projects, I was therefore ready for a greater challenge and it came in the form of a very large housing project—to be called Aranya—proposed by the Indore Development Authority. When I say very large, we are actually talking here of a fully integrated, cross-subsidized housing project for about 8,000 households across varied income categories on a site measuring 202 acres. A large number of these households included all the slum dwellers then living in Indore.

In 1954, while at Le Corbusier's office, I had already participated in an international low-cost housing competition for Delhi, where I had emphasized the issues of growth, affordability and nurturing a sense of community of those being housed. In my design, I had visualized the main streets provided with lay-by as spaces with high potential for planned and unplanned social interactions. Some of those ideas I carried in to my work for Aranya.

I decided these were going to be houses that would grow and be upgraded as required. Strengthening the socio-economic interdependence of the occupants, offering choices for self-employment and a setting for a dignified life were some of my visions for Aranya.

One of the key achievements of the project is the integration between different income groups. I have achieved this by placing the lowest income group housing in the centre of each of the six sectors that constitute the master plan. These I surrounded by layers of progressively higher income groups. The outermost being high-income, multi-storeyed housing along the sector roads and large plots for independent high-income group units.

Today, after more than 25 years, it is hard to find the modest beginnings in this project that comprised just a plinth with a kitchen and toilet provided then. These houses have grown to fulfil the occupants' needs, are well furnished and lovingly decorated. They are not houses but homes where a happy community lives. That is what finally matters.

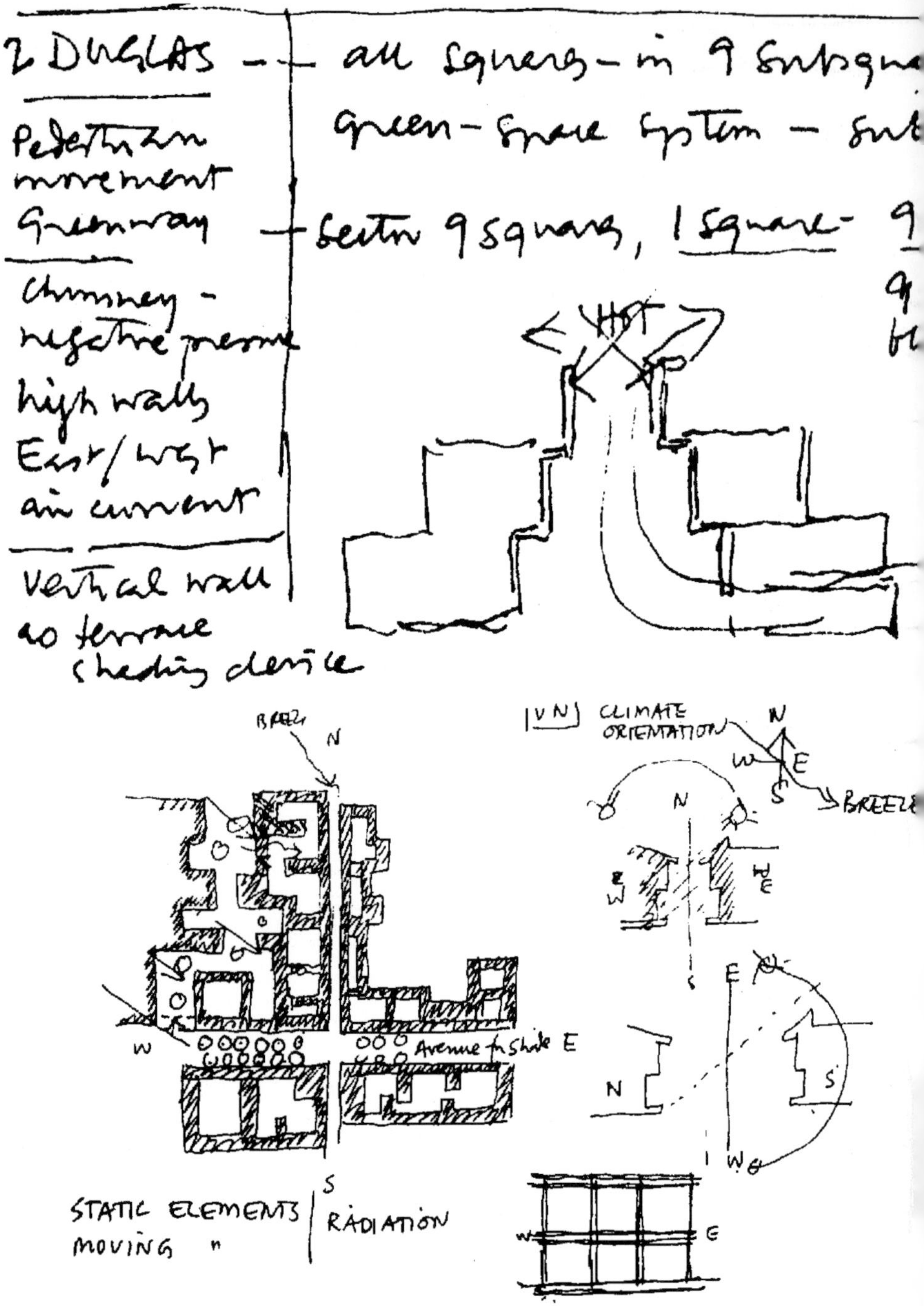
2 DUGLAS
all squares – in 9 subsquares
Pedestrian movement Greenway
green – space system
sector 9 squares, 1 square – 9
chimney – negative pressure
high walls
East/west air current
vertical wall as terrace shading device
HOT
N
CLIMATE ORIENTATION
BREEZE
W
E
S
Avenue for shade
STATIC ELEMENTS
MOVING "
RADIATION

- ~~[illegible]~~ V.N.

- major/minor – "greenway"

Us – homes square

ORIENTATION

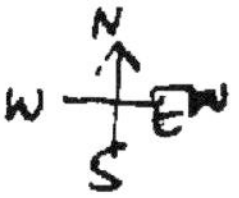

VN. 3/5/85

BREEZE
WNW
ESE

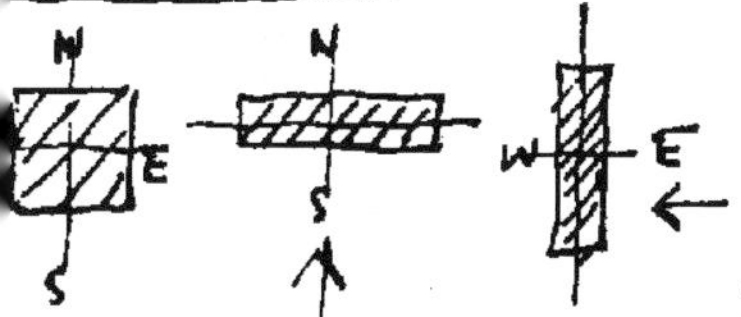

NEEDS ALT ARCH. SHADING DEVICES + PLANTATION + NARROW STRS.

– PREFERABLE

– PROVIDE MAX-HOUSING BLDG.

SQUARE SECTORS VS. OBLONG SECTORS

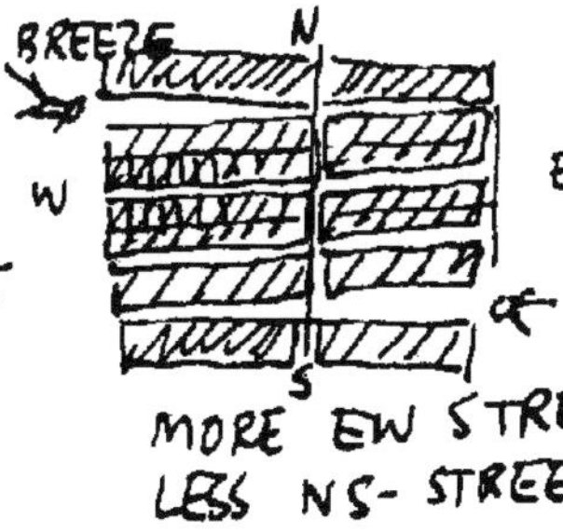

MORE EW STREETS
LESS NS- STREETS

* CHECK- INDORE LAYOUT
DOUBLE THE SCALE OF PLOTS

Another project that I am proud of is the Vidyadhar Nagar. The project, spread over an area of about 3 square kilometres, is located 2km west of old Jaipur and is well connected to its central east-west spine. Since there was a very short deadline, and I could not have spent the time required at Jaipur, the Jaipur Development Authority set up a special office for me at Ahmedabad.

We undertook several preparatory studies before we began planning for Vidyadhar Nagar. For case studies, we analysed Chandigarh and old Jaipur in great detail, which included field work on planning and urban-design aspects, the cost of development, energy-saving responses, and impact on the environs. We also carried out studies in transportation, demographics, employment trends and patterns, infrastructure planning and environmental issues.

This led to preparation of a comprehensive development plan that went much beyond the conventions. We asked questions such as: Can we minimize motorized travel and maximize walking and cycling? Can we change the conventional land-use patterns and provide for mixed land uses? Can we create opportunities at various scales where everybody can work together? Can we find an optimal transportation network? We also developed architectural controls since different architects would design the buildings in the city over several years.

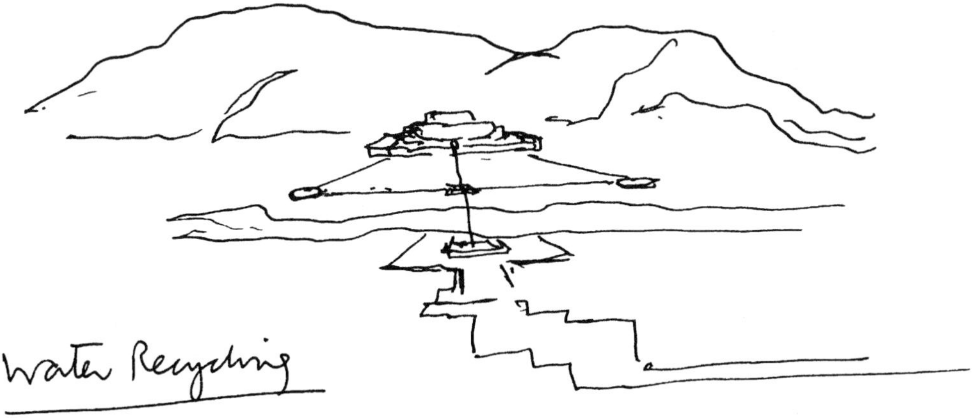

We prepared detailed plans for a sustainable development through reforestation of the surrounding region by water harvesting, recycling waste, encouraging small-scale industries, integrating natural elements such as water, solar energy and wind with housing and work areas, and creating alternative models for revitalizing the inner-city cores as well as peripheral expansion of the cities built so far.

These principles and models have guided several of our projects since then, and each of these projects has helped improve and fine-tune them. Among the significant projects are plans for revitalizing the core areas in Hyderabad and Ahmedabad (Charminar and Bhadra precincts, respectively), Cyberabad, a new high-tech city on the periphery of Hyderabad, and Kharghar, a new independent node at New Bombay spread over 2,006 acres for a population of 44,000, to give some idea about the scale of the project.

India is fortunate that most of its cities are very old, some more than a millennium and others few centuries at least. Thus, each city has a core area that is its most valuable heritage. Core areas are the hearts of a city and they work like one too. When congestion occurs, the heart fails and so do core areas. One by one, the elements of the heritage, the quality of the traditional bazaars and daily life deteriorate. Gradually undesirable activities and elements move in, encroach upon the public space and unattended properties and take over the core area.

Development then moves into peripheral areas, which now receive more attention and development funds, leading to further decay of the core areas. Over the years, this cycle perpetuates this phenomenon, constantly adding to the periphery consuming precious agricultural land, adding to transportation time and costs, pollution, etc.

If we need to conserve heritage, if we need to save resources including energy, if we value virtues of mixed and multiple land uses and if we wish to promote heritage tourism, we must revitalize our city cores. We are following this strategy in the work for Charminar and Bhadra precincts. Happily, we have received tremendous support from the citizens residing in these precincts because only those who have stayed back know the value of the heritage.

Thus, over the last 60 years or so that I have practised, I have been very fortunate to work on a whole range of projects of varied scales, complexities and contexts. I am also happy that most of these have been pioneering works in India. They have allowed me to traverse the length and breadth of this diverse country and experience first-hand its people and cultures. However, architecture remains most dear to me and it is in these projects that I now find myself most absorbed. Now, it is the psychic and spiritual experience of architecture that fascinates me more than the mundane.

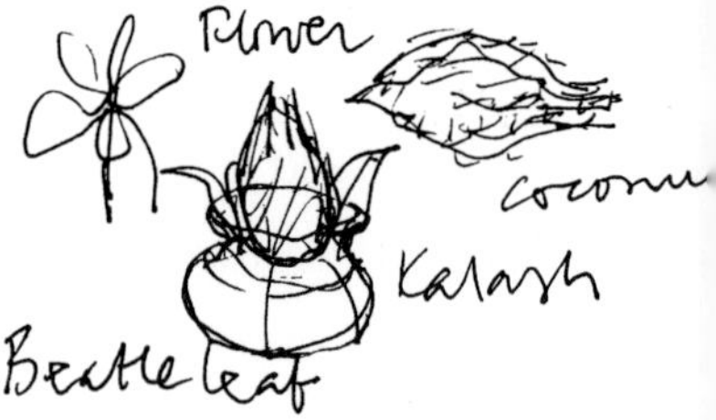
Flower
Coconu
Kalash
Beatle leaf

I believe the supreme among architectural experiences are those which occur along the routes of movement in spaces that could be characterized as pauses or ambiguous plural spaces. These spaces activate the human psyche and induce it to gravitate towards the centre; the mythical world of man's primordial being. Time and space are then internalized and a deep-rooted personal identity with the built form is established. Such space-psyche experiences become memorable and are cherished by the individual and the community at large. These experiences are then passed onto the next generation as cultural heritage.

I have had the good fortune to meet Dr Stella Kramrisch, a renowned scholar and an art historian in Philadelphia. When I met her, she was already 85 years old, and had spent a major part of her life studying Indian art; she was head of the Department of Art in Philadelphia Museum. Over time, we became well acquainted and talked at length whenever possible. She once explained to me the significance of a Hindu temple:

'The temple is a living being and the Indian *sthapati* must be a yogi. He must feel the breath of every object and material he works with. The *pran pratishtha* ceremony that is undertaken as part of the consecration ceremony after the temple is complete is intended to infuse the breath of life in the inert matter and make it come alive.'

I have never forgotten this observation made by her. Thereafter, my interest in studying the spiritual aspects of buildings has increased manifold. I believe that form, structure, surface, material and density are all of much value but they have to be harmoniously related to each other if the buildings have to become living entities; it is like giving birth to a new life.

Once that happens, silence prevails. Intangible actions and reactions between them create the energy field, allowing the soul to enter into the idol of the deity. Hindu architecture works this way. That is *vastu*—everything living, everything related, everything in harmonious relationships. When all the relationships come together in right proportions, creation happens.

I once asked Shilanand Swamy, after he had renounced his leadership of the Dhuniwale Baba's sect, as to how should an architect conduct himself to become a good architect and a happy man. His answer was short and simple, 'Design every building as a temple of God.'

While one is moving, the body becomes dynamic. When one is moving with something held in the hand which needs balancing and yet continues walking, one becomes aware of each of the steps. Turning all the time, moving down, up, the movement is rhythmic. One becomes conscious of the feet, the hands and what one holds in the hands. There is complete balance among the body, eyes, breath and movement.

Experiencing the effect of temperature on the texture of limbs separately and on the body as a whole, one walks through the first threshold, hears the sound of bells close to the ears, touching heavy metal and pushing the gong, one hears the sound Om. Chanting penetrates deep within. While designing Sangath, these were my thoughts.

There, looking around as if through a camera lens, one sees the columns and statues and ideas emerge. Spiritual thoughts dominate and make one psychically subconscious. In slow movements, one's sensitivity is heightened and slightest change in the quality of light is perceived. When one is in dark places, offering garland and touching the deity, one is transported to another world, losing the sense of the physical body, chanting occurs. Quietly, with eyes closed, one is in a trance.

I remember how very quiet and preoccupied Kahn seemed when he came back from a visit to Chandigarh. I asked him what it was. His answer was, 'If there is anyone who can freeze the dream, it is Le Corbusier. I felt it in the Assembly Complex.' He continued, 'Never have I seen someone picking up various elements and placing them together, in the most unusual fashion to create an unexpected experience. The upward-turning portico, compared to the usual sloping one, the use of the truncated cooling tower placed over the Assembly chamber and an inner court transformed into a ministers' forum are brilliant gestures. I wish I could do this some day, create such experiences.'

While designing the campus for Shreyas Foundation, my discussions with Leena Mangaldas, its founder, made me aware that there are no boundaries of space or time in learning. Learning occurs simultaneously and our responses shape our lives. The present CEPT campus and its incremental growth, with all the financial constraints, made me realize the importance of gradual expansion and distinct character of each new discipline.

As a result, the campus is somewhat loosely cohesive, allowing each new faculty adequate space for expansion. Likewise, the criss-crossing movement of faculty and students makes everyone aware about the inter-connectivity of varied disciplines as well as overall environmental concerns.

Aldo van Eyck once wrote, 'The house is a small city, and city is a big house.' CEPT campus has similarly become at once a small campus and a big house, making everyone aware about his or her role in it.

For the IIM Bangalore and IIM Lucknow campuses, I reinforced this concept of unifying diverse academic activities linked to courtyards of varied sizes. I created well-defined, semi-open green corridors to link them together and loosely define the movement patterns. The integration of functions, movements, nature and the choices to accommodate diverse activities simultaneously are the distinguishing features of the campus at Bangalore today.

Design of the headquarters for the Madhya Pradesh Electricity Board at Jabalpur offered an unusual challenge. In contrast to the flat terrain in most of our projects, the site here was undulating with plenty of very large boulders. We had to work around the boulders and the slopes and configure site circulation and disposition of dozens of building blocks to create a large administrative complex.

Hierarchies of classified functions and unpredictable growth in the board's various administrative departments called for a self-supporting but independently growing organization of the campus. I had to devise a way of connecting all of them together as if it was a cluster of some plant rooted to the ground but free to breathe freely as it rose.

The use of stone as a local material and octagonal office block subsequently took form, in which varied heights and terraces provided scope for expansion. As a result, this campus has become a part of the surrounding population. A newly created large water-body along with an auditorium, restaurant and a marriage hall, have made it a busy city centre for the people of the city.

They say the stars influence our lives in unpredictable and mysterious ways.

I experienced that when, as a challenge, I accepted one of the most demanding projects I had ever undertaken, that of designing the Bharat Diamond Bourse located in the Bandra Kurla Complex (BKC) in Mumbai.

To share the project's responsibilities, Rajeev and Radhika decided to join me. And to provide their expertise Mr Mahendra Raj, an internationally known structural engineer from Delhi, Dr Prem Jain, equally known HVAC consultant from Delhi, and Sanelac Consultants from Bangalore agreed to form a consortium.

The Indian diamond-trading community, being one of the most aggressive leaders in the global diamond business, was then spread in several different neighbourhoods in Mumbai. To consolidate their work needs and shared amenities, they decided to build a single trading bourse for 4,000 members on a 20-acre plot at the complex. Their mandate visualized a unique complex, which would attract traders from across the world and make their presence felt strongly in the global diamond trade.

It was to be a high-tech, state-of-the-art complex providing work places for 30,000, parking for 3,000 cars and banking and customs facilities within a very secure environment. For me, the challenge was to demonstrate a completely new approach to urban design and create a visionary model.

Such a task I had never undertaken before. Since the project was to come up in the heart of Mumbai, it meant fully building up to the permissible limit of floor area. This called for providing more than 300,000 square metres of space with nearly 4,000 individual offices with sizes

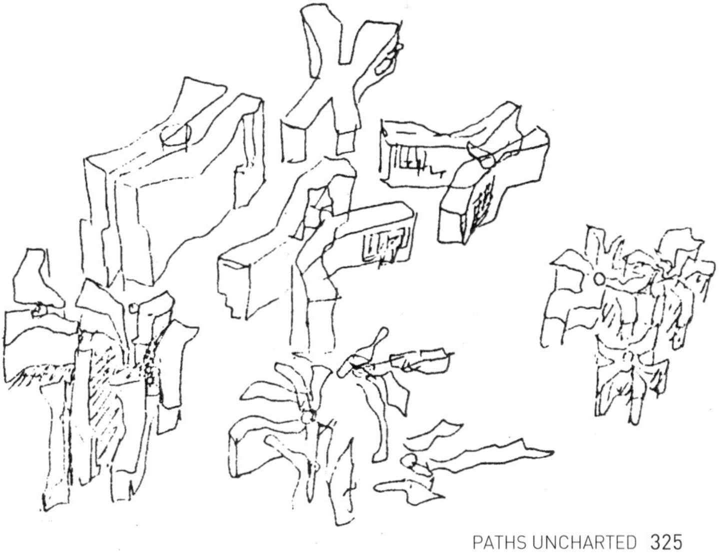

varying from just about 25 to as much as 1,000 square metres. Then there was also a time limit of just four years from the stage of design to its execution.

I thought of all the work I had done and all the concerns that had preoccupied me until then. These involved working for the poor, designing institutions in the larger context, a search for an individual and group identity etc. However, I told myself, designing offices for rich diamond merchants and a diamond-trading bourse called for a very different set of concerns.

It occurred to me that diamonds are crystalline in nature and form. Starting from that, I conceived a crystalline multi-faceted row of 12-floor high towers overlooking the north–south direction, and placed them parallel to each other to suit the irregular shape of the site. Facing north, each office in the building would receive glare-free daylight, save lighting costs and provide an unrestricted view.

Concerned about the entire 296-acre site of the BKC where many

similar commercial and institutional towers would be built in time, we persuaded the local authority to reassess pedestrian access to all plots in the complex along a network of green paths. We also undertook studies and proposed amenities such as cafes, shopping and recreation for the thousands of office workers and visitors at BKC.

For close to four years, we worked around the clock on this project to realize all these objectives. Unfortunately, misunderstandings among the members about the facilities and their financial implications resulted in the project being stalled. With no solution in sight, eventually several committees in charge of the project were dissolved and, painfully, we parted company with the clients when the bourse buildings were almost 70 per cent ready and most of the materials for the rest of the construction had already been procured.

My team of consultants and I—who had been working on the project—wanted to move on and not prolong a dispute; so we decided to concede the client's suggestion and forego a large sum of fees that was overdue. Each one of us took a huge loss on the work already carried out and our dream came to a rather abrupt end.

At Sangath, we staffed and equipped the office for a long haul and turned into a 24x7 multi-disciplinary office for this project. So, with the contract terminated, we were in debt, and the office had to quickly change gears. I had to request almost all of my senior colleagues of several decades to start out on their own and gradually cut their work time until they had found a satisfactory alternative. They understood and left over the next few months.

Seeing an almost empty office and studio, I again remembered Dada, his life and the stories he told me from the Mahabharata. I recalled the lessons from these stories, and thought often of Karna's life. I felt the same pangs that my Dada must have felt after disposing of whatever I had earned.

Sangath was silent and not celebrating

work, life and architecture as before.

Nonetheless, times change, and so does luck, and when the project for design of Amdavad Ni Gufa came up, a brand new life began at Sangath, as if it was reborn.

I wanted to put the diamond bourse project behind me, delve deep into the spirit and experience of architecture, and not just go about designing as I might have earlier. Therefore, I began by asking the basic questions about the meaning and purpose of architecture.

I decided that one must experience joys and celebration of life in architecture. It must affect our inner self. It cannot be distinguished separately either as modulation of light or surfaces or supporting system or individual elements.

A good design integrates floors, walls, ceilings into one unified whole and becomes an organic space, very much like a living being, as Dr Stella Kramrisch would describe. The spaces contained within and without its surfaces should be the sources of life-giving energy.

I can never define how I could measure the sense of space or time. The spirit of Sangath appeared fluid and I was unable to hold it in my hand or touch it. But every time I participated, the current felt through my body. For me, Sangath became a tool, a commodity but not necessarily for bartering. Its peculiar configuration, with undefined contents, created its own scale as if immeasurable.

I think I have come very close to such architecture in my design for Amdavad Ni Gufa, initially called Husain-Doshi Gufa. This project happened nearly 30 years after I first met M.F. Husain, the most important modern Indian artist, at the home of Gunvant Mangaldas, an avid art collector.

Among other things, we had discussed Ahmedabad's climate and what would be the best way to deal with it architecturally. We had concluded that underground spaces offer great benefits for reasons of climate and many others. Husain recalled this discussion and asked me to design an underground space for a gallery.

We decided to call it the Gufa, literally a cave. We thought the project could also demonstrate the collaboration between a painter and an architect. Husain's agility, free spirit and unconventional attitude needed a challenge. I wanted to incorporate my work experiences of 35 years as well as mark a new phase in life.

Husain and I asked questions such as: Why should the walls be plumb? Why do we need foundations? Why is a roof always flat? Why follow normal construction methods and techniques? Therefore, we were looking forward to creating a very unusual space and building for the gallery.

After hundreds of sketches, drawings, models in board, wood and clay, there emerged a continuous, curvilinear, underground space filled with diffused light from the oculars above, defined by curved walls, floor and a few columns which were tilted, twisted and merged as if they were legs of a precariously balanced mountain goat. The Gufa was indeed experiencing a completely new world.

The experience of the space here changes continuously with the movement of the sun striking the curved surfaces within and without. This leads to a desire to be free of all inhibitions but to be with the self. Eyes tend to move, rest, ponder and close to recapitulate. The body relaxes, becomes light. To heighten the experiential quality of this project, I wrote a story of Pithora Baba, a tribal god and Vishnu's *kurma* avatar.

In turn, as if to invoke Vishnu's Sheshnag, the mythical king cobra who is holding up the earth in its place, Husain outlined a cobra wrapping around and connecting all the domes, but it was a headless cobra. He then asked me to have this cobra finished in black mosaic. Thus, we had both the tribal and Brahmanical traditions expressed there.

I am tempted to add here another instance to suggest that creativity does spring from challenges. The more unusual and demanding the challenge, more creative and innovative the response, I believe.

Once the Gufa was ready for displaying art, Husain brought a canvas but could not hang it on the curving walls. So he walked around, observed the dynamics of the continuous surface as well as the movement of the shaft of sunlight coming in from the oculars, and painted the most unusual lines extending from one end to the other. It was a revelation of how the eye can move to reveal the unfathomed volumes of the space.

Then, few months later a truck arrived, full of plywood cutouts painted black, each almost 250cm high. These he placed at strategic locations, set up a few spotlights and created shadows on walls and floors as if he was painting with light and shadows. From that moment, Gufa began to speak of its purpose.

Yet, for Husain, Gufa lacked the space to display his canvasses, especially the series named *Theorama*, his largest work. To provide a place for it, two parallel walls were created adjoining the Gufa, with a temporary canvas roof. This finally became a permanent gallery named after his American art collector and friend, Chester Hurwitz.

Years later, the entrance was brought forward towards the main road with a small office and a coffee shop. Today it has become a civic complex, truly *Amdavad Ni Gufa*. Here people of all ages share their joys, while children enjoy sliding on varied slopes and some wonder about the Sheshnag coiling around the domes.

Soon after Gufa, I was assigned a project where this playful exploration of animated spaces could be further explored. This was the design of a campus for the National Institute of Fashion Technology (NIFT), at Delhi. Rathi Jha, Director of NIFT, had come to NID for some work and on being told about it, visited the Gufa. She very much liked what she saw and spoke about me to Pupul Jayakar, the Chairperson of NIFT, who called to ask if I would design the campus.

That was the time when India was embarking on carving a name for itself in the modern fashion and garment business. I must say fashion is, in some ways, a world with no limits. It has potentially infinite relationships with cultures, time and space, just as there are infinite opportunities to reinterpret time, space, tradition and style. I clearly saw this project as an occasion to create architecture as a setting for the fashion designers to express various times, space and styles in their designs.

I conceived a central court to emphasize the inner search as reinterpretation of a *kund*, a water tank usually found near temples, to exaggerate multi-directional views from within the courtyard. The central courtyard here is defined by building blocks, which seem like fragments of a larger whole. Each of them has a strong individual identity and serves as connectors of the external and the internal worlds.

To explain my proposal, I wrote a story as to how there was an entire village built around a sacred water tank with mysterious healing properties. Over centuries, I said, this village came to be dissected and modified by modern developments and was left to the vagaries of nature until NIFT happened. It also explained those building blocks around the central court as actually the remains of the original village homes surrounding the tank, now renovated for the needs of NIFT.

As luck would have it, this myth of the 'sacred water' was narrated during the inauguration of the campus and the Board of Directors of NIFT thought it was real. So they asked, 'Why can't we sell this sacred water?' When I told them it was just a story I had fabricated, they did not know what to say!

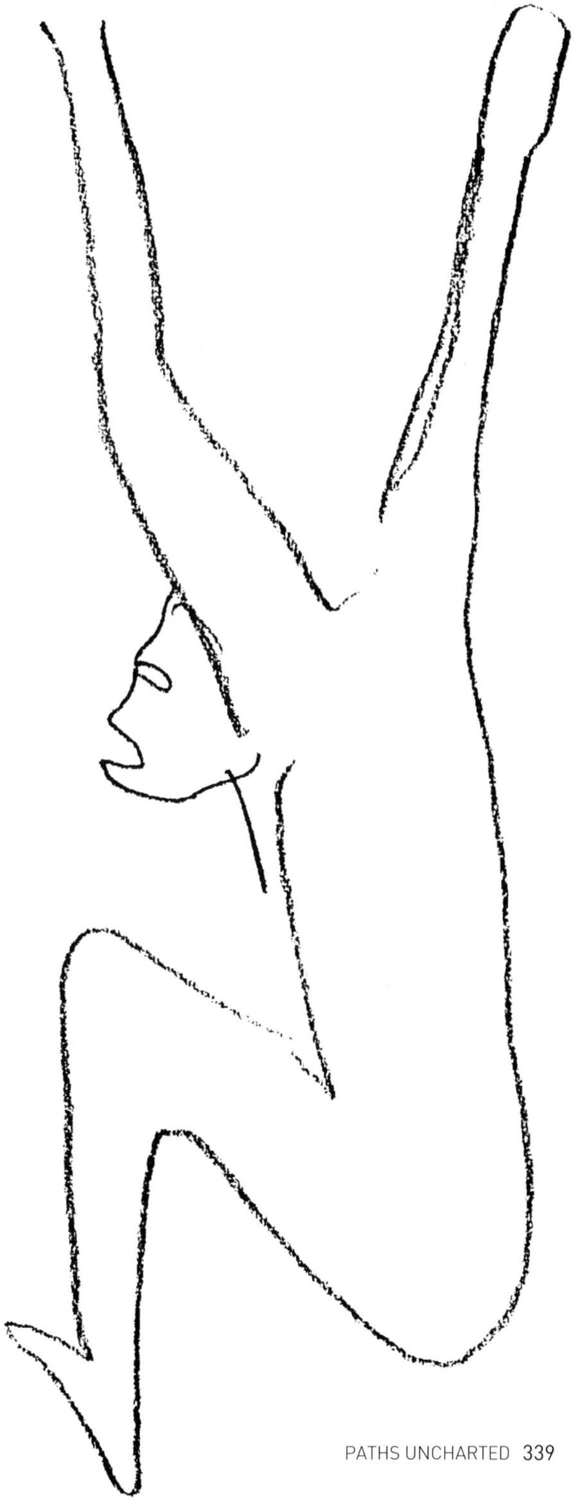

Practicing
is an obsession
involvement,
you grow
you are and
product:
between
creative urge
unspoken

architecture,
and a lifetime
the older
the more mature
the better is your
a marriage
the personal
and fulfilling
dreams of clients.

I have been fortunate to work at all the scales of city planning, urban design and architecture. And I have also been fortunate to be living and working in Ahmedabad for a very enlightened group of visionary clients. In India of the post-Independence period, they were among the most understanding, generous and adventurous clients. They may make a dozen inquiries before choosing an architect or a designer but once chosen, their faith in the architect was complete. As a result, one experiences in Ahmedabad a good harmony of culture, social life, and pursuit of the unknown.

Ahmedabad is a modern and ancient city at the same time. Its people are very frugal in their personal habits and yet generously contribute time and money for public institutions. They are very pragmatic and yet would support something completely new if they see it as good for the future.

The city's richness owes itself to the cooperation between the citizens and the leaders of industry and culture, locally called *mahajan*s. This partnership between them to conceive and create a textile industry in spite of the lack of coal, cotton and the required levels of humidity speaks volumes about their genius.

The old city of Ahmedabad is full of exquisitely carved wooden buildings; they are fine jewelled boxes. Yet, it was in this city that the most path-breaking modern architecture occurred. Ahmedabad boasts of four masterpieces by Corbusier namely Sanskar Kendra (the Cultural Centre), Ahmedabad Textile Mill Owners' Association (ATMA office), and Sarabhai and Shodhan Villas and, of course, the IIMA campus designed by Louis Kahn. It is here that one can experience a healthy interplay between money and culture.

Corbusier brought world attention to India and Indian clientele through his works at Chandigarh and Ahmedabad. It broke the spell of time and cultural constraints. Such sudden jumps into the unknown opened unexpected doors and nurtured new visions.

Because of projects by Corbusier and Kahn in Ahmedabad, many famous architects and planners from India and abroad have visited the city and continue to do so. In turn, these works have influenced several new projects in the city that continue to attract students, researchers, artists and architects from all over the world.

Their itinerary always includes the CEPT University campus where, through their lectures and discussions with students and teachers, these visitors have enriched the educational and professional scene in the city. In turn, this has helped the whole country to keep abreast of the international developments in the field of architecture and planning.

I live in paradoxes. As a result, there is a constant struggle to confine, to find security, to create walls around and then try to open them with windows and doors to see outside or go out. The choice I make is to be in and out at the same time.

Conscious and unconscious pull towards past and present; regular contacts with the east and the west enrich my practice. My efforts are to combine the virtues of diametrically opposite ways. Meandering streets and pedestrian scales of Indian villages have to come to terms with high-speed lane traffic.

Quiet life of the early morning and late evenings in courtyards, under the trees, on platforms, has to accommodate the sounds of television or motorized two-wheelers. Similarly, socio-economic transactions between extended families and communities have to be viewed with the impersonal credit cards or electronic banking.

I have always liked working with minimal resources and constraints. I consider it a challenge. It leads to very creative solutions. Limitation of resources takes us to unusual inventiveness. Lack of resources, economic uncertainty, and lack of continuous development leads us to an architecture, which suggests in its plan and expression the ambiguous nature of our life today.

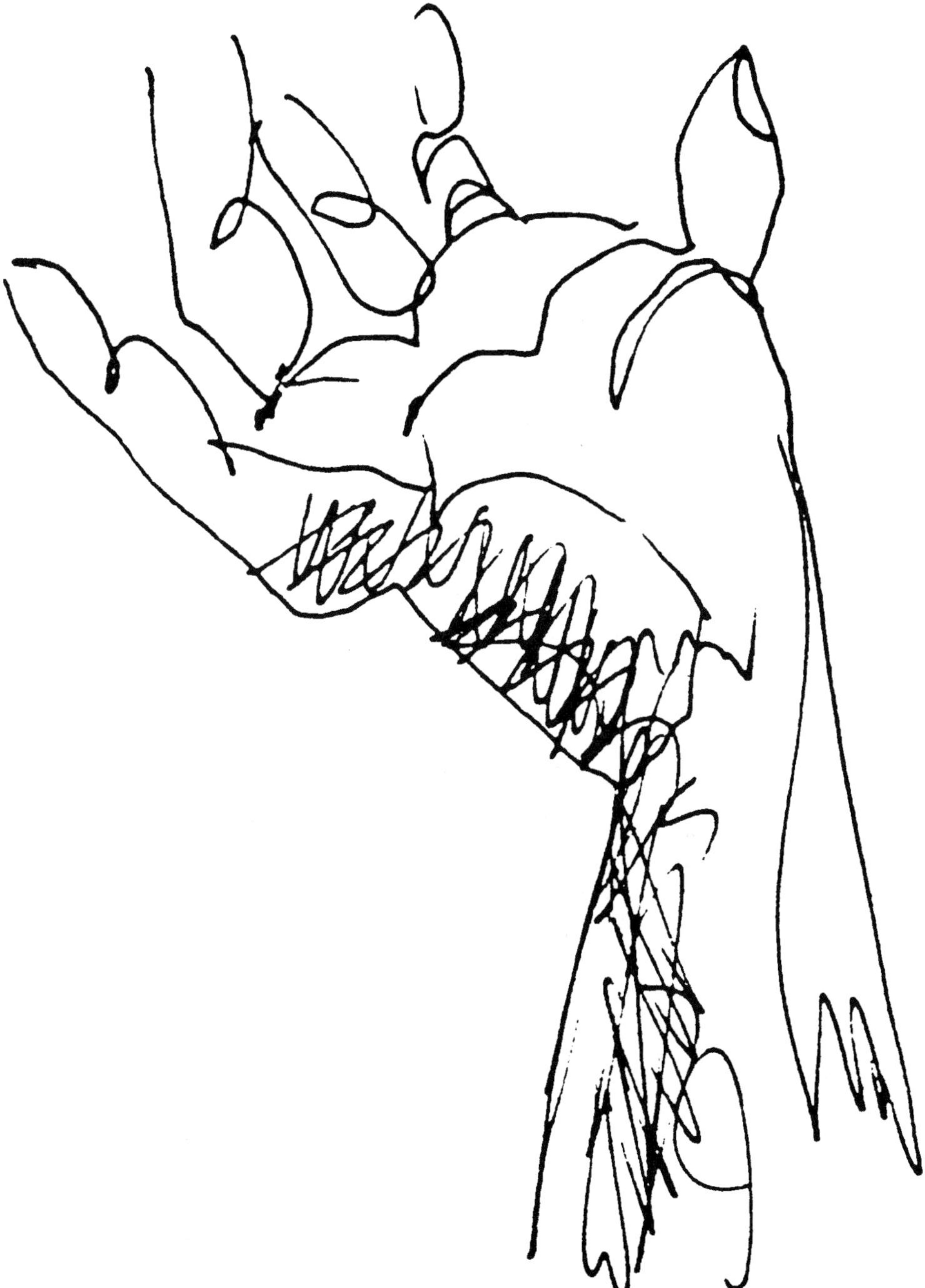

This concern was very much on my mind when we began work on Kharghar, and Cyberabad and Charminar area in Hyderabad. We began with a new understanding of sustainability and inter-relatedness with the people as the focus. The scope of our practice ranged from a modest house to large new towns.

For me, every project has a seed potential and after comprehensive studies, each project suggested to us a solution that achieved more than was called for in the original brief. Dry, denuded lands, disintegration of smaller cohesive towns into new isolated and incongruous developments became our concerns. Our proposals became extended developments.

I began to remember my guru Le Corbusier and Dada, my grandfather, who always talked about the virtues of cosmic galaxies. Interlinked hierarchies made us realize the virtue of varied scale developments where movements were minimized and activities multiplied to save time and energy.

Without my consciously realizing it, all these concerns were reigniting the fundamental questions I had always posed for myself. These are the eternal questions, which have to do with meaning and purpose of all forms of life and their physical, social and spiritual needs.

With passing years, I increasingly thought of the four terms Rasikbhai had mentioned: *vikas*, *vistaar*, *kshobh* and *drav*. He had explained these as when something blossoms, it expands; thereafter, there is a churning and ultimately it melts and evaporates, and the cycle begins once again.

If I might call them so, my spiritual experiences at places such as Kailash and Meenakshi Temples helped me to see the unity between the finite and the infinite. I often wondered if as an architect I could design a space that could offer such an experience. Luckily, an opportunity arose to design a small temple dedicated to the Mother, the spiritual head of the Aurobindo Ashram.

I well remember a visit to the Ashram decades ago. I sat there in meditation with my eyes closed near Shri Aurobindo's samadhi at Pondicherry. The air I breathed was fragrant from the flowers placed on the marble platform of the Samadhi, and the smell of incense added another layer.

Suddenly, when I touched my forehead, I felt a shiver and realized later the value of silence and peace. Sitting far away after prayers and watching the silent movement of devotees climbing steps and descending, I felt like I was observing a silent movie. The soft, almost divine, sunlight made me conscious of my eyes and the act of sitting there for a long time made me aware of all my body parts.

I was thinking of such experiences when I began to design the Mother's Shrine at Matar in Gujarat. Could I create a space that could induce spiritual experiences in people who come there? I had never before asked this question because it was never thought of as any concern of architects.

Architecture is not only about materials that we use or the size and scale of our works. What really matters is the process that begins with arrival in a space or a building and ends with a silent yet fulfilling departure. No measurable activities need to have taken place in the space for that experience except for a sense of becoming. I asked myself how one could achieve this in architecture.

I remember visiting the Pantheon, the temple without an icon, conceived by Hadrian. Although it appeared insignificant at first from the street, once inside, its interior stunned me. Its scale, proportions, volume and especially the light cast by the oculus in the dome made it a divine experience.

I just stood there looking at the shaft of light for almost an hour, unable to walk through it and across. Mesmerized, I just kept observing its movement within the space and resultant play of shadows on the walls. I then knew that great architecture such as these temples speak about time, its passing, its cyclical and yet eternal dimensions.

At Matri Mandir at Matar, I sought to create a similar experience, it was quite a challenge to create pure experience without using an image. To me such an experience meant witnessing only the varied nuances of light. Working with a small budget, I began by designing a conical space with an oculus at its apex. From the oculus, a shaft of light reached down to relics of the Mother enshrined in a circular marble platform decked in flowers. I then provided space for the devotees to sit around the platform and to meditate surrounded only by silence and light.

Here I recall what the respected Gujarati poet Sundaram, the prime mover behind the project, told Kamu in response to her query about the proposed shrine. He had said, 'Kamala, everything is already here, the shrine, the light, the flowers. What you need to do is close your eyes and be silent. Slowly images will emerge. Experience will follow. All you need is trust and faith.'

Sadly, these days, temples have been reduced to centres of debased rituals. Pilgrims come there as if they were going to a bazaar, priests and others who help them to run the affairs do so in return for a livelihood, as if it was drudgery and not service to the divine.

For me, every place we visit should be a place of discovery, both of the self and those embodied in that space. Our learning and awakening happen simultaneously, both randomly and in a regulated way. The choice is made spontaneously, and it is the impulse that dominates our action. Architecture of such a place should be as if it was an archaeological site with large volumes, some hidden below the ground and some above which cannot be grasped easily, like in ruins. The passages that one moves in offer glimpses of what is beyond as we arrive, yet they become mysterious when we move within. This provides occasions for us to either pause or skip, search for another and discover the unexpected.

In a temple complex, these searches are our treasures, constantly awakening different cells of our body, connecting ultimately together into an experience that we carry home. This indescribable journey and the memory we harbour are the story of the temple.

Echoes of all these experiences and efforts at recreating them are what make Sangath my best work. It expresses in sum total a bit of all the experiences of places I have visited, lived and worked in. All of my memories are embedded in it. That Sangath is so much a part of me as not only a place of work but also an extension of my personal life is evident in the fact that it was the chosen venue for the marriage ceremonies of all of my daughters.

I saw these weddings at Sangath as being similar to the celebration of joyous events I had experienced in Pune when the spaces of Dada's furniture workshop and our ancestral home became one. Our home is not very far from Sangath and between the two lies the CEPT campus. Every day, the act of walking or driving to school or Sangath reminds me of my childhood visits to Dada's workshop and a temple not so far away.

I am now almost as old as Dada was, when I first became conscious of the world around me, I try to see through his eyes at the ways my life and my own family has grown. We are now some 40 members strong spread over five or six cities and a dozen homes. Strangely, I find that my own children have followed, in a manner of speaking, the same pattern of breaking free and doing what they felt as the right thing to do.

Our eldest daughter Tejal was studying at NID when she met the man she married, Geev Panthaki, and it was during a dance party held at the School of Architecture. He is a Parsi and was then studying at St. Xavier's College and had nothing to do with architecture. Our second daughter Radhika, after graduating from CEPT, met her husband Rajeev Kathpalia, a Punjabi, in New Delhi. Our youngest daughter Maneesha, an artist, married her teacher Vasudevan Akkitham, a Malayalee, while studying at the Faculty of Fine Arts in Vadodara. My granddaughter Khushnu, an architect from CEPT, is married to Sönke Hoof, a German whom she met at Sangath. Another granddaughter, Jessica, is married to Vineet Nair, who is half-Malayalee and half-Gujarati.

These multilingual and multinational wedding ceremonies brought my entire extended family together, reminding me of Dada's role and place. As I am the eldest member of the family, all these celebrations took place at my home and at Sangath, amid trees, flowers and fountains. Life thrives while sharing joys and being together on such occasions. Rituals and celebrations are the connecting thread in our family; the temple and the kitchen are the bedrocks of our house.

I had spent half of my time during the diamond-bourse project in Bombay. There, seeing the city's chaotic transport network, the ever-growing number of slums right next to multi-storeyed and commercial hubs, I often wondered about the hinterlands and the poorer half of the population and what we could do about it.

I remembered Corbusier's statement about making a 'Pact with Nature'. Is there a way to reformulate our tasks as architects and planners? Should our practice not be simultaneously both at the macro and micro levels? Should we not look into a multi-disciplinary practice with expanded focus? To achieve this, I invited both Rajeev and Radhika, who had been practising independently, to join me in 1992. We started a new company and named it Vastu-Shilpa Consultants, recalling the association of the name and its meaning as explained by Motabhai.

I have always tried to discover another way of doing the same work, different from what I had done before. Either it is about the structure, or services, or material, or technology or the final expression. This has been my continuous search. My processes begin with some mundane thing I already know.

For instance, my daughter Maneesha's house began as an ordinary row house sharing walls on both the sides. Then I looked at half of my own house and looked at it as a row house. So I studied half of my own house and started exploring it as a row house.

Slowly, my own house was transformed in a home for Maneesha. The four central columns of my home were aligned in a single row, and the house came to be sandwiched between two mango trees on the site. There was indeed a lot of development and reworking in the process. Finally, the house acquired a character of its own and emerged as a home very different from mine.

However, it took me three long years to reach a point when we could start the construction. I believe there are no measures of time, energy or cost in making something the best you can. People often tell me that it is not viable that I take so long to complete my projects, in this case three years to design one house. My answer to them is that my life—and, therefore, my time—has no economic value as such. What is valuable to me is the joy from a work well done, and that is what I seek.

As to can one ever actually value the time of our lives, that was best conveyed to me by Buckminster Fuller one evening at my home. I had asked him, 'Bucky, tell me, how did you conceive ideas such as the geodesic dome, dymaxion car and other inventions?'

Bucky said, 'After completing my army assignment as a marine engineer I had come back to Boston and joined my father-in-law's construction business. I could not do what was expected of me and everyone saw me as a failure. Married with two kids and a life of misery, I withdrew into my room and spent a few days alone reflecting on myself.

'I realized one day that the average life span of an American was 42 years and I was actually 42 then. So I told myself that, for all practical purposes, I could be dead. Suddenly I said to myself that if this be the case, I am already dead. I am not there for anyone. I am free! Why can't I do something radically different? That is how I started on a new life, with new thoughts and new vision for the rest of my life. That's how the geodesic dome and other things happened.'

When I narrated this incident to Louis Kahn, he said, 'Great man, Bucky is. We have been close friends for years.' Then he said, 'I ran into Bucky on 5th Avenue in New York one day. He was wearing shoes without laces, and no buttons on his jacket. It was during the Great Depression. I stopped and asked him how things were. He said, "Great, nothing could be better. My dymaxion car is ready but I cannot find anyone to manufacture it. But Lou, how are you?" I said, "I just lost another commission in Philadelphia. Otherwise, nothing can be better. Wandering and thinking."

Such persons remind me of Dr Hiren Ghose. He was a chiropractor and a devotee of Shri Aurobindo. His life was very unusual, without any concern or care for tomorrow and fully committed to working for the poor. When I asked about his fearlessness, he had said, 'No work is less valuable. You should only do what your heart wants you to do and leave the rest to God who pervades your physical and spiritual being and he will provide for you. If you are doing the right thing, you will never go hungry.' I had often observed while at Villepatti near Kodaikanal that Dr Ghose and his wife, Roshan Vajifdar, a well-known dancer, hardly stocked any food but never went hungry either.

‘There is no greater teacher than intuition. All other learning helps physically but not so spiritually.

Intuition and dreams depict our spiritual being because they emanate from the source.’

How our routine anxieties and daily preoccupations block our future visions and how unknowingly we are trapped in the daily grind is not a deep mystery. Like Bucky Fuller, if we think of being dead, would we not do things differently including those we had sometime just dreamt about? Working on Amdavad Ni Gufa with Husain gave me a chance to think of an architecture I might just have dreamt of. Perhaps, it was my reincarnation, without any baggage from my past.

Walking from home to CEPT campus and Sangath allows me to reflect on my own life and life in our cities. I recall reading the Gita and its lessons about my duties and responsibilities towards the community.

I see the ever-growing chaos on the streets, air and noise pollution, crowding, the lack of concern for others and neglect of public space that makes me shudder. There is an increasing apathy even towards our own selves. It is at this junction that providence brought me to visit Auroville, a 21st-century City of Dawn conceived by the Mother near Pondicherry.

Here it is envisaged that a community would live in total harmony with nature and without any monetary economy. So far they have done an admirable job of transforming the parched, barren earth into a green, fertile world which is what we see today. Focussing simultaneously on both inner and outer worlds, balancing through compassion, sharing, reverence, tolerance and gratitude, the existing community, though very small, strives to express Mother's vision.

This association with Auroville has rekindled a lot of questions that I have always asked. I recalled all of my travels, meeting people, observing marvels of human creations but also wondered about how and where we take this new road. Can we constantly expand without being in harmony with nature and not even take time to check if we are doing it right? Why do we value appearance and form so much? Why have the processes, which give deeper meaning to life, taken a backseat?

Can our cities be revitalized from within and learn to recharge from without? Why can't our educational system develop tools to create self-sustaining society?

Perhaps CEPT has the potential; it has now become a large banyan tree but needs to become the 'university of forest' Rabindranath Tagore thought of in Santiniketan. Perhaps it should devote itself to training barefoot architects and reconsider studying history books and other ideas, which propound growth, but without questioning the very purpose of growth.

I believe that I have learnt much from these encounters and lessons. I have learnt not to be afraid of following your own dream, taking risks, breaking out of one's comfort zone readily and not being complacent. I have learnt from all these people how to ignore obstacles and failures and convert them into virtues.

This reminds me of another incident while I was with Corbusier. One day when he came back, after a marathon meeting for the Unite d'Habitation at Nantes, he seemed dejected, but full of rigour.

When we asked him about the meeting he said, 'The committee wanted to assign me the project provided I changed the floor height of the kitchen and other rooms and modified the tubular layout. I told them, "Gentlemen, I would prefer to let go of this project rather than make those changes."' So Xenakis asked, 'Monsieur, what would you do now?' All Corbusier said was, 'Take revenge by working twice as hard.'

I remembered this incident when the site engineer for Sanskar Kendra, K.M. Kantawala—under advice from the structural engineer—decided to change the character of the non-load-bearing wall expressed in the museum facade. I refused to budge from what Le Corbusier had designed, and resigned.

For almost 10 months that left me only with the Shodhan House assignment on a monthly fee of Rs 125. Visits to Bombay to see the doctor for my colitis, his fees; Rs 65 for house rent and being just married, it all meant a tough time. Even so, I knew I was up to a challenge and I stuck to my position to honour the architect's decision. Kantawala finally conceded my position. 'Battle won,' I thought Corbusier would have said.

Looking back, I realize that it was not an easy task advocating Modern architecture and being a Modern architect of whatever hue in those days.

Another time, during the inaugural ceremony for ATMA building, the chief guest, Morarji Desai, Chief Minister of the state, seemed very surprised, if not shocked, seeing the exposed concrete and the independently placed toilet and staircase blocks. He said, 'Is this what modern architecture is all about? With inside organs exposed?'

I well remember similar stories about Picasso's paintings I had heard in Europe. To deflect such views and arguments of the clients and their project executors, I resolved to concoct bizarre stories so that no one ever could discuss the issue of generous spaces and the monumental scales of Le Corbusier's buildings.

For example, in the case of Sanskar Kendra, I would say, 'Do you know that the Municipal Corporation had actually asked Corbusier to design a milk dairy and that is why he has provided this ramp for the buffaloes to reach the main floor? The mezzanine floor is for storing their feed and the square punctures in the ceiling have been provided to spread the feed on to the main floor, which is where the buffaloes will be. This is why it has this blank facade.'

Thinking up and narrating such stories, which in a way denigrate my guru's work, was the mask I had to wear to face subtle, not so subtle, and, at times, outright hostility and condemnation of the completely new architecture I stood for or represented. The only time I was comfortable was when dealing with Kasturbhai, Vikram Sarabhai, and very few others who understood the spirit of the new times and the need and emergence of new expressions in arts and architecture.

As to how path-breaking those projects were, I was witness to their significance, yet again, just about a year ago. Frank Gehry, an architect from the US, was going to be in Ahmedabad for few hours along with Tom Pritzker.

Rajeev Sethi, whom I have known for long, called me from Delhi saying that Gehry would like to see the ATMA building and also meet me. To save time, could I meet him there itself? Would that be possible? Therefore, we met there and as I accompanied the two around, Gehry told Pritzker, 'This is the fountainhead of architecture. And I have come to pay my respects.'

So despite what anybody said of the architecture that I stood for in those days, I knew that I was on the right path and personally very happy with my life and myself until then. I now knew that all the risks I had taken, each time I embarked on an unknown path, were worth taking and the joy I derived from my work was unbelievable.

I felt I was treading cautiously, just as Corbusier had warned us at the Atelier in Paris. There, one day, when were gathered around him, he drew a star. Then pointing at the star, he said, 'This is your dream.' Then he drew a cloud under the star. And said, 'The dreams often get clouded.' Then he drew a dagger below the cloud and said, 'Remember, no dreams are realized without overcoming the obstacles. You have to be always watchful and expect the unexpected. Then only you will realize your dreams.'

In the 1950s, there were many occasions when I would be very disturbed over the way most people looked at modern architecture and modern architects. These were really disturbing events.

I distinctly remember one of these, which went beyond merely using harsh words. One day Kasturbhai, his brother Narottambhai, the building contractor and I were visiting the IIM site just after the construction work had begun. At that point, owing to both the quality of local bricks and the mason's lack of skills, the brickwork was not of satisfactory quality.

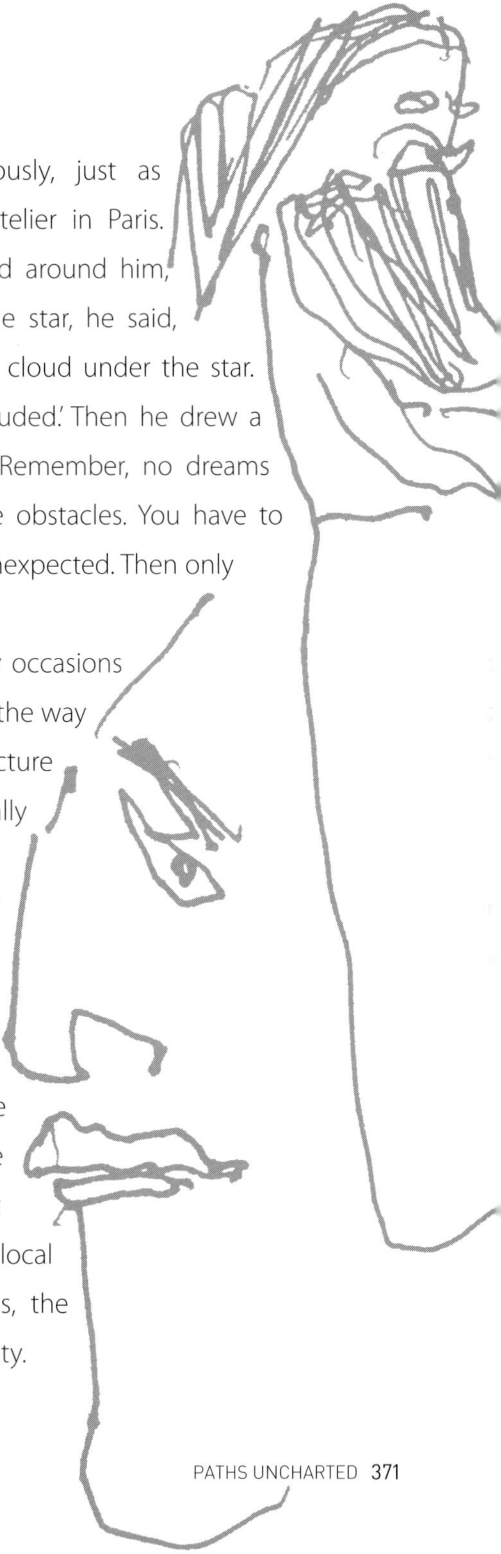

Kasturbhai and I had noted that, and we were discussing to better understand the underlying causes and how to deal with them. Narottambhai was some distance away and joined us at what may be called a wrong moment—when Kasturbhai was clearly agitated about the brickwork and was voicing his concerns.

Suddenly, Narottambhai removed one of his sandals and holding it in his hand came towards me to hit me, saying, 'You are betraying my brother with such brickwork. It is ugly and far from our expectation as suitable for an international management institute.' Just in time, Kasturbhai stopped him before he reached me but that was a close one and very unnerving.

Honestly, I did not realize the power of that simple diagram Corbusier had drawn until I faced opposition and ridicule about the new architecture. I will never forget a few of these instances. One of them concerns Shodhan House, which is built using exposed concrete and for people used to seeing buildings plastered and painted, it meant as if the client had run out of funds to finish it in the proper manner.

One day, while riding the local bus, I overheard two passengers looking at this building. One of them was saying, 'Why do people build such large houses if they have no money to finish them? I hear that now the owner cannot even afford installing doors on the bathrooms.'

I often felt like leaving Ahmedabad but remembered the 'star' behind the dagger and the cloud that Corbusier had cautioned us about and I just worked harder.

People have commented on my work all along just as they do about everything else around them, I guess. I listen to people. I think everybody has a right to express his or her opinion. When somebody says something, there will be a purpose, a lesson there for me, however trivial.

I also seek out comments, feedback. Finally, I do what I want to do but I enrich it with lessons from those comments. Whether I am writing, or sketching, or photographing or designing buildings, I am likely to miss something or the other. So why not listen to others, get it right, and even do better the next time? Learning can happen only when you absorb and reflect. It is not about being humble but open to new and different ideas, views.

As an example, I can mention this phase around 1988, when I felt that Sangath was good but its interiors needed better expression. The spaces in Sangath, e.g., the pit at the lowest level, I felt should have colours to make it a more dynamic space. Similarly, the triple-level mezzanine at the reception needed colours to exaggerate the quality of light in the space.

I felt I had become more cautious or guarded in the use of colours and needed to go back to a forceful use of colours to make the spatial experiences more dynamic.

I recalled my feelings when I visited Palazzo del Te by Giulio Romano in Mantua with its large frescoes all over the walls and ceilings that diffused the character of spaces. I also remembered the colours I used on my return from Paris and wondered how I had forgotten all of that. Sometimes I felt I was even afraid to see colours in buildings.

I thought a lot about how I got here and wondered if this had anything to do with Louis Kahn. In any case, I resolved to break free of that state and immerse myself in colours. That is how the colours one now sees at Sangath came about and continue to be an important tool of design.

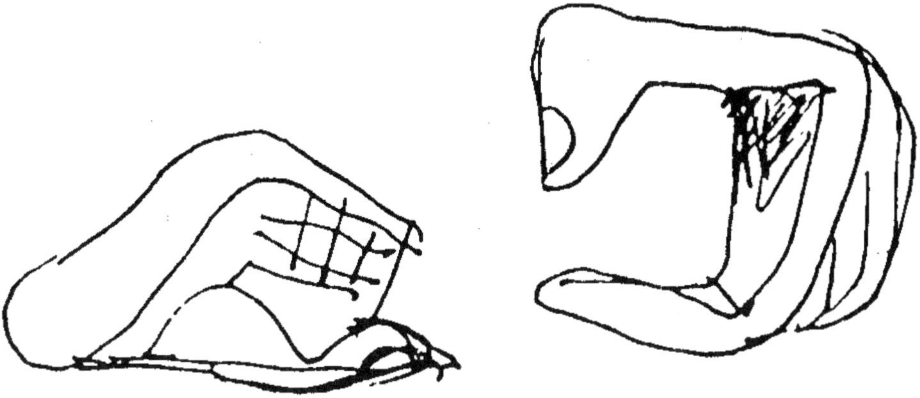

In retrospect, I wonder how I must have negotiated the two rather divergent attitudes to architecture represented by Corbusier and Kahn. For example, Kahn had rejected the quality of early brickwork at the IIM campus, even though it was more precise than the one I had supervised for Corbusier's buildings.

Corbusier liked the random cement filling between joints. He felt it made the design appear rustic. He preferred an informal, slightly chaotic approach that defied the rigidity of rules. Kahn was otherwise.

We did a few more samples for him over the next two days; he did not approve of these either. He then extended his stay for a week, worked with the masons, like in a training workshop. The samples stand there even today like a monument of brick walls, flat, segmental and semi-circular arches with buttresses and jambs on the campus.

In many ways, Sangath marks my own emergence as an architect independent of the immediate influences. It also marks my questioning of what my architecture should be like. I was then involved with the whole issue of ambiguity; I was seeking answers to the questions of life and death.

That was the period during which I started reading the Gita and understanding its lessons under the guidance of Motabhai, my uncle-in-law. I was asking him about memory, death, life, experiences and associations. From ambiguity came the idea of form and formlessness and connectedness. I said I do not want to make a building that looks like a building. In that sense, Sangath can be seen as exploration of several abstract concerns and ideas about what is a building.

Of all the projects I have designed, Sangath remains the most unusual experiment. While working on it, I was so anxious that I would ask all those who visited the place their opinion about it. 'What is it that you feel about Sangath?' I would ask them.

Most responded by saying that it seemed like a building, which was familiar and yet unfamiliar. 'It's difficult to describe in words,' they often said. This is what I learned. Experience touches the inner core.

When asked, artist Bhupen Khakhar said, 'The domes (he did not call them vaults) remind me of ancient buildings. There is something about it which gives me the feeling of being in an Indian village.' When I asked my gardener what he thought of the outdoor studio space I had built first on the site, he said, 'It looks like my village temple.'

Perhaps that has something to do with the way the building relates to the ground and the proportions of the vault in the overall image of the form. This observation made me realize that the icons of Hindu gods have a big crown resting on a small face. May be it is these proportions that lend them dignity.

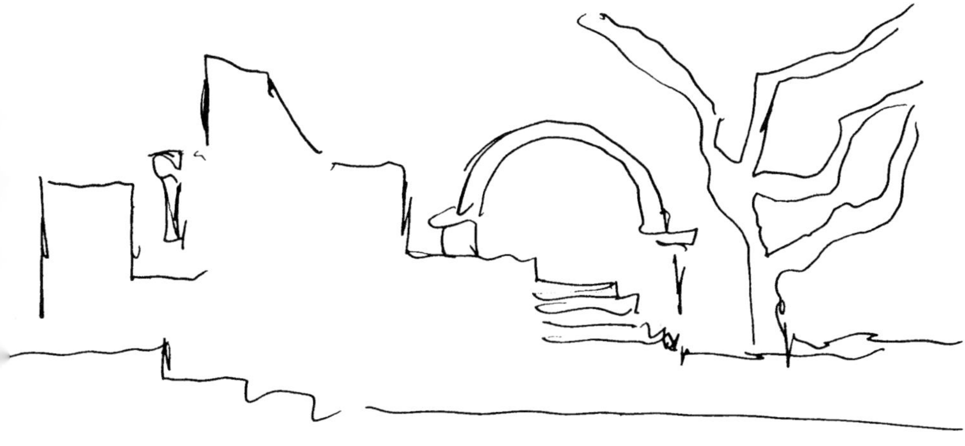

I have earlier explained the vaulted roof at Sangath as an outcome of the curved asbestos sheets I borrowed from my neighbour to quickly construct a building there to dodge the stringent provisions of the proposed urban land ceiling act. That is true. But I now suspect it actually stemmed from my earlier designs for ATIRA Staff Quarters and Peons' Quarters, which employed semi-circular brick vaults. On the other hand, maybe it was inspired by the Nissen shelters I had seen in my childhood which were built for the army with a similar roof system in Pune.

These designs must have remained latent, kind of forgotten deep in my memories, and surfaced while thinking of the roof form possible from the curved asbestos sheets for the outhouse. These again forced their way when Sangath was designed some 20 years later.

Many other spaces at Sangath recall Corbusier's studio, not to forget making the entire wall at the front end of the studio as a blackboard. Architecturally, this building owes a lot to him in terms of scale, proportion and methods. In spatial connotations, it manifests very much what I learned from Corbusier and what I experienced in old Ahmedabad.

Compact scales have been on my mind since a very early time. In

particular, I remember my visits to old Ahmedabad with Corbusier. Once we had gone to Manek Chowk, the historic market in the city surrounded by three-storeyed town houses having extremely small rooms, some just about 180–240 cm wide. As soon as he entered one such room, Corbusier stretched out on the floor with his head touching the wall on one side and his feet the opposite wall. All he said was, 'Wonderful scale! What proportions! What a measure!'

When we visited the Sarkhej Complex built in the 15th century, he said, 'Why do you need to visit Acropolis at Athens? You have it all here. Study it.' Until Corbusier spoke in such terms about our domestic and public architecture, I had not realized the significance of our own heritage. In some ways, I did feel vindicated about my own experience of the first visit to the Acropolis described earlier.

Perhaps memories shape more of our designs than we may like to believe or realize. The pool at Sangath, I believe, has come from my visit to Frank Lloyd Wright's studio in Taliesin West, which has played a role in the decision to build my own office. His earth-hugging architecture, with its emphasis on the horizontal, heavy base, reminded me of the Hindu temples bound to the earth and the sky at the same time.

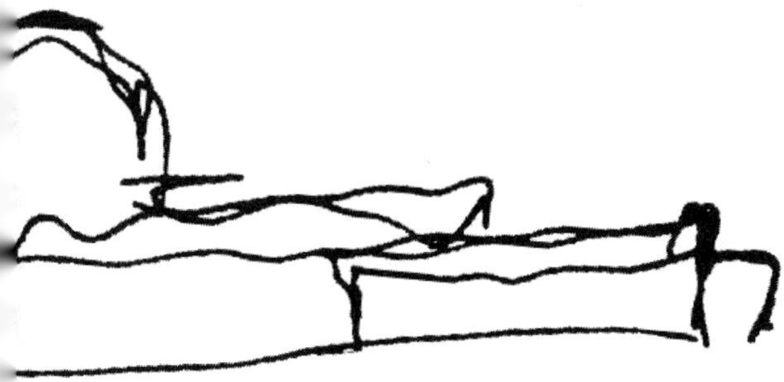

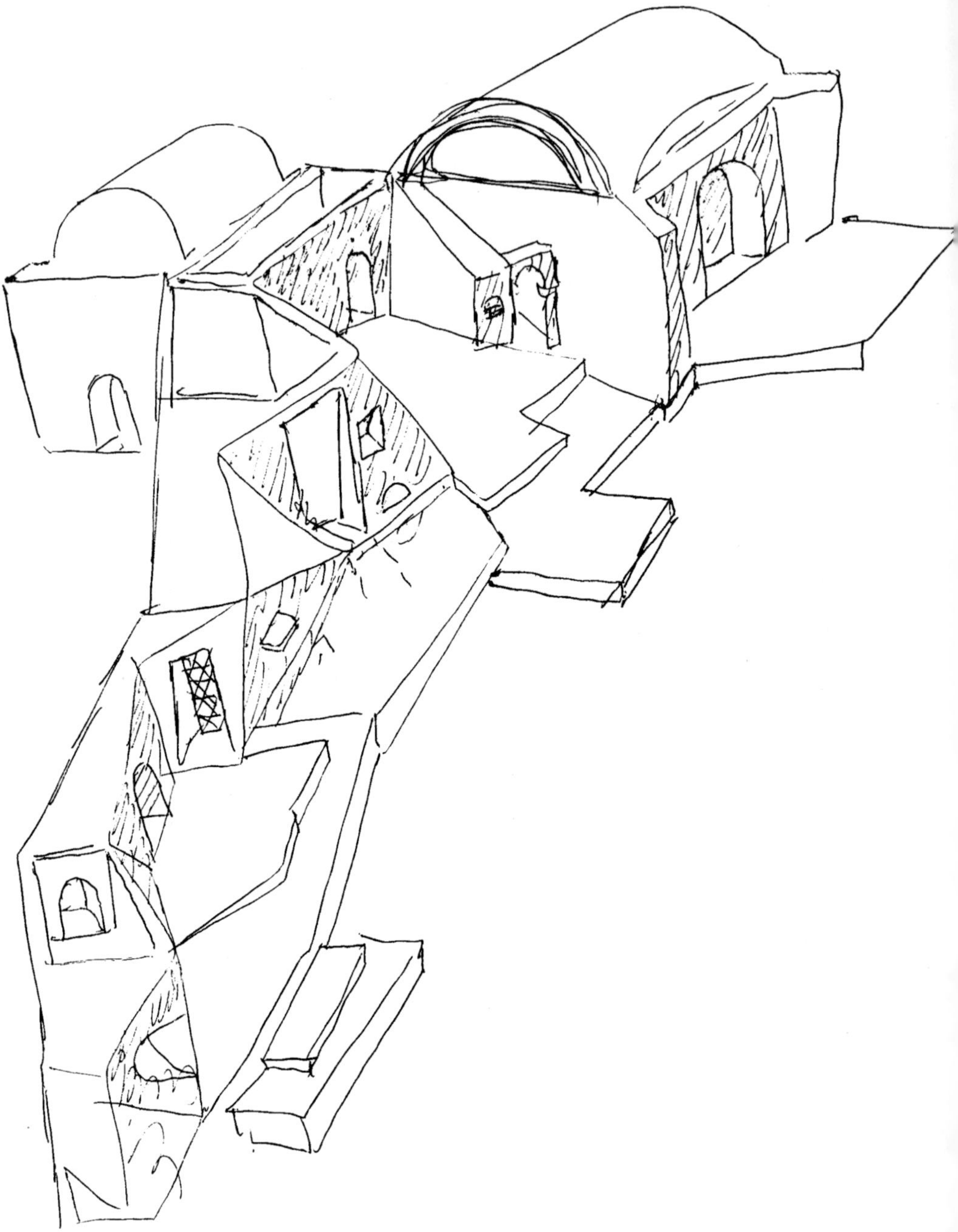

The message that Sangath's vault always conveys to me is of something Indian, something from a village, something from our traditions. When you look at it sometimes, it looks like a dome from a distance. The low base and the high roof vaults evoke the proportions of a deity's face, with the crown and the tall shikhara of a temple with a low base. The sunken floor level at the lower entrance summons the experience of entering ancient caves. The roundly articulated edges of the vaults and other surfaces accessible from the lower terraces generate a firm relationship with the ground like that found in a Buddhist stupa.

Incidentally, even in my sketches and the drawings, there is a deep-rooted longing, a connection and an intense fascination for a village. The platform, steps and spaces at Sangath are of a village square while the water-body and steps give an idea of connecting life around a village. I created it to be used by the public, which must get its due share. There is nothing very private, but nothing is very public either. However, you transact your business and then leave before a subtle threshold. This threshold is established by your own inner and outer worlds, your social and your personal worlds. All these are undercurrents of desire. Its manifestation is influenced by the experiences of buildings that I have experienced.

The final concept of Sangath came from what I saw near the pyramids of Giza in Egypt. It was a studio of sculptor Ramses Wissa Wassef. The way light entered the studio, which was dry, all sand, and his buffalos were there too, I still remember. Young children came to learn carpet-making. It was really a village place, living on art. I went there and sketched. There were the fabled Nubian vaults, centenary vaults. And under all this, there was a celebration going on, a celebration of light and life. That is what I wanted to create at Sangath.

What affected me the most was remembering the Great Pyramid of Giza, a solid overwhelming powerful mass expressing its eternity. At the other end was the Wassef studio, like a small village, which was animated with life and rich with human compassion. Is not this our true calling? To counterbalance the present-day temptation of creating mega-structures by silent murmurs full of vulnerable but sacred activities?

Our cities are increasingly becoming taller, denser, crowded, noisy and inhuman. To feel happy and proud, should not our cities combine our minute but meaningful work? Experiencing the old cities and observing

their expanding peripheries, should we not find alternating breathing and celebrating public spaces with their slow movements, chatter and micro-scale transactions? If we can achieve this, we will surely save our energies by conserving travel time, our green pastures and breathing more fresh air.

Creating a settlement, which gives meaning to our diurnal activities, should be our duty as urban planners. We need to provide pauses and porosity. Even though the surrounding properties around Sangath will one day be high multi-storeyed buildings, I wish there would be many others like Sangath, giving the area a human touch.

After my Cairo experience, I tried to build a similar parabolic arch with locally made *guna* tiles. These are vertically split half-sections of conical terracotta tubes made by the village potter for use in roofing. But they crashed under their own weight. The form too did not satisfy my desire to feel the full circle. So I switched to hollow ceramic, bottle-shaped tiles used for large-scale spans in the factories. They also perform better for insulation and strength.

The Sangath building has three different, closely interlinked structural systems. One comprises load-bearing brick walls carrying the vaulted roof, the second has a retaining wall and brick column structure of irregular shape supporting a flat roof, and the third employs load-bearing brick walls combined with a post and beam structure to carry heavier loads. Each system has been optimized to create a variety of spaces that are needed there. Likewise, three different ways of allowing light into the interior were devised. One through normal windows punctured in the wall, another through a skylight, and the third through direct penetration from the flat roof through glass bricks.

I wanted to experience life through my studio. It is both fragmentation of daily activities and its synthesis, the incomplete and the complete. Building to me is not the mere planting of a box on mother earth, but an organism that is rooted there. It is not merely a solid mass, but a mass formed out of many interrelated parts. These parts are not merely elements but organs performing several functions, like our limbs. Besides, it is supposed to evoke memories, associations and indirectly suggest our connections to nature and legacies. Growth and evolution being fundamental to living organisms, buildings have to be porous and open-ended.

Sangath is partially buried in the ground to connect it with the ground and be rooted. This way, it depicts the earlier notion of three vertical divisions of a building, as I had done at the Institute of Indology. The heavy long plinth of Sangath creates a continuous mass with apertures to create solidity and porosity. By adding the semi-circular vault to the plinth, not only does the importance of the plinth increase but it also heightens the prominence of the vaulted roof.

This is very similar to the way our temples are designed, distinguished by a heavy plinth and tall shikhara resting on the mother earth. I wonder sometimes if the enigma of what is buried within the high plinth is the essence of curiosity, which is very similar to our step-wells, buried deep within the earth, with no hints of its deeper connections on the surface level.

They say that under the ocean there is another world which is full of silence and sounds. I believe it. When you sit alone in the dark hours of the early morning, you slowly become aware of the distant sounds of birds, insects and become conscious of the vastness of the space.

Sangath also recalls our rented house in Pune. There, I lived with my brother and his wife for almost eight to 10 years after my father remarried. The corner house was linear like a train, with a narrow corridor on two outside edges enclosing tiny spaces. This is reflected in the central narrow linear space and the staircase. Adjoining the main studio space, my office reflects the small room of my house and the hostel I stayed at in Paris.

The protruding basement is the extension of an ancestral home, amorphous and ambiguous. The studio reflects the long and narrow Corbusier's Atelier. Scale of the building with the ground and the roof and the skyline has come from my childhood experiences of platforms and open spaces for *garba* and other folk dances as also from the subterranean Pataleshwar Temple in Pune.

My memory of Antoni Gaudi's work is manifested in the form of china mosaic finish, curved walls and several details at Sangath. I have seen his buildings and have been very impressed by those articulations. Louis Kahn's attitude towards the expression of the humane in a building affected me a great deal due to its similarity to that of the Hindu approach. The structural clarity about there being a main structure and a substructure comes from my discussions with him.

For Kahn, Corbusier was like a distant, remote guru. Being shy, he consciously avoided meeting Corbusier. This is very much like the story of Eklavya in the epic Mahabharata. In the story, the guru does not accept him as a disciple but Eklavya makes a clay statue of the guru and practices archery as if he was there in flesh and blood, and masters the skill.

Aware of this, I often felt that these two giants should meet each other sometime. Alas, Corbusier died in 1969, before that could happen. I had gone to Paris to pay my respects and from there I went to Philadelphia. When I met Lou at his studio, no sooner had I entered than he said, 'Did you hear?' 'Yes,' I said. 'I was in Paris two days ago. He is no more.' Lou said: 'In all these years I have worked, I have constantly felt his presence and wondered if he would like my work if he saw it.' He then added, 'Now for whom shall I work?'

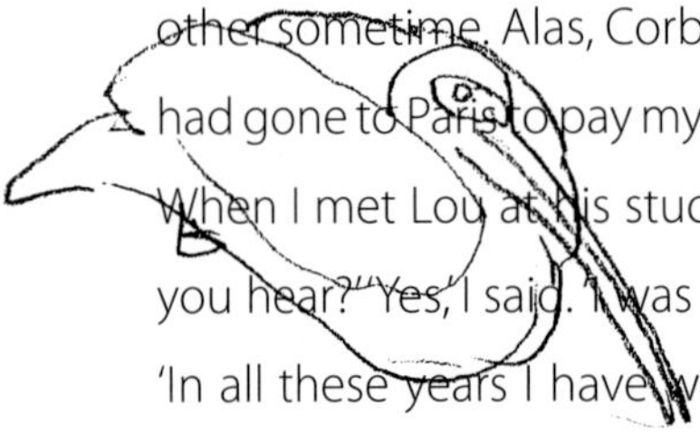

That question haunts me too: For whom am I working? It is not an easy question to answer because, in turn, the question asks who I am. Vaguely, the answer I have often reached is that I am the sum of all the memories I have gathered over my life. These memories comprise not only of my architectural training and influences, but also the life I have lived right from childhood until today; as someone rightly said: 'Isn't memory a vast library in alphabetical disorder?'

I often recall my childhood memory of the first rain. It was stuffy and damp. It was very hot and very humid. Everyone expected showers but there were no indications yet. There was an oppressive silence and restlessness resulting in great discomfort.

Suddenly, we could smell the fragrance coming from far away of wet earth, a wonderful sensation after the scorching heat of summer. Then the sky was overcast with dark clouds, the sun disappeared, and it was a different world once it started raining. We felt rejuvenated.

Next, one heard the rain drops falling on the metal roof of the veranda, then the rainwater gushing along and down the gutter from the roof edges. Children ran out to bathe under the biggest shower in the world and the elders rushed from deep within the house to the veranda.

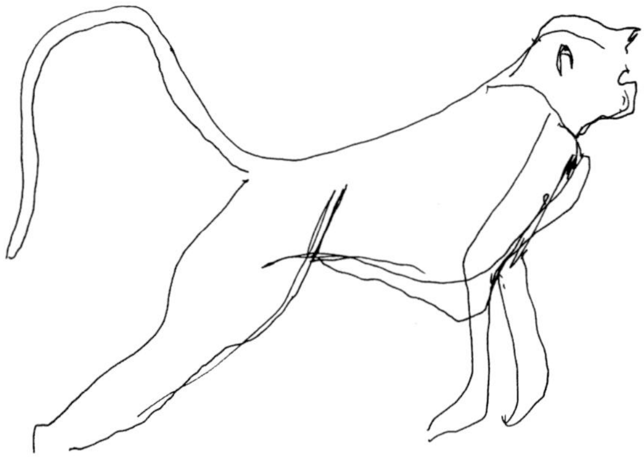

Some of them would be busy shuttering the side windows from the lashing rain. My brother would find old newspapers to make paper boats and we would try to race them in the streets. Cool relief from hot summer would call for hot tea and deep-fried savoury *bhajia*s, and—for a while—it would be like a festival.

Wet earth, swaying trees, buildings washed clean and shining, the changing patterns of clouds—it was a live tableau, a theatre. When the rains stopped, the water dripping from the trees, the roofs and the temple walls continued to create rhythmic sounds of changing intensity.

Once it was all clear, the sun shining on the mouldings of the temple made me aware of the reasons for their being, to cast shadows and drain water away. The projections also changed the nature of the surfaces creating a delightful texture under the sunlight. When dry, the patterns changed again, and the life seemed more sober.

It was years later, after I became an architect, that I realized what architecture can do. Besides physical needs, architecture and the contexts of sky, rain, wind, foliage, overhangs, speak another language. Architecture responds to seasons, to cosmic forces and makes us aware of joys that we normally overlook. Psychologically it creates associations that we cherish for life.

Architecture too can become a backdrop, when it responds to cosmic forces and human beings. It is about everything and belongs to everyone, not just for our specific, mundane requirements.

Around 1963, Gira Sarabhai had asked Kahn a simple question: 'What is architecture?' Not wishing to give a simple answer, Kahn asked for a day's time to answer. Next day he brought a small piece of paper with a statement reading 'Architecture though what I feel is its spirit, when asked of its nature I have no touch with it. The pool, a chain, a school, a palace or factory has the light of its presence if that is what it wants to be. So it can reach the heart, be it ever so simple, just so its essence is; its life is art.'

Nature demonstrates that the process of creation goes on, and often in spite of us. In fact, we are also part of nature. We are not separate. Most of our functioning is only guided, not controlled by us but we do not realize it. Creation has to be self-realizing. One has to become consciously subconscious to share one's skin and allow the manifestation to happen, in whatever form it wants to.

You ask a great musician, artist, architect, even a businessperson, or a politician, 'What is your best work and how did it come about?' He will tell you, 'I don't know how it happened.'

Le Corbusier wrote about this saying, 'Creation is a patient search. When I start painting and I begin with blue, but I don't know how in the end it becomes red.'

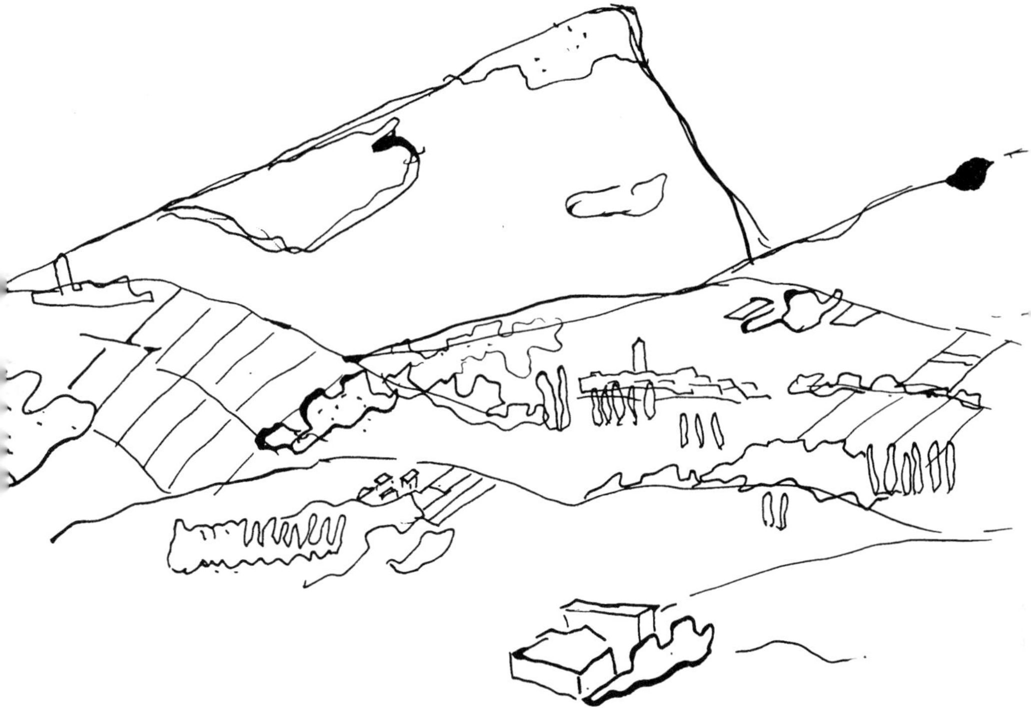

It is not the struggle; it is the virtue, the situation. It is like a river meeting the ocean. That is time. Identity is not there but one becomes universal, natural. That is *swabhav*. That is what my work is constantly striving to be.

Once looking at the photo of a blackbuck in a magazine, the colour pattern of its coat caught my eye. It looked as if the blackbuck wore a jacket over its body. Amazing! Why does nature do that? Because it wants to be more sensuous and joyous. The eyebrows and ears are functional but there is something more to that than meets the eye. The articulation is there. When articulation happens, celebration takes place.

The Japanese often maintain a miniature garden on a small tabletop, with bonsai plants and trees. They do this to help them detach from the physical world, to connect to the spiritual world and discover the secret of happiness. One is wonderstruck. What cannot be grasped, what is infinite is made human in a small place. When you look at those natural trees, and the big tree miniaturized, it affects the mind in many ways.

For the Japanese meditation is connectivity. The faraway wall is close by, so is the neighbour's street. They all belong to you. The more you miniaturize, the more expansive you become. You are looking at it in its totality. What you cannot grasp, you may now grasp and what you cannot touch, now you can, provided you see its connections. Thus, nuances appear, relationships blossom and the mind plunges deep within. There is silence. The static begins to become dynamic and a reverse process takes place. You see the expanse because the scales have melted.

Like a batsman in a game of cricket who, after a while, does not see anything but the ball. The ball begins to look as large as a football. That is concentration. The Japanese constantly talk about going deep within to discover the real self.

The Zen stories are amazing. They unfold slowly. They stop you from experiencing the expected. When agitated, they slowly take you through a path in which you unfold what you really wanted to see. At that time, the discovery is most magnificent. Like in a Japanese tea ceremony, it is an unfolding of the universe, which you do not expect.

In the Rajasthan desert, we see the traditional mud houses and we wonder with awe. We marvel at the way the mundane hut takes roots and blossoms like a beautiful tree or a child who eventually becomes a fine human being.

We see the huts in the Himalayas and notice that they combine wood and mud to make their habitat, again of great beauty. In the US, Mies van der Rohe makes his most acclaimed glasshouses such as the Farnsworth House. All these houses are very different from each other, but the thought and work that has gone in making them are equal.

Honestly, I would not know which one to choose if I had to pick just one. A person who was fully involved in its making has made that hut. The earth, the hands, the body, the thought and the spirit—all are integrated.

With this integration, the hut becomes a living object as much as the people it will shelter and nurture. It is no longer a mere room or a shelter; it manifests what is hidden deep within the occupants. That is love. We see that passion in great works of architecture.

Now, the issue is which is timeless and which is time-bound and of what period and style? I remember observing a potter at work in Ahmedabad. I think he is the only one who, through concentration and dexterity, traps the un-trappable in the forms of his creations, which is the space.

A rigid structure is time-bound. An object is time-bound. A cloud is not time-bound. The formal is time-bound. Informal is not time-bound. It is like the human body. Our body continuously grows to its limit. It grows but not in the same proportion; the head, legs, feet, toes and the torso, each of them grows differently.

I have observed in a band of elephants carved at the base of Kailash Temple in Ellora that one elephant is facing away from the rest. He was carved thus deliberately to convey that only exceptions help to define the rules with absolute clarity. That an order has a meaning only relative to the disorder.

When you provide that exception, you break the rule to make the rule work. There is an expression of freedom. If you look at miniature paintings, one cow amongst many would be moving in the opposite direction.

Rules are required, but flexibility within the structure is important. The clock is supposed to be the servant, a tool to inform us about the time. It cannot rule our life. Our tools cannot become our masters.

This is also true of other aspects of our lives. These include the conventions that we have constructed as a society as well as the luxuries masquerading as needs in our lives. I am a strong believer in absolute freedom; that we have to realize our full potential as human beings and whatever we have chosen as our vocation—be it architect or carpenter.

Just before I left for Ahmedabad, Corbusier told me this story that captures these conflicts and dilemmas we face and the choices we may make.

The story is about a hungry dog who was once searching everywhere for food. Suddenly he saw a very well fed dog in a house. He asked the dog as to how he managed to be so well-fed and if he could do the same to become like him. The fat dog said, 'Come again tomorrow afternoon and I will tell you.'

Next day, the hungry dog arrived there punctually but there was no sign of the fat dog. So he waited, and after waiting a long time, he barked several times to call the fat dog but there was no answer. Dejected, he left.

Next day, he went there again, saw the fat dog, and asked, 'Why did you not keep your promise to meet me?' The fat dog answered, 'I very much wanted to, but my master was sleeping.'

'So what?' the hungry dog asked.

The fat dog replied, 'You see, he had chained me.'

It was then that the hungry dog noticed the chain around his neck tethered to a post.

'Is this permanent?'

'Yes'

'Don't you have a choice?'

'No. Otherwise why would he feed me?'

The hungry dog thought for a while and hurriedly left the place saying, 'What a price to pay! It is better to starve than be controlled.'

Like many other lessons I have learnt from my gurus, the lesson of this story has stayed with me all my life. There have been occasions when I have acted on them and sometimes when I have not acted in accordance. Even on the occasion when I chose to differ, the lessons have influenced me. That may have indirectly lessened the number of occasions when I have had to look the other way.

Here I am reminded of an instance with Kasturbhai Lalbhai. As I have said earlier, I looked upon him as my guru and always showed a lot of deference. However, there was this time when I thought that my grace was under pressure and I had the courage, or audacity others may say, to stand up to him.

Kasturbhai had urgently sent for me so I went to his office. When he saw me, he just started speaking in a very angry tone about a project that had exceeded the budget by Rs 8,00,000, without giving me any chance to explain the reasons. I must add that in those days, it was not a small amount. However, he went on to call me a fool to have exceeded the budget without his approval, that even as he could easily afford to pay the additional expense, I was not authorized to take such a decision and concluded by saying that entrusting the design was a very big mistake on his part.

Since he was not willing to let me explain the reasons, when he stopped, I asked him, 'Can I say something?' He remained silent so I went on, 'I know I am nobody in your presence and seek your pardon if I have made a mistake. But I also believe I must be punished, and would it be alright if I pay you Rs 1,00,000 each year for the next eight years to compensate?' I doubt if anybody ever spoke to him in such terms, so he seemed taken aback and he said, 'What arrogance! Do you realize what you are saying? You want to compensate Kasturbhai?'

A long silence followed our exchange during which, I think both of us reflected on what had just transpired and how the situation got there. I felt I was pushed too far, else I would not have so responded to a man I otherwise respected so much.

I think he must have also felt the same; he shook his head to convey that the matter was over and asked me if I would join him for tea. Then he started to ask me questions about the School of Architecture as if that was what he had called me for in the first place and nothing else was talked about. I was glad that I stood by my convictions and yet very grateful to have persons like Kasturbhai who could understand and appreciate such behaviour on my part.

At this stage, the place I am most nostalgic about socially, after Dada's home, is Motabhai's home in Bharat Niwas Society, not far from my home. It was like a second home and very often Kamu, our daughters and I had lunches, dinners and our siestas there.

These would provide occasions to talk about religions, philosophies and creative arts with Motabhai and other scholars, poets and theatre personalities who often joined us there. We would discuss the classical Indian and Greek theatres along with the contemporary, in contrast to the folk theatre and especially the Ramlila, the folk retelling of epic story of Ramayana over nine full nights with its unusual innovation to tell the story most simply and effectively.

Sometimes, we would be discussing the element of time, season and space in classical Indian music as conveyed by a particular *raga*. These discourses with artists, dancers, musicians and literary persons helped me to understand the Indian theory of rasa, depicting several moods to connote emotions and express the ultimate essence of life.

I sometimes wonder if, over the last 60 or so years, I have acted more often wisely or otherwise. May be I have made more mistakes than not. I also wonder how my life would have turned out if my circumstances were different. However, one thing I am sure about is that I have lived my life and carried out my work, on my own terms.

If you want freedom break
away from the normal
conventions. Become like
a child. See things afresh,
work more with your *feel*ings
than intellectual & rational
thoughts, Because they are
fed & given to you by others
to make you One of Them.
Look how children paint,
draw figures, how they see
& put colours – They have
nothing to do with absolute
reality – Because reality is
also *an* illusion. But your
education and age has made
you think that way. Reality
is what you and others perceive
externally and similarly.

For example, how can form, colour, structure, order be accepted because historians say so.

Break away from all the rules - Forget history books. Go back to your inner perceptions. See things as if you are noticing them for the first time.

Then only you will be able to do something of your own.

L Baker May 27/89

(after seeing Khushnu's drawing of a face)

(Excerpt from a letter to Tejal, Radhika and Maneesha)

VRIKSHA SAR

In spite of a seed so dark and small,
How come you grow so beautiful and big?
In spite of the onslaught of the elements
How come you are ever so fresh, silent and poised?

In spite of the hurdles and the mighty gravity
How do you balance your twists and turns?
And rise so tall?
In spite of their acts that threaten you
How come you offer shelter to those unwanted souls?

In spite of neglect and uncaring
How come you participate joyously in celebrations?
Blossom so profusely and offer flowers and fruits?

In spite of reluctance, even anger at the follies of man
How come you continue to restore the ecosystem?
That too with a nod and a smile?

In spite of your wisdom ages old
How come you bow so low, so humbly?
And offer all you have for the purposes unknown?
And lastly, O revered tree
Tell us the essence of your being.

I am extremely fortunate that Kamu has supported all of my dreams and whims. To say that I have struggled alone would be wrong. In all that I chose to do because I wanted to, or did not, because I did not want to, she had an equal stake in the consequences, good or bad.

Yet, she allowed me and supported me. She may not have liked some of the choices I made, and we may have argued about it but finally she would always say, 'If it makes you happy, do it because it is for a cause.' The one question we both ask every day is, 'Did we both enjoy the day?'

After our marriage, when there was nobody else to discuss architecture with, I would always turn to Kamu. So sometimes, I would be showing her pictures of Ronchamp Chapel or some other building that I liked and say, 'One day, I would like to build like this.' She would be somewhat amused but the smile on her face would be an assuring one, saying, 'Go ahead, I am with you'.

Together we have travelled all over the world several times. In our hearts, in our travels, in our moments of joys and in dealing with hardships, we have together discovered many hidden doors to the treasures of our lives.

Next year will mark our 64th wedding anniversary. Now our discussions encompass religion, values and about the worthiness of things around us, what is meaningful and what is not. We are of course, happiest when we hear our grandchildren and great-grandchildren constantly asking to be with us at their *Maa-gher* (great-grandmother's home), our Sadma Society home, for a great time. They are the future and we hope their future will be as exciting as that of ours turned out to be.

Epilogue

This act of reading my own journal entries from over 60 years and editing them has meant revisiting all the places, people and the crucial life-events for me. It has allowed me to reflect on what I did and reassess the whys of choices and decisions I have made. In turn this has helped me to discover my own strengths and how I dealt with the opportunities that came my way.

Earlier in the prologue, I have tried to capture the essence of why and of what I believe has been a rather wonderful journey not only professionally as an architect but also personally. I am now sure both these are closely intertwined. Traversing the transition from my tradition-bound roots in Pune to a globalized Ahmedabad via London and Paris and then all over the world, I wonder if I could have even imagined that when I was a child.

I am indebted to the few key persons for such a joyous and meaningful life. Foremost among them is Dada, whose early grooming made me aware about the spiritual significance of life and duty towards one's commitments.

I am indebted to Le Corbusier for setting me on the path to write, sketch, design and paint and to Louis Kahn for widening my understanding of the more abstract and philosophical aspects of life and working as an architect. I am also indebted to Kasturbhai Lalbhai for constantly supporting me morally and professionally, especially during my initial years when the School of Architecture was set up.

I will always remain indebted to Ba for demonstrating the virtues of frugality and contentment. Finally, I am indebted to Motabhai for making me aware about Gandhiji's philosophy and my social responsibility.

All of them have inspired me to lead a holistic career. This has required constantly learning about new developments in all fields, disciplines and that without preconceived ideas. All my life and even now, I have lived like a student, open to new information, ideas and knowledge.

This openness and acceptance of the new, being flexible but not dogmatic, comes from my growing up in a large extended family where multiple activities, multiple uses of places, spaces and things are a normal course of life. This calls for constantly accommodating attitude to changing situations.

In my early experiences, an extended family provides a large safety net. Since one's basic needs are taken care of, one learns to take risks, big and small. If something does not work, one can always fall back on the safety offered by the family, to the old position.

However, so much has changed since then. Of all the changes, I consider the changes in the family and social structure the most crucial. Besides their impact on architecture and city, I believe they have also affected how people view their present and future.

Living in nuclear families in a highly competitive environment has taken a great toll on what a child aspires to do and actually ends up doing all his or her life. Now rather than break from the traditional family with the assured safety net, one is made acutely aware of the risks of failure and the attendant consequences.

This makes people only pursue vocations that are seen as safe career choices, in safe environments and move amidst colleagues with whom they feel safe. Therefore, they quickly identify a comfort zone and then do not venture out of it.

This means they cease to be open and flexible to all kinds of new opportunities that come their way for a meaningful work and life. Hence, currently the visions are narrower; a result of looking at only short-term benefits. Over time, even the measures have changed, and the benchmarks are constantly lowered. This is observed all around us and not just in architecture and planning.

Every time I visit and experience our great timeless heritage, be it the built environment or the cultural traditions, I wonder if we are leaving behind equally inspiring body of work and traditions for the generations to come. What will they say about us?

Earlier I said I was very lucky to have persons such as Dada, Corbusier, Kahn, Kasturbhai and Motabhai as my inspiration and as persons to measure up to in terms of the work I was doing and the richness of the life I was leading.

From them I have learnt a lot. I have learnt to understand the need to define limits for worldly desires and material success. I learned the value of doing one's duty without expectations; for that alone leads to ultimate happiness. I learnt that hardship is normal in life and that one must learn to adjust and be patient if one wants to achieve the desired goal.

I also learned to value action over speculation of the kind that philosophers indulge in, which may be described as the difference between a thinker and a doer. Speculation generates more thoughts and along with it more analysis and many doubts, while in action, a person actually experiences each stage of action and sees the results in stark reality. This he can evaluate in the real world and then with his instinct go on to improve. This also means that action is crucial to fulfilling a life.

Salvation depends upon how much one has understood from all experiences and how does one react. The first thing I do when I enter my own study at Sangath is to stand before a special alcove like in a prayer. It has pictures of Dada in his traditional attire, Le Corbusier standing like a warrior in front of the High Court in Chandigarh, Goddess Durga reminding me of my mother's signals, and Lord Ganesh guiding my actions.

Over time, I have realized the value of discharging my responsibilities and creating interdependent growth opportunities. To move in a desired direction, one needs freedom without baggage. Only then can one guide but not control; advise but not rule and lead others without asking others to follow.

I have learnt so much from these four persons, two of them brilliant architects with very different inclinations, the third a worldly-wise, perfectionist furniture-maker and the fourth, a dedicated Indology scholar. It does not matter if I was good or slipped at times, but I knew what was right and what was wrong, how far and high I should aim.

That leads me to the question I seem to be asking frequently these days, 'Are there such role models around or amidst us that can inspire the young?' I mean role models that are as inspiring and uncompromising as these four persons were. As we live and work every day, we create history but only the future will judge how well and responsibly we went about doing that.

Path Ahead

When I look back on my life, as I have just done, I find so much to be happy and satisfied about. It has been a wonderful life in every respect. I feel blessed to have received so much love, respect and recognition, far beyond what I might have dreamed of when I was growing up in my ancestral home in Pune. On many counts, I think I have proved Kadam, my brother's friend, right.

However, I also wonder if I am being complacent when I say I am happy and satisfied. Am I judging myself by a lower benchmark than I should, as I spoke of the world around us a little earlier? What about the challenges I had posed for myself to provide everyone a decent way to lead life, with food, clothing and shelter? What about the expectations my mother had for me? Why did she call me Balkrishna?

I realize that, despite my modest contribution through projects and the role I have been able to play in the area of education, much more work remains. Sincerely, I do not know how much of that I may achieve in the years to come. However, as a beginning, and as the least I must do, I have written this note which I have called the Path Ahead.

I would like it to be a reminder for myself that I must traverse this path in the years to come. I am also hoping, by sharing it with young professionals and students, that it will serve as inspiration to attain what I am tempted to call Swaraj for Indian architecture and planning.

As we all know, India has been an urban civilization for much more than three millennia by now and most of its cities, towns and villages have existed for several centuries at the least. So it is no surprise that there existed a well-developed and efficient draught animal and pedestrian-based network across the country linking all its urban centres and the rural communities.

This network also linked the daily, weekly and monthly markets located at distances easily traversed on foot, on horseback or in a bullock or camel cart. I like to think of the interplay of these two networks as something as naturally harmonious as our galaxies. In that world, one did not move beyond the immediate needs thus saving time, energy and ultimately resources.

All that changed some 200 years ago, following industrialization and the consequent rise of industrial cities much to the detriment of the rural communities. This process has now created a stage where traditional communities in hinterlands are completely neglected, and pressure on towns are now creating a new divide where mega-structures come in place without the support system, creating an unhealthy hiatus.

Mahatma Gandhi talked about the virtues of such cohesive national networks as the basis of our nation as his idea of Swaraj, a little more than a century ago—in 1909, to be precise. For several decades and certainly until the 1950s, his concept of Swaraj served as a beacon for guiding the national development and attracted all the right-thinking people, including architects and planners of the time, to shape the human habitat accordingly.

The architectural profession was then looking simultaneously at the needs of both rural and urban areas. The training of an architect began with housing for the poor; only much later in the course did it deal with design of institutions and such buildings. Now, with exposure to global happenings, all that has changed dramatically, with many students producing designs as if they were clones of celebrity architects without any regard for the land and cultural contexts.

Unfortunately, we did not consider setting up architectural and planning schools in the hinterlands. Consequently, today, every major city has more than required institutions while there are none in small towns and villages. It is not just our contemporary practices but our attitude to the heritage that also needs much introspection.

I wonder,

Why are our institutions and practices failing to fulfil this minimum task?

Why are our great works eventually getting abused or forgotten?

Why is our younger generation unaware about our heritage and culture or even about their responsibilities to themselves and to the world around them?

Why do our professionals not think beyond their own isolated commitments?

Why can't we accept critical evaluation of our works or our philosophy?

Why do we not readily support or recognize the worthy?

Why don't we provide our younger generations the inspiration to follow role models?

Why don't government agencies and real estate developers consult us to achieve a common goal for the greater good?

Why are our public institutions ineffective in their vision and do not seek guidance from the best?

Why do our leaders constantly refer to Shanghai, Singapore and Dubai, etc., which were developed purely for commercial purposes?

Why is it that we do not develop our own appropriate strategies of development suitable to our system?

Why can't our profession create a movement similar to that of Mahatma Gandhi?

Why don't we use the latest technologies to develop and exchange ideas, and develop virtual platforms for distance sharing and learning?

The cities we have developed adversely influence our habitat, diminishing the values that the traditional neighbourhoods, the street, the town-centre and the market-place represented. Earlier, even though the institutions were limited in number and variety, there was a healthy reliance on cooperation for social and economic sustenance.

As professionals, rather than encouraging the real estate developers to create socio-culturally ideal habitats, we have isolated ourselves and allowed them a free hand. The developers, realizing that the land in our cities has become unaffordable, are now moving into towns and the hinterlands. We are now like a big banyan tree, with self-centred social, economic and cultural institutions as branches to support our own growth but have restricted our outlook and life within our controlled areas, while allowing the rise of deserts all around.

An inverse economic and commercial invasion is taking place now as compared to the migration of population in search of work earlier. Until a few decades ago, even though our cities had begun to become crowded, we had at least not abused the hinterlands, which are essentially the sources of our needs. I wonder why we never thought of people who bring us all our daily necessities from small hamlets located a few kilometres away.

However, this need not be so. Today, the Internet has reached every household, everyone is connected, and, with wireless technologies, this has happened in many cases without electricity or a road. While meeting students and the youth from remote areas, or watching them speak out on television, one is impressed by their talent and their hopes for a fulfilling life. However, for the architects and planners, they do not even seem to exist. In spite of all this connectivity, our profession does not see beyond our immediate interests and commitments.

Real society is like cosmic galaxies, full of hierarchical networking uniting them. However, we have shattered this unity into fragments out of sheer avarice and control. This attitude is not only limited to economic development but it is also true of our educational and cultural scene. Sacredness, reverence, tolerance and cooperation have been our cherished values.

We have always professed a balanced life and pursued values, which nurture emotional, psychological and social harmony. We have always tried to live with nature and not against it, nor tried to control it. If we do not pursue holistic development, what we would have is what the developed countries have lived through to repent now.

After seeking ever-faster transportation to reduce commuting times, building energy-guzzling mega-structures and concentrated power-centric development strategies with emphasis on more production, more consumption and constant growth, the prophets of 'bigger the better' now realize that the right way of the future is sustainable development. This is what living with nature is all about, that is what the traditional way was after all.

So what do we do next? As I have said a little earlier, I value action more than mere speculation. Therefore, I believe this is what we need to do.

Foremost, we need to begin with a very strong network based on

digital media connectivity. This is the age when Internet-based communities have been far more successful and effective than others and this potential must be harnessed most effectively by the Indian architects and planners. The time of physically attending meetings to share views and tasks and sending out old-fashioned paper-based posts is history.

Let us then create such a community to disseminate and advocate establishment of a habitat based on the principles of Swaraj as propounded by Mahatma Gandhi. The major task of this community will be to generate debates in all the major languages of India about our contemporary habitat conditions vis-à-vis the traditional habitat, their strengths and their weaknesses.

Following from the debates, we need to undertake a sincere and critical assessment of what we have and what we need to have. This must cover all the aspects of architecture and planning to attain the goal of Swaraj. There is a pressing need to prepare policies for a balanced regional development, urbanization, settlements planning and its constituent architecture. These would include role and responsibilities of the architects and planners, the contents and methods of their education and their professional obligations, be they to serve rural communities or the urban poor and all other disadvantaged sections of our society.

We have seen how effective the public agencies have been in the last few decades and with little hope for a change in them, we need to set up a network of non-governmental organizations at all levels from that of the national to the smallest of the hamlets to execute our plans for Swaraj.

Let it also be clear that execution here does not imply actually implementing the plans to the last nut and bolt. The people themselves must do that, which is the basic premise of Swaraj. All that is needed is to demonstrate the goodness of architecture and planning based on the principles of Swaraj, through teams of dedicated volunteers. Finally, these demonstrations will serve to educate the people who will then work to attain true Swaraj and realize the dream of Mahatma Gandhi.

This is what I hope to do now.

Notes

Glossary

avatar: incarnation or Lord's descent on earth.

bhajias: an Indian savoury made of chopped vegetables mixed in a spiced batter and deep-fried. From Hindi *bhājī*, fried vegetables.

Brahmanical: of a Brahman. The term designates the first of the four Hindu castes of traditional Indian society, responsible for officiating at religious rites and studying and teaching the Vedas.

chhajja: projecting or overhanging eaves or cover of a roof, usually supported on large carved brackets. It was used extensively by Hindus for thousands of years, and then more recently borrowed by the invading Muslim empires into the common vocabulary of "Mughal Architecture."

chetna: that which gives man awareness or consciousness, as well as the faculties of perception.

darshan: the deliberate beholding, of an auspicious person or thing brings blessing, since the sight of the beneficent object infuses the beholder with its own virtue.

dhaba: local restaurants generally serving local cuisine, also serving as truck-stops and most commonly found next to petrol stations, and most are open 24 hours a day.

dhoti: traditional men's garment in the Indian subcontinent, a rectangular piece of unstitched cloth, usually around 7 yards long, wrapped around the waist and the legs and knotted at the waist.

Diwali: popularly known as the "festival of lights" is an important five-day festival in Hinduism, Jainism and Sikhism, celebrated between mid-October and mid-November. For Hindus, Diwali is one of the most important festivals of the year and is celebrated in families by performing traditional activities together in their homes.

Doge (of Venice): "military leader", often mistranslated as Duke, was the chief magistrate and leader of the Most Serene Republic of Venice for over a thousand years. Doges of Venice were elected for life by the city-state's aristocracy.

drav: melting.

garba: an Indian form of dance that originated in the Gujarat region, traditionally performed during the nine-day Hindu festival of Navarātrī.

guna: conical clay cylinders made by a potter on a wheel which, when cut in to half, yield two of the traditional country tiles used in most parts of India for roofing.

Holi: a religious spring festival celebrated by Hindus by throwing coloured powder and coloured water at each other. Bonfires are lit on the eve of the festival, also known as Holika.

Indra: the chief and the king of the gods of the Rig Veda.

Indraprastha palace: The palace of the Pandavas in their capital Indraprastha on the banks of the river Jamuna, near modern-day Delhi. The palace was constructed by the *asura* architect Maya and had such wonderful flooring and ceilings that visitors could not distinguish between crystal floors and pools of water.

Ise Grand shrine: a Shinto shrine dedicated to goddess Amaterasu-omikami, located in the city of Ise in Mie prefecture, Japan.

Jamuna (Jamna, Jumna): the Yamuna in Sanskrit literature that rises in the mythical Kalinda mountains. On the banks of this river lies the city of Delhi as did the ancient Indraprastha.

karma: the principle of universal causality resulting from action. A term of wide application, karma is used in various contexts to mean action, deeds, destiny, causality, effect, product, result.

Karna: the illegitimate son of Kunti and the Sun-God Surya before her marriage to Pandu.

kshobh: churning.

kund: well, water reservoir or stepped-tank built as part of a temple complex in Indian temples, used to store water.

Kurma: in Hinduism, Kurma, the tortoise, was the second avatar of Lord Vishnu.

lota: an Urdu and Hindi word for a small, usually spherical water vessel of brass or copper or plastic used in parts of south Asia. It is commonly used to store or transfer small amounts of liquids like milk or water.

La Sagrada Familia: a large unfinished Roman Catholic church in Barcelona, Catalonia, Spain, designed by Catalan architect Antoni Gaudí (1852–1926).

Laxmi (Lakshmi): Goddess of Wealth, consort of Vishnu. In the Vedas, the term *lakshmi* occurs in the sense of "auspicious" and is also applied to a fortunate woman.

Le Poeme de l'Angle Droit: "The Poem of the Right Angle" is a series of 19 paintings and corresponding writings composed by the influential Swiss architect Le Corbusier.

maa-gher: grandmother's home.

maya: illusion; the energy of the Supreme Lord that deludes living entities into forgetfulness of their spiritual nature and of God.

Mahabhinishkraman: The Great Renunciation. Prince Siddhartha, later known as Gautama Buddha, left the royal palace and his family in search of truth at the age of 29. In Pali literary traditions, this particular journey of Siddhartha is known as Mahabhinishkraman.

Mahadev: one of the names of Lord Siva.

mahajans: trade guilds in India with ancient traditions.

moksha: liberation, salvation, literally "release", is the liberation from *samsara* (world) and the concomitant suffering involved in being subject to the cycle of repeated death and reincarnation.

namadhikaran (naamkarana): traditional Hindu naming ceremony performed to formally name a baby. The ceremony is considered to be the first step in establishing the identity of a newborn. It is also a joyous occasion for the family to welcome their new arrival.

Navaratri: a Hindu festival of worship of Shakti, and festivities. The Sanskrit word *navaratri* literally means "nine nights", *nava* meaning "nine" and *ratri* meaning "nights".

Neti, neti (not this, not that): In the Upanishads, Lord Brahma is said to be beyond all description. Whatever is said of him may be rendered as *neti*, *neti*; hence many of the epithets and titles of Brahma are in the negative.

Om (Omkar): the sacred syllable that represents the Absolute Truth.

pagadi: turban, specifically refers to a headdress that is worn by men and needs to be manually tied each day.

Pandavas: the five sons of King Pandu—Yudhisthira, Bhima, Arjuna, Nakula and Sahadeva.

Pandu: the brother of Dhritarashtra and father of the Pandava brothers.

pran pratishtha: the Hindu rite or ceremony by which a *murti* (image of a god) is consecrated in a temple or place of worship.

pukka: properly or perfectly done, constructed, permanent.

Ramleela: the folk retelling of epic story of Ramayana over nine full nights with its unusual innovation to tell the story the most simply and effectively.

ragas: from Sanskrit, meaning 'colour' / 'tint' or 'passion'; each of the six basic musical modes in Indian classical music that express different moods in certain characteristic progressions, with more emphasis placed on some notes than others; so named because each raga is believed to create a specific emotional effect that 'colours the mind of the listener, and put him/her in a certain mood'.

rasa: the essence of taste.

runanubandh (rinanubandha): a term denoting that a relationship exists between all living beings on Earth. This relationship forms the basis for the various bondages in one's life both physically and emotionally.

samadhi: trance; complete absorption in God-consciousness; the term is also used for the edifice erected over the burial place of a holy person.

sat-chit-anand: a compound of three Sanskrit words, *sat*, *cit*, and *anand*, meaning (the Eternal) 'truth', 'consciousness' and 'bliss', respectively.

Satyanarayan Katha: the Satyanarayan Puja, with the accompanying *katha* (telling of the story), is a Hindu ritual performed before/on any major occasion like marriage, house-warming ceremony, etc., and can also be performed on any day for any reason.

seth: head of trade guild, any big financier, merchant, or mill owner, the leader of a *pol* (traditional housing clusters in north Gujarat).

Sheshnag: a celestial serpent that is the seat of Lord Vishnu in the underworld.

shikhara: a Sanskrit word translating literally to "mountain peak", refers to the rising tower in the Hindu temple architecture of India.

shilpa: the nearest Sanskrit equivalent for the term 'art' is *shilpa*, which means 'diverse' or 'variegated', and was first used for the decorative arts, but subsequently covered all skills, including architecture.

shringar: love, called *sringara*, employed in Hindu mysticism to symbolize the love of the human soul for the divine.

smorgasbord: a type of Scandinavian meal served buffet-style with multiple dishes of various foods on a table, originating in Sweden.

sthapati: an architect, a master carpenter or builder.

stupa: originally, a primitive burial mound, the stupa was developed and elaborated by the Buddhists, and became their most characteristic architectural structure.

swabhav: intrinsic nature, ownness or essence. Implies that each conscious being has its own innate disposition for which certain forms of living, livelihood, duties and ways of conduct and behaviour are appropriate.

swaraj: Swaraj can mean generally self-governance or "self-rule", and was used synonymously with "home-rule" by Mahatma Gandhi.

tilak: a mark put on the forehead in the space between the eyebrows. The Hindu symbol tilak stands for victory, success and good fortune.

Unite d'Habitation at Nante: the name of a modernist residential housing design principle developed by Le Corbusier. The concept formed the basis of several housing developments designed by him throughout Europe with this name.

upashraya: building that serves as a resting place for Jain monks and nuns.

Vaishnava: appertaining to Vishnu or worship of Vishnu.

vastu: the total environment around us.

Vastushastra: *Vāstu Śāstra*, "science of construction".

vikas: blossoming.

Vishnudharmottara Purana: a Hindu text, encyclopaedic in nature. Along with the narratives, it also deals with cosmology, cosmogony, geography, astronomy, astrology, division of time, pacification of unfavourable planets and stars, genealogies (mostly of kings and sages), manners and customs, penances, duties of Vaishnavas, law and politics, war strategies, treatment of diseases of human beings and animals, cuisine, grammar, metrics, lexicography, metrics, rhetoric, dramaturgy, dance, vocal and instrumental music and the arts.

vistaar: expansion.

yoga: a physical, mental, and spiritual discipline, originating in ancient India, whose goal is the attainment of a state of perfect spiritual insight and tranquillity.